Saving Cinderella

*What Feminists Get Wrong About Disney Princesses
And How To Set It Right*

Faith Moore

For my parents, Ellen and Andrew Klavan

Contents

Introduction 9

Chapter One: Snow White 17

Chapter Two: Cinderella 38

Chapter Three: Aurora...................................... 58

Chapter Four: Ariel... 79

Chapter Five: Belle.. 98

Chapter Six: Jasmine 119

Chapter Seven: Pocahontas............................. 137

Chapter Eight: Mulan 152

Chapter Nine: Tiana 169

Chapter Ten: Rapunzel 188

Chapter Eleven: Merida 209

Chapter Twelve: Elsa and Anna....................... 223

Epilogue 241

Acknowledgements... 245

About The Author.. 247

Introduction

Picture this: Disney's Rapunzel leaps off a cliff and swings by her hair down to the ground. Then a real little girl leaps onto the uneven bars in gymnastics class. Cut to Merida, from *Brave*, scaling a cliff-face, then a real little girl rock climbing. Pocahontas running, a little girl in a race. Ariel swimming, a little girl snorkeling. And on and on and on. "For every girl who dreams big," a smooth, confident voice tells us, "there's a princess to show her it's possible." A pause, and then: "Dream big, Princess!"

This is the keystone ad in Disney's "Dream Big, Princess" campaign, launched in 2016. Like all the ads in the campaign, this one is expertly done — the way Disney does everything — with a catchy hip-hop song over soaring violins, lots of swooping camera work, and panning shots of beautiful scenery from beloved Disney princess movies. It's epic. Intense. Inspirational. Or meant to be. In fact, it's so well done it took even a Disney traditionalist like me a minute to realize what's wrong with it. But there's definitely something wrong. Very, very wrong.

Sure, at first glance, it seems like the princesses are doing what they've always done: inspiring girls to be the best version of themselves. But are we really supposed to believe that Rapunzel's most inspiring quality is her ability to use her hair as a zip-line? Is Ariel's most important feature her ability to swim? She's a *mermaid*, of course she can swim! I mean, how shallow (pun, unfortunately, very much intended) do you have to be to think that this is what these characters have to offer?

Once upon a time, Disney princesses embodied bravery, compassion, loyalty, and heart. Their stories were about their inner lives — their struggles and their triumphs — not their physical appearance or athletic prowess. In each movie, a girl with a big heart, and even bigger dreams, was stuck in a situation that kept her from realizing her true potential. Snow White and Cinderella were captives to wicked step mothers; Ariel and Belle wanted more than the life they were born to. And so on. And, throughout the course of the movie, we learned how a brave, determined girl with a strong moral core could overcome these obstacles and achieve her dreams. In essence, we learned how to grow up into strong, centered, moral women. So, what happened? How did we get from the nuanced original movies to the superficiality of the "Dream Big, Princess" campaign? *That's* what this book is all about.

The shift began with a small, but very vocal, minority of radical feminists who misunderstood the movies. Let's call them "princess critics." These princess critics took a look at the original princesses — like Snow White and Cinderella, and even the more modern princesses, like Ariel and Belle — and deemed them "anti-feminist." They called them damsels in distress, and proclaimed that they had no agency in their own lives, and needed a man to take care of everything for them. They boiled the princesses' dreams down to "husband hunting" and said they would settle for the first guy that came along. They called them "drips," said they were "boring," and branded them as terrible role models for little girls.

But nothing could be further from the truth. These ideas aren't borne out by the movies at all. In fact, it's quite the opposite. The earlier princesses had dreams of their own. They actively pursued them and worked hard and made sacrifices to achieve them. They didn't jump at the first guy who came along. They made sure their love was true and real before choosing a partner to spend their lives with. They were kind, courageous, loving, compassionate, and principled. Exactly the kind of women that I'd want my daughters to aspire to become.

But I can just picture you shaking your head at me. You think I'm crazy. Disney princesses aren't damsels in distress? They're not just after a man? *Yes they are!* you're yelling into the book. (Calm down. I can't actually hear you.) But they're not. And I'm going to prove it to you.

The problem (and the reason you don't believe me) is that the views of this group of feminist critics who got the movies so terribly wrong happen to be shared by the publishers of major news sources read by the general public. *The New York Times*, *The LA Times*, *The Washington Post*, and *Time Magazine* (to name a few) have all published articles, over the years, denouncing the princesses as bad for little girls. So that, now, this is widely accepted as truth. Modern moms, who don't want their little girls to watch "anti-feminist" movies, have banished from their homes the princesses they themselves loved as children. And Disney, afraid of losing its audience, began to cater to these critiques, thus solidifying the myth that the original princesses aren't good role models.

But I disagree. The original princesses (Snow White, Cinderella, and Aurora) and the "Renaissance" princesses (Ariel, Belle, and Jasmine) embody a set of values that allows them to live rich and full lives without compromising their morals or beliefs. They believe in following their dreams, which makes them courageous, determined, and mentally strong. They believe in true love, which makes them unwilling to settle for the first suitor who comes along, but open to

11

falling in love when they meet the right guy. And they believe in presenting their best selves to the world, which makes them kind, gentle, well-mannered, and true. It's a pretty good list of characteristics to aspire to.

Personally, I've never wanted to be the CEO of a Fortune 500 company. I've never wanted to be a professional athlete, or a rocket scientist, or a marine biologist. There's nothing *wrong* with wanting to be those things. But I (and lots of other women and little girls like me) see a different sort of future for myself. A more "traditional" future that includes a partner to love, a home to keep, and children to raise. It's a dream that, in the narrative of the princess critics, is often seen as outdated — a product of an oppressive culture that kept women in the kitchen, catering to their husbands' every need. And perhaps that *is* how it felt for some. But for lots and lots of others, their "big dreams" are quite a bit closer to home.

Some might argue that the princesses *made* me feel this way. But that's not it at all. I didn't choose to get married because I watched Ariel kiss Eric on board a boat. I didn't decide to be a homemaker because Snow White sang "Whistle While You Work" and made it seem so appealing. I don't enjoy wearing pretty dresses because of Cinderella's ball gown. I'm not who I am *because* of the princesses. It's the other way around. I see myself *in* the princesses. They represent something that's already inside of me — inside of so many women, if we're honest. I see the sort of kindness, gentleness, and optimism I feel within myself. The kind of bravery, determination, and boundless love I hope to harness and embody. I see *womanhood*.

I know I'm not alone in this. So many women and little girls love the princesses too. They recognize the same things in them that I do. They see their own womanhood reflected back to them and know somehow that this *matters*. These days, women who love Disney princesses often feel ashamed to love them because of the false narrative about them. They worry that Disney princesses are *bad* women — that they portray a passive, oppressed, two-dimensional view of women. But we don't need to be ashamed. Because the movies don't portray that at all. And this book will prove it to you.

It's radical, I know, to say this, but Disney princesses aren't anti-feminist. And they're certainly not boring. The good ones aren't, anyway. And they're relevant, even now. For little girls looking for role models. Who want to know how to grow up, discover who they are, move away from their parents, and follow their dreams. And yes, even to find love.

A minority opinion, based on misinterpretation, has pulled the wool over our eyes. It's made it hard, even for those who want to believe, to see how these antiquated heroines could have anything to offer girls in the modern world. So, let me be your guide. Let me show you what the Disney princesses of yesterday taught me.

Each chapter in this book covers one of the eleven "official" Disney princesses (plus Elsa and Anna from *Frozen*, who aren't yet "official"). In chronological order we will explore the themes, tropes, and symbolism of these movies, and the ways in which the princess critics have influenced our perceptions of them. And we will examine how the princess critics' misguided complaints have caused Disney filmmakers to ruin the princess narrative. By the end of the book, I hope it will be clear how wrong the princess critics are to malign the early Disney princesses, and how detrimental to young girls the new "feminist" princesses really are. And, armed with this knowledge, I hope that we — in our conversations with our daughters, and our attendance at the box office — can finally save Cinderella.

Part I

"A Dream Is A Wish Your Heart Makes": The Original Heroines

Chapter One: Snow White

Okay, I'll admit it, Disney's Snow White is kind of weird. She moves like a ballet dancer suspended in water, her eyes are almost never open (even when she's awake), and her voice sounds like a chipmunk on helium. When I look to the Disney princesses for inspiration and encouragement (as I frequently do, judge me how you choose), Snow White's general affect doesn't give me much to work with. I mean, if I waltzed into a room, one arm extended gracefully out in front me, the other suspended behind me, with my head cocked to one side, and my feet doing a sort of prancy-glidy thing (that's a very technical dance term, by the way) it would probably be assumed by all who observed me that I was off my freaking rocker. And, if I began to speak in Snow White's signature high-pitched warble, it would then be assumed that I was, actually, on some sort of psychotropic drugs. Because a *real* (sane) person would never, ever act like Snow White.

But of course not! Snow White is a princess in a fairy tale. And fairy tales, by their very nature, are unrealistic. Animals talk, people are physically transformed, fairy godmothers watch over orphaned girls, and witches cast magic spells. Even though Disney's *Snow White and the Seven Dwarfs* is a full-length movie, rather than a two-page-long story, it doesn't stray from the fairy tale mode of storytelling. In fairy tales, key tropes — like princes and princesses, witches and magic — tell a story that is deeper and more meaningful than the sum of its parts. A fairy tale is a very specific kind of story. A kind of story that *Snow White*'s original audience in 1937 would have been intimately familiar with but which, judging by their reactions, the princess critics know nothing about.

According to some studies (like one published in the Royal Society Open Science Journal in 2016) fairy tales are some of the oldest stories known to man, dating back, perhaps, almost 6,000 years. And, until people like the Brothers Grimm began writing them down in the nineteenth century, these stories were almost exclusively oral — passed down from generation to generation for thousands of years. Which means that there is something about these stories — something about the themes and elements they contain — that is essentially, and fundamentally important to the human experience. According to child psychologist Bruno Bettelheim in his book *The Uses of Enchantment*, fairy tales offer a child "a moral education which subtly, and by implication only, conveys to him the advantages of moral behavior." Fairy tales boil down the key elements of the human experience into manageable stories which offer a kind of moral roadmap with which to navigate the complicated and confusing terrain of life. They teach life lessons, caution us against life's pitfalls, and metaphorically represent universal life transitions. And, because they have remained, largely, the same for so many years, we can infer that the themes they address have resonated with human beings since time immemorial.

All human beings, it seems, except princess critics. According to *them*, Snow White is "a drip" and "a bore." Out of pronouncements such as these, an entire narrative about Snow White was born. And this narrative took such hold in the public imagination that it has become the prevailing idea about Disney's Snow White. In an article for *Hello Giggles* called "The Evolution of the Disney Princess — From Dainty Damsel to Badass," Kit Steinkellner says, "Snow White is about as passive as a heroine can be. She sits around a wishing well waiting for her prince to come, then after getting tricked into going to the

18

woods to get almost-murdered, she sits around the dwarfs' house cleaning up after them. Then she's poisoned and lays around in a glass coffin waiting for true love's kiss." Seriously?! Apparently, according to princess critics, thousands of years of essential human experience has been in error. I mean, really, what hubris!

It's criticism like Steinkellner's that proves that the princess critics know nothing about fairy tales. But fairy tales work in a very specific way. If you were to boil *Snow White* (or any other fairy tale) down to its most basic elements, you would be left with a series of tropes which represent a kind of fairy tale shorthand. A shorthand which symbolically represents universal human concepts. As Marina Warner puts it, in her book *Once Upon A Time: A Short History of Fairy Tale,* "fairy tale consists above all of acts of imagination, conveyed in a symbolic Esperanto; its building blocks include certain kinds of characters (stepmothers and princesses, elves and giants) and certain recurrent motifs (keys, apples, mirrors, rings, and toads); the symbolism comes alive and communicates meaning through imagery." A prince, for example, represents true love, a witch represents the underlying tensions between mother and daughter, a dark forest is symbolic of transformation, etc. Each symbol, and what it means, remains constant from fairy tale to fairy tale so that the listener implicitly understands the story's moral underpinnings and gleans the fairy tale's lesson. Within this framework, fairy tales are able to delve deeply into complex human issues, offering nuanced and emotionally accurate depictions of life events, within a very short and simply worded narrative.

Snow White is no exception. Both the original fairy tale and the Disney version use this specific fairy tale shorthand to excellent effect. The symbolic elements of *Snow White* draw together to represent an important (and often frightening) aspect of a young girl's transformation from childhood to adulthood: puberty. Just as they do today, mothers hundreds (if not thousands) of years ago sought to allay their daughters' fears and demystify the physical and emotional

19

changes that would happen as they grew. Fairy tales were a memorable and easy-to-digest way to explain a woman's journey. A mother's gift to her daughter. What do you think princess critics? Can we all be on board about the usefulness of *that*?

*

There's no doubt, even among princess critics, that *Snow White and the Seven Dwarfs* is a cinematic masterpiece. It was the first-ever feature-length animated film. Before this, cartoons were simplistic, childish, and full of sight-gags and humor aimed at kids. Clocking in at around six minutes, they usually preceded the newsreel at the movie theater and weren't taken seriously as an art form at all. As Roger Ebert explains in his 2001 review of the film, "What could then be seen in *Snow White* — and what is now much more difficult to keep sight of in retrospect — was the transformation of a one-time novelty into an art form."

Even though *Snow White* changed the perception of what a cartoon could do, it's also a product of those earlier animated shorts. All you have to do is watch an old Betty Boop cartoon to understand that Snow White, and all her weirdness, would have been totally familiar to a contemporary audience. And the veritable zoo of animals that follow Snow White around, and seem sort of like overkill to us, would have been expected by an audience who held Mickey Mouse as their standard for cartoon entertainment.

But, while contemporary audiences would have recognized key elements from the earlier cartoons, everyone who saw *Snow White* understood that this was something else entirely. Ebert explains, "At a time when animation was a painstaking frame-by-frame activity and every additional moving detail took an artist days or weeks to draw, Disney imagined a film in which every corner and dimension would contain something that was alive and moving." So it *looked* different (impressively so) but it was also a totally new way of telling a story. Animation wasn't just for silly six minute shorts anymore, it was a new and legitimate mode of storytelling. But the *type* of story it told wasn't new at all. As Walt Disney, himself, said the story is "basic, all the way through."

It was only later, when the princess critics, looking for something to complain about, turned their misguided eyes back on the original Disney princesses, that anyone began to question whether Snow White was a "good" woman. Before this, Snow White would have been seen in much the same way as she would have been perceived by children listening to their mothers tell them the tale of *Snow White*, or by readers of the fairy tales by the Brothers Grimm. They would have instantly interpreted the fairy tale shorthand, understanding that Snow White was a pure and virtuous woman.

But let's give the princess critics the benefit of the doubt. Let's assume that they are simply misguided and uninformed, rather than arrogant and egotistical. Let's assume that, in spending all their time in women's studies classes, they simply haven't had time for English literature. And, because of this, one of their many misconceptions is that Disney princesses (particularly the early ones like Snow White, Cinderella, and Aurora) were meant to be seen as real, flesh-and-blood (pen and ink?) women. They want us to judge Snow White for marrying the first guy she meets, being foolish enough to eat the witch's apple, enjoying housework, and being frightened by the woods at night. And even though none of this is fair — because all of that (the guy, the apple, the housework, the woods, and the fear) are metaphors that play out within the overarching allegory that is the story of *Snow White* — let's humor the princess critics and evaluate Snow White as a real woman.

Because, even on their own terms, the critics are wrong. In her book *Cinderella Ate My Daughter*, Peggy Orenstein says, "I had purposely kept [Snow White] from [my daughter] because, even setting aside the obvious sexism, Snow herself is such an incredible pill." But that's completely untrue. If we view Disney's Snow White as a real person, we'll find that she is far from a passive participant in her story. In fact, we'll see that she's an industrious and courageous girl who

21

longs for a better life but doesn't let her difficult situation break her. Weird chipmunk voice aside, I wouldn't worry one bit about a modern girl who held Snow White as her role model. So, first we'll prove that — even as a real woman — Snow White has merit and once we've done that, we'll go back and discuss what this movie is *really* about.

*

The main problem that princess critics have with Snow White is that she's "passive." Janet Maslin of *The New York Times* says, "Aside from her great daintiness and her credentials as a fervent housekeeper, Snow White has no distinct personality. She exists only to be victimized by her wicked stepmother." And entertainment website *Flickering Myth* says "Snow White is young and beautiful, but appears to have no real motivation in life other than finding a handsome prince." So is it true? Does Snow White just sit around staring into wishing wells and singing strange, high-pitched songs while the action unfolds around her? Or is there more to her than that?

When we first meet her, Snow White is trapped in an impossible situation. Her step-mother (we have no idea where her father is, he seems to be out of the picture, or at least unable to help her for some reason) sees that Snow White might one day surpass her in beauty, so forces her to dress in rags and become the castle scullery maid. Snow White is a child, she has been enslaved all her life, and has nowhere else to go. She has no choice but to submit. Here is the princess critics' first issue with Snow White. In an article for *Stylist* which ranks all the Disney princesses from most to least feminist, Kayleigh Dray says of Snow White, "she is still an archetypal Damsel in Distress, waiting to be rescued by her very own Prince Charming and be whisked off into the sunset." Princess critics view the fact that, when we first meet her, Snow White hasn't done anything to escape her situation as proof that she is just waiting passively for rescue. And the almost immediate entrance of The Prince seems to support this. But let's look a little deeper.

Snow White is a girl whose family has failed her. Her father is absent, her mother is dead, and her step-mother is *literally* a wicked witch. What Snow White is waiting for, when we first meet her, is not rescue, but *love*. And while it would be nice to imagine that she could somehow find parental figures that would care for her and love her the way parents should, that ship has sailed for Snow White. In Disney's version, Snow White is fourteen — just on the cusp of adulthood and unlikely to be adopted by anyone else. All human beings need love. We long for human connection, and to be valued for ourselves. This shouldn't be a controversial concept. And, since Snow White is loved by no one, she longs to find someone who *can* love her. *And* since she's too old for new parental bonds, so she naturally turns to the next stage of love: romance.

"I'm wishing / For the one I love / To find me/ /Today," Snow White sings into the wishing well, when we first meet her. And there, as if on cue, is The Prince. (Yes, his name is just "The Prince" — or Prince Florian if you delve deep into Disney fandom. We'll discuss The Prince's namelessness later but, just in case you were wondering, it doesn't mean he's a total rando that Snow White fell in love with because of something superficial like the jaunty feather in his hat.) When The Prince turns up he is the literal embodiment of Snow White's need for love. "One heart / Tenderly beating / Ever entreating / Constant and true," The Prince sings to Snow White. He loves her, he will always love her, and he won't abandon her. And, in fact, he loves her even in her ragged clothing, proving that he's not concerned with her physical appearance or her status, only what's in her heart.

When she sees him, Snow White doesn't throw herself at him, crying and beating her fists against his chest, begging him to take her away from this horrible place and make her his wife so she can be rich and live in a castle and have nice things. (Isn't that what she'd do if she was just waiting around for some guy to save her?) Instead, she is happy to see him, attracted to him, but shy. In fact, she ultimately runs away from him, unsure — in her girlish inexperience — what to do with his advances. (How many of us, in our teenage awkward phase, ran away from the very person we actually had a crush on? I sure did.)

By the way, it's worth noting that this may not actually be the first time that Snow White and The Prince have met. Snow White sings about wishing that "the one I love" will find her "today." It's as if there's *already* someone she loves, and she hopes she'll get to see him on that particular day. The Prince takes Snow White by surprise, appearing next to hear as she sings into the wishing well, and finishes the last line of the song with her. She is (understandably!) startled, since she didn't see him come in. "Hello," he says. "Did I frighten you?" He's speaking to her as if he knows her. As if he expected her to be as happy to see him as he is to see her. But, instead, Snow White runs away. "Wait, please! Don't run away!" he calls after her.

Sure, it's a cartoon fairy tale, but you can imagine this happening in real life, right? A high-school girl is caught unawares by her crush (who she's been flirting with lightly all semester but hasn't actually had a real conversation with) when he comes up behind her and says "Boo!" as an excuse to be near her. And she, unsure how to handle these completely male attempts at connection, swats at him playfully and then runs off to tell her friends all about it. It's the sort of innocent flirtation that holds the promise of becoming more, but hasn't gotten there yet. It's possible we're just catching Snow White and The Prince in the moment in which he finally declares his true feelings for her, telling her that this isn't just a schoolboy crush, he's in love with her. And she, though she runs from him at first (initially startled by his sudden interruption), comes back to the window to accept his declaration, sending him a white dove which carries her kiss.

But even if this *is* the first time they've met, we can still confidently assume that Snow White and The Prince are truly and legitimately in love. Why? Because this is a fairy tale. And, in fairy tales, love at first sight is another one of those shorthand elements. The Disney movie, as well as the original fairy tale, is telling us that

The Prince is Snow White's one, true love. That he embodies qualities that make him worthy of her — loyalty, bravery, passion, strength. It *isn't* that Snow White falls for the first guy she meets. It's exactly the opposite. We are being told, in the language of fairy tales, that she has found her perfect match. And, if we weren't sure about this, his song tells it to us clearly: "One Song / My heart keeps singing / Of one love / Only for you."

The princess critics' worry, as voiced by *Flickering Myth*, is that "young girls will see the film as a model for life, wherein beauty takes precedence over personal ambition and all of life's problems can be solved by finding the right man, or 'prince'." But *that's* not what they see at all. Mothers who despair over their daughter's obsession with "true love" have got it all wrong. The message here is this: find the man who is your soul mate — your heart's true match. Settle for nothing less. And when you find him, cleave to him, because human beings need connection, and this is the most powerful connection of all. *That's* what fairy tales are telling us when their heroines fall in love at first sight. *That's* why The Prince is a *prince*. The point is not how wealthy and powerful he is. The point is that he is the worthiest of men. Just as she, even in rags, is a princess — the worthiest of women.

So, Snow White is someone who is (understandably) looking for love and she has just found her prince. If she was simply looking for rescue (or for the richest guy she could find) this would be the time to pack her bags, leap into his arms, and ride off into the sunset. But she doesn't. She stays where she is. He loves her and she loves him, but this is still just the beginning of their young relationship and she's willing to wait. Looking at Snow White as a real girl, it's clear that she views The Prince's role in her life not as rescuer, but as lover. And, either because we believe that they have met many times before, or because we understand the fairy tale shorthand, we can assume that their love is built on something that is satisfying and real to both of them.

Very soon after this encounter with The Prince, Snow White is told that The Queen (presumably a powerful figure, who would have influence over the people that Snow White might meet in the outside world) wants her dead. The Evil Queen's magic mirror has proclaimed that Snow White, not The Queen, is suddenly the fairest in the land. Unwilling to accept this, The Queen sends her huntsman to cut out Snow White's heart. But the huntsman, overcome by Snow White's innocence and purity, can't go through with it. "Run away," the huntsman entreats her, and "never come back." So she does. She *must*. She has no time to pack a bag, or make a plan, or think things through. If she confronts The Queen, she'll die. The Queen has powerful magic which, presumably, Snow White knows about given that she's been living with the woman for most of her life. The Huntsman can't help her, he's employed by The Queen and might (it would be reasonable for Snow White to assume) change his mind at any moment. So she runs. And at first, like we probably all would in her situation, she panics. But then, when she's calmer, she thinks things through and makes a plan.

"I'm so ashamed of the fuss I've made," Snow White tells the animals, when she comes to her senses. It isn't like her, this tells us, to be so hysterical. She is determined to pull herself together and find a way out of this. So she asks the woodland animals to help her find a place to sleep. They lead her to a little cottage in the woods. Snow White goes inside and finds the place in shambles. But when she sees what a mess the cottage is, she comes up with a plan. "I know!" she tells the animals. "We'll clean the house and surprise them. Maybe then they'll let me stay." And she begins to industriously and efficiently tidy up.

"Snow White will always make scrubbing and scouring seem the pleasantest of chores," complains Maslin. When princess critics look at Snow White's behavior upon entering the dwarfs cottage, they despair. Because, to princess critics, an affinity for housework is the surest sign of a woman's oppression by the patriarchy. And Snow

26

White, seeing a messy home, gets straight to work, singing a cheerful song. Maslin, and others, believe that Snow White's cheerfulness in the face of adversity somehow conveys that the adversity is fun. But that's ridiculous. No one *wants* to be afraid for their lives in a cottage in the woods instead of safe with people who love them. Her cheerfulness is not indicative of her *enjoyment*. It's indicative of her *strength*. She won't let her hardship get her down. Her cheerfulness is an act of defiance. *You will not break me*, she is saying to the world. I am stronger than you. "There's no use in grumbling / When the raindrops come tumbling / Remember, you're the one / Who can fill the world with sunshine."

Snow White *doesn't* like housework. She doesn't like it at all! When we first meet her, in fact, she is scrubbing a flight of stairs and sighing forlornly about how many more stairs there still are to scrub. If she loved housework, wouldn't the vast number of stairs excite and motivate her? And here, while tidying up the dwarfs' cottage, Snow White sings the now-famous song "Whistle While You Work" which princess critics use to show how much Snow White loves chores. If she's whistling while she works, she must love it, right? No, no, wrong again, no.

"Just whistle while you work / And cheerfully together we can tidy up the place / So hum a merry tune / It won't take long when there's a song to help you set the pace." Snow White doesn't like this. It's tedious, boring work and she'd rather be doing something else. But she whistles, and puts on a cheerful face, because what's the use in complaining? "When there's too much to do / Don't let it bother you / forget your troubles / Try to be just like a cheerful chick-a-dee." The song is not *because* of the chores, it's *in spite* of them. The song allows Snow White to find some joy in a difficult and boring task. It's what the British call "stiff upper lip." She's been handed a raw deal and she's got two choices: she can whine, complain, and swoon (rather like a damsel in distress); or she can buck up and get on with doing what she has to do. And she chooses the latter.

27

One thing Snow White *does* do is take *pride* in her work. Which is very different from liking it. Like many women in America today (myself included) Snow White believes in keeping a neat and orderly home. Condemning anything a woman does towards the upkeep of her home, and the smooth running of her family is harmful to the many, many girls who yearn (as I did) to grow up to be wives, mothers, and homemakers. If feminism truly means letting women be anything they want to be, then homemaker has to be on the list of acceptable life paths. No, not *everyone* has to be a homemaker, but those who do oughtn't be condemned for it. Wife and mother is a valuable and worthwhile (perhaps the most worthwhile of all) life path. So don't knock it.

When the dwarfs finally arrive home, Snow White is ready with her bargain. She tells them, "If you let me stay, I'll keep house for you. I'll wash, sew, sweep, and cook!" She's making a deal: keep me safe and I'll cook and clean for you. This is not the behavior of a passive heroine. In fact, it's pretty resourceful, if you ask me. Contrary to all the princess critics' complaints, Snow White has actually found a workable solution to her problem all on her own. In essence, she has saved herself. Here, again, looking at her as a real woman, the way the princess critics want us to, she comes out looking pretty good.

But, oh dear, this simply will not do! For princess critics, Snow White's bargain with the seven dwarfs isn't resourceful at all. In fact, for them, it's the height of passivity. Because, even though Snow White has orchestrated her own rescue by using her marketable skills (which princess critics should approve of wholeheartedly) she has done it using housework. And housework, as we've already seen, (no matter its purpose) is the epitome of oppression. But think this one through carefully, feminists. Would you rather Snow White becomes a freeloader in the dwarfs' cottage? Should she throw herself on the mercy of *men*? Should she expect them to save her? To hide her and care for her for nothing? Isn't that *exactly* the problem with Disney princesses according to princess critics? That they expect men to save them? But Snow White doesn't expect that at all. She sees that she would be asking something of them, and she offers them something in return. Something they actually need. It's a bargain, and a mutually beneficial one at that.

Snow White is someone who is using the resources available to her to find her way out of a difficult situation, and who takes pride in the work she is doing. "She cooks, she cleans, she sews on buttons, she makes men feel good about themselves," scoffs Dray. But far from simply waiting around for her prince to show up and rescue her, she spends her time industriously engaged in providing for her own future. Once the dwarfs accept her bargain, Snow White spends her time in the cottage, not elegantly draped over furniture sighing "woe is me!" but, rather, engaged in the difficult task of keeping house for seven slovenly men. Not because she feels the need to attend to the needs of every man she meets, but because she is earning her keep.

Looking at Snow White as a real woman, as the princess critics insist we do, reveals her to be resourceful, brave, and fiercely determined. Sure, her daintiness and her treacly sweetness may not appeal to everyone. And yes, she's certainly not as fully realized and internally nuanced as the princesses Disney would create in the early '90s. But, remember, Snow White was the first. She's the blueprint for a Disney princess. Her kindness, her strength in the face of adversity, her unwavering determination to follow her dreams, and her understanding that love must be true in order to be worthwhile set the precedent for all the princesses to follow. And, when you look at the list of qualities she actually embodies (not the ones the princess critics want to mistakenly ascribe to her), it's easy to see why so many young girls gravitate towards Disney princesses. And easy, too, knowing what we now know, to let them.

So, what about the fact that Snow White then gets duped into eating an apple by a literal wicked witch who looks about as trustworthy as a guy wielding a chainsaw? And what about the fact that this apple causes her to fall into a "sleeping death" from which she is only awakened *after* the wicked witch has been vanquished? This final sequence of the movie leads princess critics like Maslin to conclude that Snow White, "exists only to be victimized by her wicked stepmother." It's the same old Snow-White-lacks-agency argument. But we've just proven that Snow White *isn't* passive. That she's a strong, resourceful young woman, who's in love with The Prince but not reliant on him for her ultimate survival. So what's going on in this final sequence?

Well *this* is where we have to look to the film's true meaning. We need to view it as a fairy tale, and interpret the fairy tale shorthand of this final sequence and the story as a whole. Because even though, as we've just proven, Snow White has a lot to recommend her as a real woman, she actually isn't one at all. That's not what's going on in this film. It's actually something much deeper than the princess critics are willing (or able) to see. *Snow White* is an allegory.

*

All Disney princess narratives are about the transition from childhood to adulthood. As legendary Disney producer Don Hahn explained it, "Disney films are about growing up. They're about that day in your life when you have to accept responsibility." And, while the later Disney films tackle this idea in a much more literal way, the original Disney princess narratives stick much closer to their fairy tale origins, and depict this transition almost entirely metaphorically. The story of *Snow White*, both the original fairy tale and the Disney version, is a clear, concise, and obvious (if you're looking for it) allegorical tale about puberty. It tackles the intense, confusing, and sometimes frightening transition that all girls must go through as they morph from an innocent child to a sexually mature adult woman. And this story, like so many others, is meant to help girls process this transition and approach it in a way that is healthy and mature.

But here come the princess critics screaming at us again (hush princess critics, we can hear you!) *Healthy?! Mature?! She falls asleep! She waits for a man to save her! She's powerless! Passive!* Or, in a lovely little piece of victim-blaming, the *FeministFiction* blog declares, "She's so insufferably good that it's no wonder the Evil Queen wanted to kill her." Poor, misguided princess critics. That isn't it at all!

When the story begins, The Evil Queen looks into her magic mirror and asks, "Who is the fairest?" And, initially (as the slave in the mirror has told her every day up until this point) the answer is that *she* is. She, an adult woman who has already reached sexual maturity, is the fairest in the land, even though a very beautiful girl is living in her home. It is at the exact moment when The Prince declares his love for Snow White that the mirror changes his tune. Suddenly, Snow White is the fairest, *not* The Queen. In her book *Spinning Straw into Gold,* Joan Gould explains, "Snow White's body has begun to change by the time her story is under way — we know this from the violence of her stepmother's reaction to her beauty." The spark of romance that has been kindled between Snow White and The Prince is only possible because Snow White is beginning to mature. The Prince wouldn't be attracted to *a child*. And it is *this* that suddenly transforms Snow White into the fairest in the land — usurping The Queen, who may be getting close to menopause.

And, of course, princess critics want to whine about the emphasis on physical beauty, claiming that it sends the wrong message to little girls, but remember, it's *The Queen* that's obsessed with Snow White's physical beauty. The Queen. The bad guy. Snow White has absolutely no interest in her physical self. As Gould says, "her self-awareness hasn't taken into account the biological upheaval staring to take place inside her." She's not aware of these physical changes, and doesn't indicate in any way that she holds beauty as an important element of her character. In fact, as we've already seen, she is much more concerned with being industrious, cheerful, resourceful, and brave. The whole "fairest" thing is the symbol for the changes of puberty. She is transforming from a girl to a woman. It's not about how nice she looks while doing it, it's that she's doing it at all. She becomes "the fairest" at precisely the moment when the change has begun.

So we get this first indication that Snow White's transition into puberty has begun. And it is this that causes the mirror to make its fateful proclamation which, in turn, causes Snow White to have to flee the only home she's ever known. A young adult having to leave home. Sound familiar? The onset of puberty and the inevitable push to adulthood means that, eventually, the girl will have to leave her family and find a way to make it on her own. Since this is an allegory and not a realistic narrative, the leaving home follows immediately on the heels of the revelation that puberty has begun. And, in leaving home, Snow White encounters the next metaphorical element in the story: the dark forest.

Bettelheim explains that, in fairy tales, the forest "symbolizes the place in which inner darkness is confronted and worked through; where uncertainty is resolved about who one is; and where one begins to understand who one wants to be." The forest represents Snow White's teen angst. It's the dark, confusing, frightening teenage years in which, as parents often lament, a sweet, well-behaved child becomes a moody, rule-breaking terror. It's the time in a girl's life when she has to come to terms with the fact that she must leave her childhood behind and become a woman. She *must*. Her body, if nothing else, makes that very clear to her. The forest metaphor is present in so many fairy tales (*Hansel and Gretel, Rapunzel, Goldilocks, Little Red Riding Hood,* and on and on and on) and it always means the same thing. In fact, there's an entire musical (*Into the Woods*) based on this metaphor and what happens to the characters during their time in the forest.

As happens in many fairy tales, Snow White's narrative pauses in the woods. It's the moment Bettelheim describes, of confronting the inner darkness and beginning to figure out who she will become. At first, Snow White is frightened. Things that she thought she knew and understood (trees, and leaves, and animals, and branches) are suddenly transformed into frightening creatures with evil eyes. And, as we've already seen, she panics. The woods is the metaphorical embodiments of Snow White's "inner darkness." But Snow White passes through the fear and, as with many other allegorical heroes and heroines, Snow White encounters a stopping point in the woods. A place where she must do her soul searching.

And here, in the cottage, she finds seven little men. This cottage is the place where Snow White is going to practice being the woman she will one day become. But *OMG!* the princess critics are screaming. *The kind of woman she'll become?! But she's cooking and cleaning and taking care of men!* Or, as Chelsea Mize says on *Bustle,* Snow White is practicing her "trophy wife skills." But that's not it at all! Regardless of whether Snow White wants to become a rocket scientist, or a lion tamer, or an activist for democracy (given the current situation with the monarchy), the skills she is practicing while in the dwarfs' cottage are precisely the skills she'll need for what her body is preparing her to achieve: motherhood.

So, yes, for Snow White, homemaking will probably be her lot in life. One that she (and so many modern women) will be happy to embrace. One that she aspires to and takes pride in (as I do, as so many of us do). But, in the context of this allegory, that's not the point. The *point* is that puberty quite literally prepares a woman's body to conceive and carry a child. So, by the time she has fully transitioned (whether she actually decides to become one or not) she will be ready (at least physically) to become a mother. So the thing that she must metaphorically come to terms with in the cottage is not her *career* path, but the inevitable fact of what her body is now capable of. And this is represented in the story by Snow White preparing for motherhood (and wifehood, too, since you can't biologically become a mother without some kind of interaction with a man, much as feminists might like it to be otherwise).

So these dwarfs are men, but they're not *really* men. The characteristics they embody (as represented by their names) aren't the characteristics of fully-grown men. Men aren't bashful, dopey, and sleepy. They're brave, loyal, and passionate. Like The Prince. *These* men are actually more like children. And Snow White treats them as such, scolding them for not washing before dinner, and not allowing them to eat until they've submitted to her will. But, in other ways, they *are* men, who are affected by Snow White's beauty and desirous of her physical affection. When it's time for them to go to work and Snow White gives each of them a goodbye kiss on the head and they all react with a swoon.

It is Grumpy — who embodies a trait which, to a child, might seem more masculine than the other dwarfs' demeanors — who Snow White spends the most time trying to win over. Before bed, she prays to God that Grumpy will like her and, while the dwarfs are at work, she cooks a pie with Grumpy's name written across the top. It is the dwarf that is least childlike that Snow White focuses her attentions on, trying out her newfound romantic abilities on this practice man. And, in the end, she wins him over with a kiss — the physical representation of her new role as a sexual being. Snow White's kiss renders Grumpy initially disoriented and, later, evokes the kind of loyalty and protectiveness indicative of an adult man. Snow White is practicing for her real man, The Prince, who she knows she will find again once this interlude in the forest is over.

So, in the cottage in the woods, Snow White learns to inhabit her new, adult, body and practices the womanly activities that her new sexual maturity allow her. Enter The Evil Queen. While Snow White has orchestrated her own escape and hidden herself as best she can, the Queen has consulted her magic mirror again and realized she's been duped. And, hell-bent on killing Snow White, she searches out a magic spell to get rid of her once and for all. Consulting her book of evil spells, The Queen fixes on "The Sleeping Death," a potion which, when consumed, will cause Snow White to fall asleep, as if dead. And the only thing that can wake her, according to the spell book, is "love's first kiss." Not "true love's kiss" as it is often misquoted as being. Love's *first* kiss. (More on this in a moment.) The Queen, sure that the dwarfs will think she's dead and bury her, is confident that this will get rid of Snow White for good. And so, the potion ready, The Queen dips *an apple* in it, ready to take to Snow White.

The red apple that The Queen chooses as the vehicle for Snow White's "sleeping death" is another metaphor in the story. The apple's redness is important because of the traditional symbolism of the color red. "Above all, sex is red," Gould explains, "as in Eve's apple, a virgin's 'cherry,' Persephone's pomegranate or the Devil's cloak, the red-light district, red shoes, red satin boxes shaped like hearts and filled with candies to be licked on Valentine's Day, or a Scarlet letter A for adultery, embroidered in gold on a Puritan gown." But the apple itself is important too, as was Eve's apple in Genesis. Gould again: "After a single mouthful, Eve was overcome by knowledge and left innocence and the Garden behind." Biting the apple is the metaphorical representation of Snow White's acceptance of her new role as a sexually mature woman. One bite of this sexually-charged object changes everything for Snow White. Literally *and* metaphorically.

Princess critics hate the fact that Snow White falls asleep. They think it represents her ultimate passivity. She's literally immobile until The Prince comes to wake her up. But the sleep is another metaphor, of course. Snow White falls asleep at exactly the moment when she accepts the symbol of her sexuality. And, similar to a caterpillar going into its cocoon in order to emerge a butterfly, the sleep that immediately follows the acceptance of her new self is symbolic of this final transformation taking place within Snow White. And the kiss that The Prince bestows on her is not, as Dray suggests, an act of "necrophilia" performed by "some stranger" while she's "dead" (gotta love those princess critics), but the metaphorical representation of Snow White's readiness to emerge an adult.

The kiss that The Prince gives to Snow White is not "true love's kiss." The point here is not that she's been waiting all this time for the right man, and if only he would come along then all her problems would be solved. She's waiting for "loves *first* kiss." The kiss is the symbol of Snow White's readiness to be a romantic being. And we've already established that Snow White and The Prince love each other and that he isn't a stranger. He's the adult man who represents the natural counterpart to her as a (now) adult woman. The fact that The Prince has no other name marks him as a symbolic representation of Snow White's readiness to be a woman. Rather than her single-minded desire to be rescued by a man.

See, the princess critics want us to view The Prince's namelessness as further proof that Snow White has pinned her hopes on a totally random guy she doesn't even know. That she's just passively waiting around for any guy at all — even one with no name whatsoever — to rescue her. But it's actually the opposite. The story is about *her* internal transformation. *He* isn't really that important. He's the symbolic conclusion of Snow White's transformation to adulthood and sexual maturity. Not because all adult women need men to complete them (although a fulfilling romantic relationship *is* part of a complete adult life), but because the completion of puberty means that she is now able (whether she is emotionally ready to do so or not) to bear children. As Bettelheim puts it, "the central motif of 'Snow White' is the pubertal girl's surpassing in every way the evil stepmother who, out of jealousy, denies her an independent existence." See, princess critics? It's a completely female story. A woman's journey. The man is almost irrelevant. Doesn't that make you happy? Don't you want to change your mind about *Snow White*? Oh never mind.

*

Snow White was a huge critical and commercial success when it came out in 1937, and it remains one of The American Film Institute's top 100 movies of all time. In the Disney canon, Snow White is precedent-setting. She's the first in a long line of princesses, each trying to depict a woman's journey from childhood to adulthood. And while she certainly is a product of her time, and while it may be debatable whether the allegorical mode of storytelling hits its mark with modern audiences, there's no doubt in my mind that Snow White is a good role model. She's strong, brave, resourceful, and true. She depicts, in a way that children can process and begin to comprehend, the transition to adulthood. She demonstrates how to stay strong and true to yourself even in the most adverse circumstances. Sure, she walks kind of weird, and she sounds even weirder. But those things are only on the outside. A true princess's beauty is on the *inside*. Regardless of what princess critics believe.

Chapter Two: Cinderella

When I was in grad school, studying to be a teacher, I got a job babysitting an adorable two-year-old girl. She loved Disney princesses and so did I, so we got along well. And every day, for months, we would act out the fairy godmother scene from Cinderella. It always went the same way. First, she would run into her room and fling herself facedown onto her pink princess armchair. "Cee-bella so sad!" she would lisp from inside the cushions. Enter the fairy godmother — me. "Don't cry, Cinderella," I would say. "You *shall* go to the ball!" And she would lift her little angelic face from the chair, her blonde hair in disarray — her features still arranged in a two-year-old's facsimile of sadness — and gasp. A light would enter her eyes, her eyebrows would raise in timid hope, a smile would adorn her lips (she was really an excellent actress) and she would stand. I'd lift my hand, wave my magic wand, bibbidi bobbidi boo, and she was transformed. And then we would do it again.

Cinderella is inarguably Disney's most iconic princess. Even if you haven't seen the movie in years (or at all!) you can probably still picture the moment that Cinderella's pink rags, are suddenly, spectacularly, transformed into a glittering white ball gown. You *shall* go to the ball! Even though princess critics want us to favor "feminist" princesses, like Mulan or Merida — because of their "strength" and their "agency" — Cinderella is actually Disney's most popular princess. It's true. A poll conducted by the secret-sharing app Whisper that asked a whopping 80,000 people to reveal their favorite Disney princess crowned Cinderella number 1. Mulan and Merida didn't even make top five. In fact, Elsa from *Frozen* was the only "feminist" princess to make the cut.

It isn't surprising. Almost every culture in the world has a Cinderella story. According to The American Library Association, more than 500 versions of the tale have been documented in Europe alone, with its roots dating as far back as the ninth century. Clearly, there is something about *Cinderella* that deeply resonates with us. Something powerful that speaks to a universal human experience. Otherwise it wouldn't have endured for so long or become so meaningful to its listeners. So what is it? What truth does *Cinderella* illuminate? What secret longing does it help fulfill?

Don't try asking the princess critics. They have literally no idea. "Cinderella is another unfathomably popular princess," says Kayleigh Dray from *Stylist*, "considering she doesn't do or say all that much to help herself in this movie." Okay, thanks for that Kayleigh. Literally everyone for thousands of years has been wrong and *you're* right. Jeez. But Dray is not alone. Princess critics hate *Cinderella*. They, like Mary Grace Garis from *Bustle*, think it's about a girl who sits around until "a rich guy she just met decides she's hot enough to marry." Or Chelsea Mize, also from *Bustle*, who thinks it's a story about a girl who's "pretty enough to grab the prince's attention." Shoes and a dress. For princess critics, that's what *Cinderella* is all about. A girl who sits around doing nothing until a magic lady shows up and solves all her problems by giving her a pretty dress, some fancy shoes, and sending her off to the ball where she can meet a rich and powerful man who will save her from her mean stepmother and stepsisters. Yup, that must be it princess critics. All human beings, for over a thousand years, have been obsessed with fashion and its lifesaving capabilities.

The problem with the princess critics, of course, is that they take everything so literally. It's true that, compared to *Snow White*, Disney's *Cinderella* is a much more realistic movie. Thirteen years had gone by between the release of *Snow White and the Seven Dwarfs,* and *Cinderella*, which came out in 1950. And, in those intervening years, Disney had made an additional twelve feature-length animated films including classics like *Pinocchio, Dumbo,* and *Bambi.* This art form that was a daring experiment when Disney tried it out on *Snow White* was now an established filmmaking technique. Roger Ebert notes a "general smoothing-out of the character's appearances" such that they look less "odd." The whole thing seems much more "normal" to modern eyes and ears. The characters don't look so different from the animated characters that we're used to from the late '80s and early '90s. The voices sound somewhat old-fashioned, but not weird like Snow White's. The characters' movements and dialogue are much more realistic. So, if we were in a particularly forgiving mood, we might excuse the princess critics for forgetting everything we learned in the last chapter about fairy tale shorthand and symbolism. But they'd be wrong to forget it. Of course.

It should be obvious to everyone (including princess critics) that, at its most basic level, *Cinderella* is a classic rags-to-riches narrative. That's one reason it has endured for so long and in so many cultures. It's the oppressed winning out over the oppressor. The plucky little guy triumphing over the bully. The American dream. As folklorist James Deutsch explains in *Smithsonian Magazine*, "the story of Cinderella tells us that virtue is rewarded and evil is punished. You rightly deserve your prince (or princess)." It's humanity's most basic wish-fulfillment dream. We all believe we can be more than what we currently are. That we *deserve* better. Justice will be done. Vengeance will be ours.

But there's even more to *Cinderella* than this. In fact, I believe that Disney's version of this classic tale does two key things that the princess critics — and therefore most viewers — miss. The first is to expertly employ the fairytale shorthand inherent in the story of *Cinderella*. And the second is to *use* that shorthand to make a bold and very specific point that is Disney's own. Even more than being a rags-to-riches story, *Cinderella* is the story of someone becoming who she truly *is*. Yes, she bests her wicked stepfamily by getting what the stepsisters were after — the prince — but it's not *just* that. *Cinderella*, like *Snow White*, is a fairy tale and employs the exact same fairytale shorthand. The dress is not a dress, the shoe is not a shoe, the prince is not just some guy. They're all symbols for Cinderella's inner self. Even a two-year-old could tell you that. You don't have to understand exactly what each item symbolizes to feel the resonance of the story. When my little friend was asking me to repeat the transformation sequence from *Cinderella* over and over again it wasn't the dress she cared about (she had lots of dress up clothes, and they never came into it), and it wasn't the prince (she never actually made it to the ball) it was something so much deeper than that. She, even at two years old, had grasped the deeper meaning of that pivotal transformation sequence — that it isn't just about rags becoming a pretty dress, it's *also* about a downtrodden girl becoming her true self. She grasped it the way we all do, intuitively, when we watch it. All of us, that is, except the princess critics. So that's the first thing I'm going to show you — what the symbols in *Cinderella* are and what they represent.

But I believe Disney goes one step further. All the traditional symbolism of the story of *Cinderella* is there in the movie. But there's an additional layer that is Walt Disney's alone. A powerful statement that would serve as a blueprint for the intention of all his princess narratives from this point onward. By intentionally coupling the established fairytale shorthand of *Cinderella* with Christian themes and metaphors Disney makes a bold pronouncement about the place of love (true love) in our lives. The traditional symbolism of *Cinderella* — which inspires us to become the truest version of ourselves — acts as a springboard for Disney to elevate that concept to a *Christian* vision of becoming who *God* intended us to be. The themes of this movie are

41

deeply religious, and they draw a clear comparison between the transformation of Christ from God, to man, to God again, and Cinderella's transformation from noblewoman, to scullery maid, to princess. By elevating the traditional meaning of the Cinderella story in this way, Disney equates *true* love with *God's* love, letting us know that the Disney princess narrative is not a frivolous love story between a pretty girl and a charming prince. It's so much more than that. It's a map which, if followed, leads to the deepest fulfillment we can achieve on this earth. That's the second thing this chapter will explore.

If Cinderella is Disney's most popular princess, we ought to be able to love her proudly and openly. We shouldn't have to confess our love for her only on anonymous secret-sharing websites — literally whispering that this iconic but unfairly maligned princess is really our favorite. By the time we're done, you'll know that Cinderella's popularity comes not from the sparkliness of her dress, but from the glittering purity of her character.

*

So, who is Cinderella really? Let's begin by delving into the fairytale shorthand of *Cinderella* and the way that it plays out in Disney's retelling. Princess critics think Cinderella is a poor girl, dressed in rags, forced to be a household drudge and comply with the every whim of her evil step mother. But if *that* was who she was, there'd be no point telling her story. See, that isn't who she *is*, that's what she's *doing*. In fact, that's one of the very first things we're told about Cinderella: "Though you're dressed in rags you wear an air of queenly grace / Anyone can see a throne would be your proper place." (That's from a song that plays during the opening credits of the movie.) The rags (and the drudgery and the servitude) are a disguise, hiding Cinderella's true self. Who she *really* is, you see, is a princess. Not a literal princess, a symbolic princess. She embodies the highest virtues a person can possess. She's the perfect woman. But she *looks* like lowest of the low. She's a dirty scullery maid dressed in rags. Her

42

journey won't be through — her story won't be complete — until the inside of her and the outside of her are a match.

This idea of being a princess is one of the most important fairy tale symbols. And it's vital to *us* because . . . well, because this is a book about princesses. But *also* because the symbolism of the princess remains constant throughout all Disney princess movies (except the ones the princess critics ruined) and it means something that ought to help us understand one of the princess critics' central mistakes. In a fairy tale, the point of being a princess is not to have lots of money, lots of pretty things, and a handsome prince to marry. The point is that a princess is a high-born lady. She represents the highest, most true, most virtuous elements of womanhood. She is perfect. Strong, brave, kind, determined, patient — everything we wish we were. You can be a princess even in rags. Cinderella is. We're explicitly *told* that she is. It's a symbol: an external, concrete image of an internal, intangible quality. *That's* the mistake the princess critics make over and over again. The external beauty of a fairy tale princess is shorthand for her *inner* beauty. As Gould explains, "In plays and movies, we understand the visual code that says the good must be beautiful while the wicked are ugly." Disney movies (and fairy tales in general) aren't telling little girls that they ought to be literal princesses. They're telling them to be the best possible versions of themselves.

So, other than the fact that the movie explicitly tells us so, how do we know that Cinderella is actually a princess (in the fairy tale sense of the word)? Well, she shows us. Like Snow White, Cinderella is in an impossible situation. Her doting father has died, leaving her alone with her wicked stepmother and cruel stepsisters, who force her into servitude. Princess critics want us to believe that Cinderella's submission to this situation, like Snow White's, is indicative of her weakness. Garis says, "The problem with Cinderella has always been a lack of genuine motivation. At any point in the 10 or some-odd years that Cinderella works as a housemaid she could've just been like, 'NOPE' and bailed, but she doesn't." But that's ridiculous. Where would she go? What would she do? Live on the streets? Hire herself out as a scullery maid to some other family? Perhaps Cinderella could invent something (an iPad? A flush toilet?) that people want and save up enough money to strike out on her own. No. She's obviously stuck there. We can't judge her based on her circumstances. We have to judge her based on how she handles them. And she handles them with grace, determination, and strength.

When we first meet Cinderella she is singing about what she wants. "A dream is a wish your heart makes," she tells her animal friends. But, when asked what she was dreaming about, Cinderella won't say. If you tell a wish, she explains, it won't come true. But we have a guess about what it might be because, as she's singing, the camera keeps panning to her window where the glittering castle is pretty much the only thing that can be seen. But don't jump to conclusions! She's not dreaming of the man who lives in the castle coming to rescue her (she doesn't know him at all). She's dreaming of getting back a life that once was hers — a life of luxury, comfort, and warmth. A life she once enjoyed in her father's home where she is now a servant. A life represented to her by the glittering luxury of the castle. Cinderella wants to live, if only for a moment, the life of a noblewoman — the life she was born to. We know this because, later, when she doesn't finish her chores in time to go to the ball, it's the *ball* she's sad to miss, not the opportunity to meet the prince. A royal ball, she says to herself would have been "completely wonderful." She knows that the ball is in honor of the prince, but at no point does she hope that that prince will notice her. Unlike Snow White, Cinderella's hope is not to find romance but, rather, to reclaim the life that once was hers.

People like Mize want us to think Cinderella "was willing to continue her crappy lifestyle and never tried to escape her situation. She waited for a prince to whisk her away, and if that hadn't happened, she would have been checking out her reflection in soap bubbles for the rest of her dreary life." But that's not true at all. Cinderella is *stuck* in her "crappy lifestyle" but her dreams for the future tell us that she's longing to escape it. "In dreams you will lose your heartaches," Cinderella sings. "No matter how your heart is grieving / If you keep on believing / The dream that you wish will come true." Cinderella is not content. Far from promoting "a fetishization of housecleaning," as Alyssa Rosenberg suggests on *Slate*, Cinderella is doing what she must until she finds a way out of this nightmare and into the life of her dreams. The life she *used* to have, and longs for again. The thing she *ought* to have, because it is rightfully hers.

Like Snow White, Cinderella has resolved to be cheerful in the face of adversity. Instead of falling all over herself in self-pity, Cinderella's inner strength allows her to make the best of a terrible situation. Immediately after learning that she longs for a better life, but has resolved to make the best of her current situation, we see her interacting with her animal friends. She frees a frightened mouse from a trap, feeds him, and clothes him, and gives him a name. She takes time to visit with the horse and the dog, the mice and the birds, and make sure they are fed and comfortable. Even in amongst all her other chores that she *must* do (lest she face the wrath of her stepfamily) she finds time for chores she *wants* to do because of her care for her animal friends. She even, in an act of charity most of us would not attempt, tries to think of something good about her stepmother's diabolical cat Lucifer who is tormenting the other animals. So we know, very early on, that, in addition to being strong in the face of adversity, Cinderella is caring, compassionate, and kind.

And then we meet her stepfamily. Over and over again, from the very first time we meet the stepsisters, and on throughout the rest of the movie, Cinderella and her stepsisters are intentionally compared to one another. And through these comparisons Cinderella's true character is further illuminated. Immediately before we meet the stepsisters for the first time, we see Cinderella carrying three full breakfast trays up the stairs with dexterity and grace — one on each hand, and one balanced precariously on her head. She even, in a moment of foreshadowing, loses her shoe on the stairs, turns, reclaims it, and turns again to continue up the stairs, all without dropping a thing. And then she enters her stepsisters' rooms, where she finds them sprawled across their beds, backsides in the air, yawning loudly without covering their mouths, whining and complaining in voices that would make anyone's skin crawl. Here they are, the movie seems to say, two examples of womanhood. Take your pick.

And, if that wasn't clear enough, the comparisons continue. The stepmother, offering her daughters a traditional feminine education that is closed to Cinderella, begins a music lesson with them while Cinderella scrubs the floor. While their horrible, out of tune, voices drift down the stairs, they mingle with Cinderella's beautiful, clear tones singing the same song. "Sing sweet nightingale," the girls sing. There wouldn't be anyone listening who couldn't discern which of the girls in the house was truly the "sweet nightingale." Cinderella, we are learning from these early comparisons, inherently possesses the traditional feminine qualities of grace, beauty, and elegance that the stepmother is trying (and failing) to instill in her daughters. But, of course, this isn't enough for princess critics because grace, beauty, and elegance are all qualities of an "oppressed" woman. Not a "strong" and "empowered" one. Which is fine, because (as we'll see in a moment) Cinderella is so much more than graceful, beautiful, and elegant. But, remember, we're trying to build a picture of perfection — of a princess. Her quiet elegance, her effortless grace, her unselfconscious beauty, are all symbolic representations of her inherent goodness. So we'll add them to the mix.

A messenger comes to the door. The prince is holding a ball! But what Cinderella hears and what the stepsisters hear, when this message is read, are two very different things. "Cinderella never asked for a prince. She asked for a night off and a dress," quipped young adult novelist Kiera Cass. For Cinderella, as we've already seen, the exciting prospect is the ball — a chance to be seen as her true self. For the stepsisters, though, the exciting prospect is the prince. Contrary to all the princess critics' complaints that Cinderella's "dreams all revolve around marrying someone, anyone," (as Dray proclaims) it's the *stepsisters* — the example of what a woman should *not* be — who immediately fixate on marrying the prince. And then fall all over themselves trying to be beautiful enough to attract him — as if outer beauty was what was important here.

In this moment of learning about the ball, we not only see that Cinderella isn't obsessed with marriage and physical appearance (as the princess critics want us to believe), we also see her stand up for herself and show the "backbone" the princess critics say she doesn't have. As the stepsisters squabble and preen Cinderella realizes that the invitation is extended to "every eligible maiden" in the land and that, as such, *she* is also invited. Her sense of self is intact. She knows who she is. *She* is an eligible maiden, worthy of attending the ball. And she says so. Would a drudge — content to be a drudge, totally broken by her stepfamily, and afraid of their wrath — speak up in this moment? I don't think so. But Cinderella does. "Why, that means *I* can go too!" she says. And even when her stepfamily scoffs, and teases — "I'd be honored your highness, would you mind holding my broom?" — Cinderella stands firm. And she wins. Her stepmother agrees that Cinderella may go to the ball, as long as she finds something suitable to wear, and completes all her chores before it's time to leave. Of course her stepmother fully intends to give her so many chores she couldn't possibly complete them, but it's a victory nonetheless. And it shows that Cinderella has a strong sense of herself, and a fierce and determined inner drive to get what she wants. As Deutsch reminds us, "Cinderella is not a passive wimp who simply wishes upon a star. She makes things happen through her fortitude, perseverance, and wise decisions."

This is who Cinderella really is. A kind, caring, generous girl, who hasn't forgotten her true identity, who stands up for herself with quiet determination, and works hard to get what she wants. A princess. Not because of her external beauty or her desire to marry a prince, but because of the internal qualities which manifest — through fairy tale shorthand — in her beauty and grace. So Cinderella, who has been aided by her animal friends, comes downstairs ready for the ball wearing her mother's old gown, adorned with her stepsister's castoffs. But, when Cinderella's stepmother sees what she's wearing and points it out to the stepsisters, they rip her dress to pieces. So that, by the time the stepmother and stepsisters leave for the ball, the stepsisters are wearing their finest dresses, and Cinderella is in rags. It's backwards. The stepsisters are internally ugly, but externally dressed in beautiful clothes. And Cinderella is internally beautiful, but dressed in ugly tatters.

This is the pivotal moment. Princess critics complain because Cinderella's efforts to get to the ball on her own — with her mother's dress — don't work out. "Not only is this poor girl kind of enslaved," says Sonia Saraiya on *Nerve*, "but then pretty much everything she tries to do to make her life better blows up in her face." They see this as her attempt at agency and dislike that it is thwarted in favor of the fairy godmother's intervention. But Cinderella's agency or non-agency isn't the point here. The point is that her mother's dress, done up with the stepsisters' sash and pearls, isn't good enough. It isn't *her*. Only magic can make this right. Only magic can manifest internal qualities as external ones — can allow the world to see with their eyes something that occurs in the soul. Princess critics think the dress is just a dress. That Cinderella is a person who couldn't even find a dress to wear without magical intervention. But that's just silly. Now that the stepsisters are gone, she could have raided their closets. *That's* not the point. What happens to Cinderella is not a thing that could actually happen. Anyone can wear a pretty dress. The stepsisters were wearing pretty dresses when they left for the ball. But there isn't, in real life, a way to visually display your true self. *That's* what the fairy godmother provides.

The fairy godmother gathers together a bunch of ordinary things (a pumpkin, some mice, a dog, a horse) and elevates them to the level of the extraordinary. But, in the movie, these are not just any mice, dog, and horse. They are Cinderella's friends, who have served her faithfully and stuck by her. And so, just as *she* will, they become expressions of who *they* truly are. Faithful steeds, trusty footmen, loyal coach drivers. And when all this glittering finery is complete, it's Cinderella's turn. With a final wave of her magic wand, the fairy godmother reveals Cinderella's true self — a transformation that has stuck in the memories of countless viewers for almost seventy years. The dress shimmers and sparkles with the light of truth, and (in Disney's version at least) it's white like the purity of Cinderella's soul. And, raising the hem of her dress, Cinderella finds she is wearing slippers made of glass. Glass like a mirror. Reflecting her true image. Finally, Cinderella *looks* the way she *is*. And, in the symbolism of the fairytale shorthand, she is now transformed for all the world to see. Her internal self made visible.

Only magic could have done this. Because, not only does Cinderella's dress represent to us, the viewer, that we are now witnessing her true self, but it represents this to everyone else in the *story* too. Princess critics hate the fact that Cinderella and Prince Charming fall in love at first sight. They think it means that they're only attracted to each other physically — that Prince Charming fell in love with her because, as Mize puts it, she's "pretty enough to grab the prince's attention." But that's not the point. Prince Charming, who has been yawning and rolling his eyes through the presentation of all the other beautiful ladies, sees Cinderella in her magic dress and glass slippers and knows immediately that she is someone worthy of his love. He sees her true self. Because that's the magic of the dress and the shoes. That's what they represent.

Neither Cinderella, nor Prince Charming, expected to find love at the ball. The whole ball was arranged by the king, who wants to see his son married so that he can start creating heirs to the throne. Charming couldn't care less, and doesn't think he's going to find his true love by meeting a bunch of random women and dancing with them. Even the grand duke, the king's advisor, says the whole ball concept is "a pretty plot for a fairy tale, but in real life it was foredoomed to failure." As in, only in a fairy tale, would a prince and a princess be able to recognize each other for who they truly are just by looking at each other. It's *not* something that would happen in real life. Luckily, this *is* a fairy tale. Even with this line right there in the movie, the princess critics still miss it. They still take the whole thing literally. But they're wrong. They're so *obviously* wrong.

When Cinderella realizes that she has lost track of the time and that she must flee, the prince tries to stop her. "How will I find you?" he calls to her, "I don't even know your name!" Who are you? What is your name? He's just met the girl of his dreams and she's running off without leaving her number. Of course he's going to ask her name and where she lives. But it's also worth nothing that a person's *name* is also often shorthand for who they *are*. Their inner selves. It's a trope that appears in some of the later Disney princess movies — most notably *The Little Mermaid,* but also *Aladdin.* Prince Charming feels that he won't be able to find Cinderella again because he doesn't know who she *is.* He wants her to leave him with something that is, without a doubt, *her,* so that he can find her again. Her name. But, instead, he ends up with her slipper. Not as helpful, if this was a realistic story. I mean, if I left my shoe with a guy I met in a bar it's very unlikely he'd be able to use it to figure out where I lived. But, in the fairytale shorthand of *Cinderella,* the shoe (as we've already established) is the symbol of her true self. And *that* is why the prince ends up with it.

At midnight, the dress, the pumpkin, the horses, and the footmen all return to what they were before. The fairy godmother's gift was not permanent. Cinderella must *make* it permanent, with her actions later on. But one thing is left. Her glass slippers haven't faded away. She still has one of them. And the prince has the other. And, of course, *this* will prove integral to the final sequence of the plot. Because the shoes — those reflectors of Cinderella's true self — are the only way the prince can find her again. Not because he can't remember anything about her, or because he wouldn't necessarily recognize her face, but because the shoes are representative of who she truly is. That's why only Cinderella will fit into them. (Did you really think there wasn't a single other girl in the kingdom with the same size feet as Cinderella?) They're the perfect safeguard against the prince choosing the wrong girl. The girl who wore these slippers is the embodiment of "princess" to his embodiment of "prince." The shoe is a physical symbol of Cinderella's "princess-ness." Only the girl whose foot fits inside this shoe is worthy of being revealed as a princess.

When Cinderella learns that the prince (who she didn't intend to fall in love with, but whose own true self has revealed itself to her) intends to marry her, she immediately starts acting more like herself. She hands the dirty laundry back to the stepsisters, refusing to do her usual chores, and goes upstairs to look at her face in the mirror — not because she's obsessed with her physical appearance, but because her true self is suddenly reflected there. And this behavior finally alerts the stepmother that Cinderella is the girl the prince danced with at the ball. The minute Cinderella begins to project her true self out into the world, the world begins to see it too. And it prompts the stepmother to lock her in her room so she can't try on the shoe. But, again, the animals come to Cinderella's rescue and, after a valiant fight against Lucifer the cat, bring her the key. And so, Cinderella, in an act of agency the princess critics refuse to credit her with, rushes downstairs to announce that she is, indeed, the prince's true love. And, even though the stepmother causes the slipper to be smashed on the ground, Cinderella will not be dissuaded. She has the other slipper. She *is* who she says she is. A princess. Even in rags.

So *that's* what the fairytale shorthand of *Cinderella* tells us. It's a tale that seeks to represent a universal human need: to be seen for who we truly are. We all long, in one way or another, for the world to see our true selves and, in one way or another, we can't quite make them. And even if we hadn't thought all this through before, even if we couldn't have said exactly what all these things represented, we knew in our hearts that this story is about more than shoes and a dress. We had to. Otherwise we wouldn't have loved it as we do. The story wouldn't have endured as it has. This is not a superficial story. It's a deep and universal one that speaks to us whether we're two or one hundred and two. The only reasons we now *think* Cinderella (and other Disney princess movies) is superficial is because we've bought into the princess critics' superficial interpretation of it. We have to stop being so literal. We've got to stop listening to the princess critics.

*

The traditional symbolism of *Cinderella* is, as we've just seen, alive and well in the animated movie. But, as I mentioned earlier, there's an additional layer that is Disney's own. I believe (and will endeavor to prove) that Walt Disney intentionally meant to link the themes of *Cinderella* to the Christian idea of redemption. And, in doing so, he made a bold statement about the importance of true love. A statement that resonates down the years and provides a lens through which to view all the other princess narratives to come.

First, let's establish that Disney was, in fact, a Christian. In 1949, one year before the release of *Cinderella*, Disney said, "I believe firmly in the efficacy of religion, in its powerful influence on a person's whole life. It helps immeasurably to meet the storm and stress of life and keep you attuned to the Divine inspiration. Without inspiration, we would perish. All I ask of myself, 'Live a good Christian life.' To that objective I bend every effort in shaping my personal, domestic, and professional activities and growth." So we know that Christianity, and its themes, were very important to Disney, and that he believed that they had a place in his "professional activities." So we can at least speculate that it would be likely that Christian ideas would manifest in Disney's films.

I am not a biblical scholar. In fact, until about four years before the writing of this book, I wasn't even a Christian. But I *am* going to put forward the theory that, in a very broad-strokes and generalized way, the story of Disney's Cinderella mirrors the story of Christ. And I am going to further theorize that this connection was intentional on Disney's part, and that it says something specific about the Disney princess narrative and its intention. It's not a direct mirror. It's not just a retelling of the Christ story. But the connection is there. And it goes a long way in refuting the princess critics once and for all. So, let's begin.

Cinderella is someone who, because of the actions of her father, has come down from on high. "Though you're dressed in rags you wear an air of queenly grace. Anyone can see a throne would be your proper place." As we already discussed, this could (and should) be taken to mean that Cinderella is really a princess in disguise. (Not a literal princess, obviously, but the fairy tale symbol of princess. The perfect woman.) But this idea of "throne" could also evoke another kind of throne (a heavenly one), and, of course, the idea of "grace" is a very Christian theme. So Cinderella, like Jesus, has come from on high (in Cinderella's case, she's "high-born") and has come down to lowlier circumstances. And both of them choose to mingle with the people (or animals) that no one else will associate with (in Jesus' case prostitutes and tax collectors, in Cinderella's case mice and birds). In other words: "he gave up his divine privileges; he took the humble position of a slave and was born as a human being," (Philippians). And the people (okay, okay, or animals) they associate with, pledge allegiance to them and would follow them anywhere.

From the very beginning of *Cinderella* (in the second scene), we are introduced to a cat named (wait for it) Lucifer. Lucifer is the arch nemesis of Cinderella's pals the mice. He's always trying to spoil their plans, steal what's theirs, and, ultimately, take their lives. And Lucifer is the only person (cat) in Cinderella's whole life (which is full of pretty awful people) that Cinderella can think of nothing good to say about. So we've got Cinderella, come down from on high, to mingle with the lowest of the low, coming into contact with Lucifer.

Cinderella talks a great deal about "belief." When we first meet her, she is fervently expressing her certainty that "If you keep on believing / The dream that you wish will come true." Even in this dark situation that's she's found herself in since her father's death, Cinderella holds on to her "belief." She "wishes" and she "dreams" and she "believes." I think it would be fair to say that Cinderella is praying. She believes that if she wishes and dreams hard enough, her desires will become real. For her, there is something out there — some cosmic force — that will look out for her, protect her, and ultimately lift her out of her difficult circumstance. As Jesus says in John, "the one who believes has eternal life."

While she is waiting for her prayers to be answered, Cinderella spends her time showing compassion to those who are usually overlooked. Trying to teach them to be kind, even to those who want to do them harm, and to support one another. Cinderella specifically entrusts the care of Gus, a new mouse in the house, to Jaq, a mouse who has been friends with Cinderella for a while. Take care of each other, she teaches them, be brave, resourceful and kind, avoid the cat. They are like her disciples. The mice (and the birds) do everything in their power help Cinderella achieve her goals. They risk their lives to create a dress for her even though they don't fully understand its significance. But they don't have the power to create the kind of dress Cinderella really needs. It must come from somewhere else.

At Cinderella's lowest point — when her stepsisters have ripped her dress (and her dream of going to the ball) to shreds, and left her behind — Cinderella runs to the garden, weeping. And there, for just a moment, she has a crisis of faith. "There's nothing left to believe in," she sobs. Everything she thought was true has been called into question. "My God, my God, why have you forsaken me?" Jesus cries out from the cross. And, before you go there, please don't think I'm saying that not being allowed to go to a party is the same as dying on the cross in order to save mankind. Remember the fairy tale shorthand here. It seems that all hope of Cinderella becoming her true self is lost.

She believes she has failed. It seems that no one will help her. It seems that no one will see her for who she truly is.

It is at the exact moment of Cinderella's seeming loss of faith that the fairy godmother appears. The fairy *GOD*mother. *Hello*! "If you'd lost all your faith," the fairy godmother says, "I couldn't be here." A fairy godmother, apparently, can only appear to someone who believes in fairy godmothers. And Cinderella has never truly stopped believing. So, here, at her lowest point, comes salvation. A fairy godmother who, in Disney's version, proclaims she is here to perform "a miracle." And what is the miracle she's here to perform? She will clothe Cinderella in the garb of her true self. She will reveal her, in her true form, to the world. She will resurrect her. But only for a short time. Only until midnight.

"It's like a dream," Cinderella says, examining her reflection, "a wonderful dream come true." Her prayers have been answered. The dream that she wished has come true. Her belief has been validated. All is right with the world. And off she goes to the ball. Where no one recognizes her. Transformed, as she is, into her true self she is like Jesus risen from the dead — somehow unrecognizable to those who had known her intimately. It says in Luke: "Jesus himself came up and walked along with them; but they were kept from recognizing him." No one who knows Cinderella from her life before (her stepmother or her stepsisters) can figure out who the beautiful young girl dancing with the prince could be. But the prince, who has never met her before, recognizes her as the love of his life. The prince who, in fairy tale shorthand, is the most perfect version of manhood recognizes Cinderella, the most perfect version of womanhood. And their union is at the center of this entire transformation.

"So this is love," Cinderella and the prince sing to each other. "This is what makes life *divine*." "This key to all *heaven* is mine." "This is the *miracle* that I've been dreaming of." This is it. Heaven. The triumphant reward. The fulfillment of Cinderella's true self. Love. True love. "Wives," it says in Ephesians, "submit yourselves to your own husbands as you do to the Lord." Disney is saying that the princess narrative is not just a story about a girl and a boy falling in love. It's an expression of the divine on earth. Love — human connection — with someone who recognizes you for who you truly are, who shows his true self to you, and with whom you can be complete, is the greatest happiness we can achieve on this earth. It's the closest we can come to the divine. As Gould says, "The Cinderella story is, in its own way, a religious vision that describes the entrance of grace into our lives." When the prince and the princess recognize each other — either through true love's kiss, love at first sight, or some other, more realistic means — it is an experience akin to redemption.

So Cinderella has appeared on earth in her true form. And no one recognized her. Not, that is, until Lucifer the cat (remember him?) is shoved out the window by Cinderella's animal friends. He falls to his death, snarling and hissing all the way. Vanquished. "I saw Satan fall like lightning from heaven," it says in Luke. And, in that exact moment, Cinderella emerges from her room, pulling from her pocket the symbol of her true self: the glass slipper. Which, when it is placed on her foot, immediately reveals her true self to everyone in the room. And, the very next moment, Cinderella ascends to heaven — she marries the prince. And the story is complete.

*

You see, we love *Cinderella* because it's a story about something we all want: to become our true selves. To be *seen* as our true selves. To be *loved* as our true selves. It's not the dress. It's not the shoes. It's not the handsome prince, or the fairy godmother, or the ball. It's what those things *represent*. What we *know* they represent. The princess critics have made us forget the we know it. Their literal take on every movie they watch siphons off all the symbolism, leaving only an empty shell. That's *not* the way to view this movie. The story makes no sense without the symbolism. And we *know* that it makes sense. We feel it. A two-year-old can feel it. Don't listen to the princess critics, okay? Love Cinderella. She's worth it.

And remember this, too: Disney means for you to understand something about true love. He wants you to see that his princesses don't just fall in love with the first guy they meet. They don't wait around for a man — any man — to rescue them. They wait for a man who sees their true selves. They wait for a man whose true self *they* can see too. They wait for that man, and then they cleave to him. They complete their lives with love. Not because they can't survive without a man. But because everyone is better off with love in their lives. Because someone who knows who they truly are can find someone who completes them. True love, *Cinderella* tells us, is divine.

Chapter Three: Aurora

I hate to say this but, when it comes to *Sleeping Beauty*, the princess critics kind of have a point. The princess (Aurora) spends only eighteen minutes, out of seventy five, on screen and delivers around eighteen lines of dialogue. Not much to work with. Not to mention the fact that the movie is kind of boring. Okay, fine, a lot boring. Plus, *Snow White* was pretty much the same story, only done a whole lot better. A wicked witch casts a spell on a princess so she falls asleep and only true love's kiss can wake her up? Yup, same story. Same symbolism of jealous witches, and falling asleep, and true love's kiss. Yes, they're common fairytale tropes, and we're certainly open to another movie that includes them, but it's got to offer something more than the one we've already seen. And *Sleeping Beauty*, well, it kind of doesn't.

But we shouldn't write this movie off. Regardless of my own personal feelings about this movie, and the contemporary critics' reaction, many many people *love* Aurora. In the Whisper poll that asked 80,000 people to name their favorite princess, Aurora placed third. Try asking people you know who their favorite princess is and, before long, you'll get at least one — if not more than one — answer of "Aurora." But there is no doubt that the movie is problematic. The film received a poor showing at the box office, luke warm reactions from critics, and, ultimately, spelled the demise of the Disney princess narrative for the next thirty years

The real (and actually kind of fascinating) problem with *Sleeping Beauty* is that it's stuck between two modes of storytelling. The traditional fairytale mode employed in *Snow White* and *Cinderella*, and the more modern, more realistic mode which Disney had begun to branch out into. *Sleeping Beauty* came out in 1959, nine years after *Cinderella*. In the meantime, Disney had made *Alice in Wonderland, Lady and the Tramp,* and *Peter Pan* — three films based, not on fairy tales, but on more modern stories which didn't employ fairytale shorthand. The characters in these films, though still old-fashioned to our eyes, were much more realistic and flawed. They make mistakes, suffer jealousies, and have bad tempers. They can be petty, they play pranks, and they have checkered pasts. Think Peter Pan getting angry with Wendy for earning the affection of the Lost Boys, or Tramp's criminal history. Although these movies are still for children, they're not fairytales. And that matters.

When Disney Studios began work on *Sleeping Beauty*, Walt Disney had a very specific mission for the film. He was hoping it would be a "moving illustration," and a return to the grand scale of films like *Pinocchio* — another film based on a fairy tale. In other words, Disney, it seems, was trying to steer his team back towards the sweeping, fairytale narrative, and away from the more modern, more realistic one of the recent films. But Walt himself was busy overseeing the first of his theme parks (Disneyland) and focusing on the company's television programs, so his team was on its own when it came to fulfilling Disney's directives. The result is a pretty mixed up narrative — neither traditional fairytale nor realistic story — but, instead, something caught between the two. A mash-up of Aurora's fairytale story on the one hand, with the more realistically told story of the fairies, Prince Phillip, and Maleficent on the other. But I would argue that this mash-up is untenable. You can't have a symbolic character interacting with a realistic one as if they existed on the same plane. It just doesn't work. And it showed.

But that doesn't make *Sleeping Beauty* antifeminist, no matter what the princess critics say. What makes this movie interesting — though perhaps not entertaining — is the development of realistic, flawed, strong female characters (in the form of three feisty fairies) juxtaposed with a purely allegorical one (in the form of Aurora). The fairies (not Aurora) are the true protagonists of this movie and it is because of their heroic actions that the story reaches its happy ending. But this confusion over who we're actually rooting for — and what kind of story this really is — creates a rather rambling and disjointed tale.

So, to understand *Sleeping Beauty* we have to review the fairytale shorthand going on in Aurora's narrative, look at the development of this new type of Disney narrative, and see what the juxtaposition of these two modes does to the story. And, when we're through, we'll be able to see how the early mode of traditional storytelling *and* the more modern mode of storytelling paved the way for the Disney renaissance thirty years later. *That* is *Sleeping Beauty's* contribution to the Disney princess canon.

*

In contrast to the other two Disney princess movies that came before, we don't even *meet* the princess (except as a baby) for the first twenty minutes of *Sleeping Beauty*. Instead, we are introduced to King Stefan and his queen (Aurora's parents), King Hubert and Prince Phillip (royalty from a nearby kingdom), three fairies named Flora, Fauna, and Merryweather, and an evil sorceress named Maleficent. In a traditional princess narrative, these would all be the secondary characters — appearing at key moments to represent important aspects of the princess's journey (like the fairy godmother in *Cinderella* or The Prince in *Snow White*). Instead, they're introduced right at the beginning of the movie. The prince, whom normally we'd first meet on his gallant steed or dressed in his regal finery, is a child who looks into the cradle at his future bride and raises a skeptical eyebrow. The three fairies who, in their physical appearance and entrance in a ray of fairy dust, are reminiscent of Cinderella's fairy godmother, act more like three cozy old ladies, cooing over the baby and fumbling to get into line in front of the king and queen. And the two kings, who ordinarily would be peripheral characters (or completely absent) embrace one another and slap each other on the back like old friends. But all these secondary characters, who behave much more like real people than their symbolic counterparts, are here at this christening party to *create* a princess. A traditional one.

The fairies have come to offer Aurora magical gifts. The first is the gift of beauty. We've seen already what a princess's beauty symbolizes: internal goodness. And we've seen, too, how the princess critics miss this symbolism and assume that Disney means us to understand that physical beauty is a woman's most important asset. And they make this mistake about *Sleeping Beauty* too. The Feminist Disney Blog finds the gift of beauty "disturbing" and Leigh Butler, of *Tor.com*, says, "no one thought maybe a cooler thing to give her would be, I dunno, the 'gift of intelligence' or 'gift of hand-eye coordination,' or whatever." But those would be gifts for a *real* person, and it is clear — in the very giving of this gift of beauty — that Aurora is not a real person but a fairytale princess.

The second gift is song — another symbol. A beautiful voice means a beautiful soul. Disney movies would use voice as a metaphor to great effect in *The Little Mermaid* thirty years later, but it's the same metaphor here. A princess's voice (or anyone's "voice" really) is symbolic of her true self. So, a beautiful singing voice means a beautiful inner self. These three fairies, who seem more like three absent-minded grannies, are turning this baby into a Disney princess — complete with symbolic attributes. We don't know what the third gift would have been — grace or virtue, maybe, who knows? — because at the exact moment that Merryweather is about to bestow her gift, Maleficent arrives in a blaze of green fire.

Maleficent is easily the most interesting character in the movie. Even the animators thought so. "Nobody cared much about the Prince or Aurora," said Floyd Norman, one of the animators who worked on *Sleeping Beauty*. "It was Maleficent who was really the core of this film. And in a way it was a shame that we didn't do more with her." Her main appeal, I think, is that, while she's evil — and boy is she evil! — her motives are incredibly human. Maleficent is miffed because she didn't get invited to the party. "Maleficent doesn't know anything about love or kindness or the joy of helping others," the fairies explain. She's lonely. She wants to be invited. But, because she's an evil witch, her people skills leave something to be desired. Maleficent has the ultimate case of FOMO. How much more human can you get?

And yet, when this lady with some pretty realistic problems turns her attention to the princess she gets very symbolic. Because Maleficent has been excluded from the party she bestows a curse on the baby Aurora: "Before the sun sets on her sixteenth birthday she will prick her finger on the spindle of a spinning wheel and die." Why her sixteenth birthday? Well, adulthood of course. Before Aurora is able to fully blossom into a woman (as Snow White did) she will prick her finger on a spinning wheel and die. This has always seemed like a really weird choice to me. Prick your finger on a spinning wheel? Um . . . okay. But . . . *why* exactly? Symbolism, of course! According to Joan Gould in *Spinning Straw Into Gold*, "spinning is a metaphor for transformation" and a spindle looks "remarkably like a man's genitals." Pricking her finger on the spinning wheel, drawing blood, and falling asleep is a metaphorical representation — much like Snow White eating the apple and falling asleep — of beginning to menstruate and becoming ready to bear children. So Maleficent delivers a curse that is so symbolic as to be almost unintelligible. It is clear that, with Aurora, we are in the fairytale realm. But with everyone else? Not so much.

The fairies aren't powerful enough to reverse the curse (there's their realistic-ness again, they're limited) but they can take the edge off.

She won't die, she'll only fall asleep. And, "from this slumber you shall wake when true love's kiss the spell shall break." There's the fairytale shorthand again. True love's kiss: the recognition of two compatible souls meeting one another, the young girl waking up into her new role as woman. The same symbolism we encountered in *Snow White* and, to a lesser degree, *Cinderella*. Aurora's whole life has been mapped out for her in fairytale terms. There she is, a little baby in a world that seems populated by fairly realistic characters (albeit ones with magical powers), destined to live the life of a fairytale princess.

But Aurora's parents don't react symbolically. Burn all the spinning wheels in the kingdom! King Stefan decrees. Burn the spinning wheels??! Doesn't he understand? It's not the physical spinning wheels that are the problem, it's what they *represent*. He can't burn *that*. Stefan is attacking a symbolic problem through literal means. (Kind of like a princess critic!) And, just to be safe, they decide (along with the fairies) that Aurora must be hidden. But, again, you can't hide from your symbolic destiny. The fairies (being magical) should know that. But it is *they* that suggest the remedy: Aurora will come to live with them in the woods. She will be raised as their child and know nothing of her true parentage. The fairies will give up magic and live as humble peasant women. In essence, they will give up their fairytale-ness and live as human beings. But trying to hide a fairytale princess's true self is like . . . well, it's like dressing her in rags and expecting no one will see her for who she truly is. The fairies should have known better. But they don't.

And yet, in this rather confused plan, something interesting is happening. These fairies, who ought to be the motherly God stand-ins we saw in *Cinderella*, are displaying qualities that are normally attributed to the princess: bravery, self-sacrifice, and determination. This is a huge thing they are doing for Aurora and her parents. They are giving up the thing that makes them who they are (their magic) in order to save a girl they've only just met. They will become physically weak and vulnerable and, in doing so, show their internal grit and resolve.

Strength in the face of adversity, resourcefulness, self-sacrifice: these are all things we've seen in the princesses that came before (and will see again in the princesses that come later). Very early on we are learning that, regardless of the film's name, it is the three fairies who are really the heroines. As Butler writes, "it is Flora, Fauna, and Merryweather who make *all* the critical decisions in the film, the ones which drive the action." So we've got three old ladies who seem to embody many of the characteristics typically attributed to the princess.

And then we meet Aurora. Sixteen years have passed and Aurora is now a willowy girl, wandering dreamily through the forest, knowing nothing of her true identity. But the fairies are getting ready to tell her the truth. It's her birthday and the fairies send her out into the woods so they can prepare a special party for her. And out she steps through the cottage door. Butler describes Aurora as "basically a Barbie doll knockoff who does nothing the whole film but sing wistfully about Finding Her Man, before becoming the ultimate passive Damsel in Distress." And, in a lot of ways, this isn't completely wrong. That Aurora looks like a Barbie doll is totally true. And that's not a coincidence. 1959 (the year that *Sleeping Beauty* came out) was also the year the Barbie doll was invented. Aurora even has the slanted bare feet Barbies used to have to fit into those plastic high-heeled shoes. But her resemblance to Barbie just tells us exactly what we already know: by the standard of the day, Aurora is generically beautiful. Of course she is! She was gifted beauty at the beginning of the movie, and she has it. Because she's a princess. Outer beauty equals inner beauty in fairytale shorthand. We know this already. It's also true that what she does (pretty much the only thing she does in the whole movie besides prick her finger) is sing a song about finding a man.

It's like the traditional fairytale princess symbolism has been boiled down to its most basic elements in Aurora. She's beautiful on the outside so we infer that she's beautiful on the inside. She's becoming a woman so she's looking for a man who will represent her

64

adult self. Disney hasn't taken the time to create a character (even a symbolic one) for Aurora. She's all symbols without a person to embody them. She's beautiful, she's positive and cheerful even though her life is humble, she wants to find her soul mate. But the *reasons* for these things are unclear. Unlike Snow White and Cinderella whose difficult lives have tested their true princess-ness, Aurora is loved and well cared for (if poor). Aside from the fact that she has a curse hanging over her head (which she knows nothing about) she has endured none of the hardship of the other princesses. She has three foster mothers who love her, she has been well taken care of, and has not suffered. There is nothing that has forced her to develop the internal strength the other princesses posses (the strength the *fairies* possess in this story). So, in that sense, she *is* superficial. But not because she's just a beautiful maiden looking for a man (as the princess critics want us to think) but because the movie forces us to fill in all the blanks. They are giving us *only* the symbolism, with no character to act as a vessel for it. *That's* why Aurora comes across as rather vapid, particularly in comparison to all the more fleshed-out characters around her.

"I guess it kind of goes without saying that the relationship [between Aurora and Phillip] occurs at a ridiculously fast pace and their desire for each other is based on dreams, beauty, and the sound of singing voices," says the *Feminist Disney Blog*. Goes without saying, the implication is, because *all* Disney princesses fall in love this way. But *we* know that's not true. What *is* true, is that it happens this way for Aurora. "They say if you dream a thing more than once, it's sure to come true," Aurora tells her animal friends. Sound familiar? "If you keep on believing the dream that you wish will come true." It's exactly the same sentiment Cinderella expresses at the beginning of *her* movie. But even though Aurora *is* looking for a man, she's not looking for *any* man. "You'll love me at once / The way you did once / Upon a dream," she sings of her dream man. She waiting for *the one*. And we know, from Disney's statement in Cinderella, what the symbolism of *that* means. It's just that the movie hasn't taken the time to introduce her to the man (except as a very small child) before she expresses this sentiment. "We will walk together and talk together and just before we say goodbye he takes me in his arms and . . . I wake up." Aurora is expressing her own symbolism in a way that the other princesses don't. And, because we were introduced to Phillip at the start of the movie, we feel sure that he is, in fact, the one for her. Aurora, and her narrative, are *all* symbols.

But when the man actually shows up we suddenly pivot from the symbolic to the realistic. Instead of being the traditional, nameless prince symbolically representing Aurora's adulthood, and her connection to God's love, *this* prince has a name (Phillip) and he's a real, live person. He tells jokes, he falls off his horse, and he has to convince the stubborn animal to follow the sound of Aurora's voice by offering him extra carrots. He's a guy. A pretty regular guy. But *this* is the prince who's supposed to complete Aurora's symbolic destiny by giving her true love's kiss and breaking her curse. It's a little jarring. On the one hand, he's by far the most interesting prince we've encountered yet. For the first time, young girls are being presented with a character they might actually *meet*. Not really of course (he's a cartoon) but a *kind* of guy they might meet. He's handsome, romantic, funny, a little bit sarcastic, and not afraid to make a fool of himself for a good cause. Basically, he's totally crush-worthy, in a way the other princes aren't, because *those* princes are just symbols. But this actual guy, who we begin to think might possibly fall for *us* because we, too, are real, goes straight for the symbolic princess.

He interrupts Aurora's song (just like The Prince interrupts Snow White's) and proclaims himself to be the man she met "once upon a dream." He's her soul mate, the one she's been looking for. And she believes him (because in her world there are *only* symbols) and, in a very short space of time, finds herself resting her head trustingly on his shoulder. In one sense, it does ring a little false, in a way that Snow White's and Cinderella's quick romances don't.

Because for *them* the symbolism of the prince and his role in their narrative has been well-established in the movie. But Phillip is a regular guy. Who's to say he *is* her soul mate? But, in another sense — the sense the movie clearly wants us to perceive — we know he's her soul mate because *she* recognizes him as such. Aurora, who possesses a fairytale princess's ability to see the internal prince-ness of her soul mate has chosen Phillip. But does Phillip have that same power? Does he see the internal princess-ness of this peasant maid with a beautiful voice? Clearly he does, since he followed her voice and proclaimed himself in love with her. But it's harder to tell *why* he does this, given that we haven't necessarily established that he has a fairy tale prince's ability to discern the princess's true self. But, there it is. They're in love and Aurora is ready to tell her foster mothers that she's met the man of her dreams. She tells him to come to the cottage tonight and he runs off to tell his father, King Hubert, that he's giving up the throne to marry a peasant woman.

It's worth pausing here to point out the *very* feminist thing that's happening here. Something that the princess critics refuse to acknowledge but that's there nonetheless. Aurora doesn't *know* that Phillip is a prince. She thinks he's a peasant just like her. In her book *In Defense of the Princess*, Jerramy fine writes, "We watch Aurora wander barefoot through the woods completely uninterested in aristocratic affairs." She's not looking for a way out of her poverty by marrying a prince. She's only looking for a soul mate to make her feel complete — to help her transition from childhood to adulthood. In fact, when she learns that *she* is, in fact, a princess, she's devastated because she thinks it means she won't be able to be with her true love. There is nothing about wealth or power that appeals to her. And Phillip, who really *is* a prince and knows it, is willing to give it all up for the woman he loves. "Give up the throne? The kingdom? To marry some nobody?" his father splutters, when Phillip tells him of his intentions. And the answer, Phillip tells him, is yes.

But princess critics, obsessed as they are with the perceived anti-feminism of true love, don't see this startling reality: *Sleeping Beauty* is clearly putting forward the notion that royalty, power, and money mean nothing. No gold diggers need apply. This is another important aspect of Disney princesses. They are *never* concerned with the physical trappings of royalty. They embody only the symbolism of prince and princess that we've already discussed. And nowhere is that idea stated more explicitly than in *Sleeping Beauty*.

So, Aurora goes home to tell the fairies her good news. But, while she's been gone, the fairies have made a terrible (and totally human) mistake. In trying to set up a birthday party for Aurora without using their magic, they've made a mess of everything. It's slightly unclear how they've gone sixteen years without being able to sew a dress, or bake a cake, or clean the house, but apparently they have. Their attempts to do these things are laughably ridiculous. And so, here again, we are shown their "real-ness." These are not fairies in the traditional, fairytale sense. They are little old ladies who are doing their best but are out of their element. And *because* they're out of their element, and because they have come to love Aurora as mothers (another human quality), they decide to use their magic. And, being the little old ladies they are, they begin to bicker. Will the dress be pink or blue? And they find themselves in a magic battle, flinging blue and pink sparks around the house and, accidentally, up the chimney, where Maleficent's crow minion sees these sparks and flies back to report to his mistress that he's found Aurora.

But, hang on, this isn't how fairytales are supposed to work. It shouldn't be the magical caretakers that make a mistake. According to the fairytale rules, they are meant to be all-knowing protectors and guides. They are meant to dispense the wisdom that puts the princess on her path to discovering her true self. The *princess* can make mistakes. Snow White can take a bite of the poisoned apple. Cinderella can lose track of time at the ball. Not the *godmother*! But, in *Sleeping Beauty*, the very people who have been protecting the princess for sixteen years are the ones who inadvertently betray her. What gives?

And Maleficent, who's been harboring her very human grudge for the past sixteen years, is back in business. This, too, is unlike the traditional wicked witch. She couldn't *find* Aurora? She didn't have magic for that? She's not all-knowing? Apparently not. She's a human witch, it turns out, whose prey can escape her. Who needs help carrying out her curse. But now she's found her. And she's going to carry out her revenge.

In the meantime, the fairies tell Aurora she's a princess and that it's time for her to go to the palace to meet her real parents. Instead of being overjoyed as the fairies assume she will be, Aurora is devastated because she thinks it means she won't be able to see Phillip again. But she has no choice, so they all head off to the palace. Prince Phillip, not knowing that Aurora is gone, rides back to the cottage and flings open the door (honey, I'm home!) only to find Maleficent and her minions inside. He is promptly tied up, taken back to Maleficent's castle and thrown into a dungeon. Maleficent seems to have won. She knows where Aurora is (back at the castle) and she has in her possession the one person who could break the curse (Phillip). All she's got to do now is get Aurora to prick her finger on the spinning wheel and her curse will be fulfilled. Which is exactly what she does.

The fairies — making another mistake — leave Aurora alone in her room to weep. Maleficent takes advantage of this by placing Aurora into a trance and luring her up to a tower room where she conjures a spinning wheel (see, King Stefan, burning them was fruitless) and gets Aurora to touch it. The curse is fulfilled; Aurora sleeps.

At this point (with the exception of a weird drunk scene with the two kings as they wait for Aurora's arrival) the story then takes a drastic turn. Suddenly, the plot ricochets back into the realm of the symbolic. All the important characters — the fairies, the prince, Maleficent — go into the final sequence as their symbolic fairytale

69

selves, instead of the more realistic counterparts they've been throughout the whole rest of the movie. It's jarring to watch. But it's necessary. Because now, what must be accomplished is the fulfillment of Aurora's fairytale narrative. The spell must be broken, evil must be vanquished, true love must conquer all. And, while this could certainly happen in a more realistic way, it can't when the princess in question is nothing more than a symbol herself. This must be a symbolic rescue, not a literal one, because it's a symbolic curse that can only be broken by the symbolism of true love's kiss. And so the agents of Aurora's rescue suddenly become their symbolic selves.

Maleficent — throwing off her mean-girl, jilted persona — becomes a true wicked witch. She reveals her evil plan to Phillip (and boy is it evil). Aurora will sleep, Maleficent explains, for a hundred years and, in her sleep, she will not age. But Phillip, locked in Maleficent's dungeon will. And when one hundred years are up, Maleficent will let Phillip go, and he will ride (ancient and gray) to the castle to bestow true love's kiss on the sixteen year-old Aurora. It's truly horrifying. Maleficent, you see, wants to pervert the symbolic narrative. She's doing her job as wicked witch, working to fulfill the exact opposite of the happy ending. And she does it with a wicked witch's signature glee in her own wickedness, and a chin-thrown-back evil laugh.

The fairies, too, become true fairies. They see that they have failed and are heartbroken. They create a bower for Aurora in the tower room and tuck her up in bed. And then they cast a spell. They aren't powerful enough to undo the curse, but if Aurora must sleep, suspended in time, so will the rest of the palace. When Aurora wakes, time will not have touched her family. She will be able to live a happy life, even though time has passed. The fairies are acting as the magical protectors they are meant to be (not the human protectors they tried to become). And, in doing this, they learn one final detail from the original, more realistic plot line. As King Hubert is falling asleep, he reveals that Phillip was in love with a peasant girl — allowing the fairies to put two and two together and realize that Phillip is the one who can break the spell. It's like the realistic narrative is falling asleep, divulging one last detail, and then disappearing. And the fairies, reacquiring their princess-like inner strength, use this information to bring the plot to its symbolic conclusion.

"Without a prince who was willing to fight through a terrifying field of thorns to wake her up, Sleeping Beauty would have had a pretty boring ending," says Chelsea Mize of *Bustle*. Sonia Saraiya, of *Nerve*, says Aurora "promptly falls asleep for the rest of the film, until a man shows up to wake her up." But the princess critics can't see through the fog of their own prejudice. Without the three fairies, Phillip would have stayed in that dungeon for the hundred years Maleficent sentenced him to. And, even if he *had* escaped, he'd have been hard pressed to defeat Maleficent and all the crazy stuff she threw at him in her efforts to keep him from getting to Aurora. What the princess critics *are* onto is the way in which Phillip's rescue of Aurora doesn't totally fit into the narrative from the first three quarters of the film. It *does* seem sort of contrived and a little empty. But it isn't about needing a man to save the day, it's about the collision of the realistic and the symbolic narratives. And it's quite a collision.

The three fairies sneak into Maleficent's castle and find Phillip in the dungeon. They magically unlock his manacles and he springs up, ready for action. But Phillip, the man, cannot save Aurora. It must be Phillip, the *prince*. And so, just as they did for Aurora at the beginning of the film when they gave her the gifts of beauty and song, the fairies proceed to turn Phillip from a *regular* prince into a *symbolic* prince. With a wave of their wands they conjure the "shield of virtue" and the "sword of truth." Suddenly, and without warning, this movie becomes much more overt in its symbolism than either of the other two princess movies that came before. In *Snow White* and *Cinderella* the symbols are just that: symbols. *We* have to figure out what they mean. But here are symbols that tell you what they are. It is Phillip's virtue that will protect him from evil, and truth that will ultimately defeat it.

71

Armed with these weapons, Phillip and the fairies begin their escape. When Maleficent's minions see them escaping and mount a full-on attack, the fairies use their magic wands to neutralize the situation. It isn't Phillip who turns to fight the evil pig-like creatures Maleficent sends after them, it's the fairies. And they fight like . . . well, like fairies. They turn the arrows the minions shoot into flowers, and the burning oil they pour into bubbles. Flowers! And bubbles! This isn't a manly man doing battle, it's three magical women fighting like girls, and winning. Good, symbolically (and somewhat comically) represented by flowers and bubbles, against evil, symbolically represented by the trappings of war. But the good guys aren't off the hook yet. The fairies have transformed Phillip into his symbolic alter-ego and Maleficent is about to do the same thing to herself.

She begins by surrounding Aurora's palace in thick thorn bushes which Phillip must hack through with — you guessed it — the sword of truth! I mean, okay, I have a degree in English literature, but I'm pretty sure that isn't necessary in order to figure this one out. Truth is good, lies are evil, lies obscure, truth reveals, blah, blah, blah. What this has to do with the *story* thus far is slightly unclear. It's like Disney just suddenly throws in some generic symbolism to make it all seem more epic. I mean, the message, such as it is, is a good one. But in terms of Aurora's transition from childhood to adulthood, or the meeting of two compatible souls, or anything related to the Disney princess narrative of growing up, it kind of comes out of left field. But there it is. In order to wake Aurora up, Phillip must hack through a forest of lies with the sword of truth. And in the middle of this particular forest is Maleficent in full fairytale regalia.

"Now shall you deal with me, oh prince, and all the powers of hell!" screams Maleficent, turning herself into a truly terrifying fire-breathing dragon. Suddenly, and without warning, Disney throws in Christian themes. Maleficent, it seems, is an agent of the devil. Which, by association, makes Phillip an agent of the Lord. Virtue and truth against deception in the form of a woman disguised as a dragon — or a serpent, perhaps? Maleficent names Phillip as her adversary calling him "prince" instead of "Phillip" or even "Prince Phillip." It is prince against witch. Good against evil. "Let evil die and good endure," the fairies proclaim, enchanting Phillip's sword.

So Phillip uses the Shield of Virtue to protect himself from what we can only assume are the fires of hell emanating from Maleficent's dragon mouth. And he plunges the sword of truth into her heart. Phillip, whose wry humor and open-hearted declarations of love have allowed us to get to know him, doesn't utter another word for the rest of the movie. His battle with Maleficent has transformed him completely. He is no longer a flesh and blood man, he is simply The Prince, fulfilling his fairytale duty of breaking the spell. He makes a beeline for the tower room where Aurora lies. He leans over her and he kisses her. She, in turn, promptly wakes up, looks into his eyes and smiles. Destiny fulfilled. Aurora is awake to her womanhood, her prince by her side, and they descend the stairs and into the main hall, where everyone else is waking up too. Aurora embraces her mother and father but she doesn't stay with them. She isn't a child. She finds her way back to Phillip's arms and they dance together into the clouds.

I must confess, I find the end of *Sleeping Beauty* kind of baffling. I mean, it's epic and exciting (in a movie that's been kind of blah up until then) and Maleficent as a dragon is truly terrifying. So in that sense it's good, old fashioned fun. But what on earth has it got to do with what came before? What are we supposed to make of this highly symbolic, rather stylized final sequence? Animator Floyd Norman called *Sleeping Beauty* "the end of an era." And I think that's exactly right. Norman, being an animator, was talking about the artistic changes that took place after *Sleeping Beauty*, but I think it's more than that. I think we are witnessing the clash of Disney's original mode of storytelling (the fairytale mode), and the new and completely different mode that Disney had begun to experiment with in the movies between *Cinderella* and *Sleeping Beauty*. And this clash nearly ruined everything.

*

The thirty years that followed *Sleeping Beauty* are known as Disney's dark ages. While there were a few films that are considered classics, like *101 Dalmatians* and *The Jungle Book,* there were far more duds than delights. Although Walt Disney's death in 1966 certainly contributed to the studio's unmooring, it's clear from the contemporary reaction to *Sleeping Beauty* that they had already begun to drift off course. The 1959 *New York Times* review of the film, for example, called Prince Phillip "saccharine," said the fairies were the "maiden sisters of the misogynistic seven dwarfs," and lamented that the movie was just a knock-off *Snow White.*

For the next three decades, films like *The Aristocats, The Black Cauldron, Oliver and Company,* and *The Great Mouse Detective* became the typical Disney fare. And not one of Disney's feature films from 1960 through 1988 was based on a fairytale, or employed the kind of imagery and symbolism that elevated many of the earlier films. *Sleeping Beauty* is the turning point, stuck between Disney's original vision, and the post-Walt studio's floundering. On the one hand, it's the traditional princess narrative with a princess and prince, a wicked witch, some fairy godmothers and an epic transformation in which good conquers evil. On the other hand, it's a new kind of cartoon narrative populated by flawed characters who get by on pluck, and grit, and make jokes along the way. A narrative that would eventually come into its own, but hadn't quite gotten its feet under it yet. Can a Disney princess narrative — with all its symbolism and ideals — exist in the real world? The answer, of course, is yes. But it took Disney thirty years to figure that out.

Snow White, Cinderella, and, yes, even *Sleeping Beauty* give us a blueprint for what it means to be a Disney princess. Disney's original vision for a well-lived inner life — his map for growing up. Inner strength, resourcefulness, optimism, kindness, and courage, these are the traits of a princess. *Not,* as the princess critics want us to believe, outer beauty, passivity, and a fixation with the trappings of royalty. A princess knows her soul mate when she sees him. Her heart is open to love. She recognizes the divine power of love in her life. And she lives her life with honesty, dignity, and grace. When Disney princesses finally made their comeback in the late 1980s, this was the framework upon which the new princesses were built. And over top of it, Disney Studios shaped realistic personalities and drives that ushered the Disney princess into a new and glorious era. The Disney renaissance.

Part II

"A Whole New World": Renaissance Princesses

Chapter Four: Ariel

Here's how you play mermaids: ask your mom for a sheet (not the fitted kind, the regular kind). Fold the sheet in half (because you're only seven years old or so and otherwise it'll be too big). Then wrap it lengthwise around your waist and tie it at the hip. Next, sit down on the floor and get a friend to tie the bottom corners together, encasing your feet inside. Wave your hands around as if you're swimming.

The Little Mermaid came out in 1989, thirty years after *Sleeping Beauty*. Suddenly, out of the long-cold ashes of Disney's glory days, came Ariel. She was sparklingly real. Strong-willed, feisty, and romantic. A person, with quirks and flaws, but courageous and true-hearted. Not to mention her incredible mane of flowing red hair and her glistening green, undulating tail. It's no wonder the film made such a splash. (Ha ha, a splash. Get it? A splash? Never mind.)

While Ariel was the star, the movie also succeeded on so many other levels. It was the first Disney movie with Alan Menken and Howard Ashman at the musical helm, who meshed the songs with the plot in a new and thrilling way, due, in large part, to Ashman's lyrical genius. The animation, too, was more vibrant and more realistic than Disney animation had been in the past. And the film featured a supporting cast of fully realized characters.

King Triton, Ariel's father, was believably torn between his love for his daughter and his desire to keep her safe. Sebastian, Ariel's crab friend, embodied a relatable mixture of nervous energy and fierce loyalty. Eric, Ariel's love interest, was handsome (of course) but also kind, brave, and conflicted about his role as royalty. And, of course, Ursula the sea witch oozed a kind of sleazy seductiveness and hunger for revenge that utterly terrified us.

The Little Mermaid was a huge hit, grossing over $84,000,000 at the box office, 64% more than Disney's animated feature from the previous year. While the princess critics hadn't yet fully convinced the general public of their misguided interpretation of the Disney princesses, the original princesses (Snow White, Cinderella, and Aurora) had begun to receive some criticism for their perceived passivity. But *this* movie was not only successful with traditionalists who were thrilled to welcome a new princess to the Disney pantheon, but with more modern viewers, who were more likely to subscribe to the critics' assertions that the original princesses were anti-feminist. In fact, when the movie came out, critics hailed Ariel as a feminist icon. A modern princess for a modern age.

But times have changed. Now, Ariel is seen as decidedly anti-feminist and has joined the misunderstood ranks of the original three princesses. 21st century critics point to Ariel's willingness to give up her voice in order to get a man, her desire to be something she isn't, and her ability to win Eric's love without the use of her voice (and therefore, the critique goes, with her body) as evidence for her demotion.

But none of that is true. Ariel doesn't do *any* of the things the princess critics say she does. They're just not there in the movie. But the princess critic version is now the official narrative. It's hard to believe that Ariel *doesn't* give up her voice for a man, or fall in love based on looks alone. But she doesn't. Ariel doesn't deserve to be proclaimed unworthy of the attention of little girls simply because a few people who misunderstood the film found their way to the public arena to tell us about it. Her reputation deserves to be restored.

*

Based on the fairy tale by Hans Christian Anderson, Disney's *The Little Mermaid* is the story of Ariel, a mermaid who longs to be human. When she falls in love with a human named Eric, her father, King Triton, forbids her to ever visit the surface again. This forces her to enlist the help of the evil sea witch, Ursula. Ursula convinces her to give up her voice in exchange for legs, with the caveat that, if she can't get Eric to kiss her by the end of the third day, she'll be doomed to be Ursula's slave forever. Ariel doesn't succeed but, with Eric's help, she defeats Ursula and convinces her father that her wish to become human is more than just teenage rebellion. King Triton uses his magic trident to turn Ariel into a human and she and Eric live happily ever after.

In essence, *The Little Mermaid* is about what *all* good Disney princess movies are about: becoming who you truly are. It holds within it the symbolism from the earlier films that stuck more closely to their fairy tale origins, but it also tackles this question head-on in a much more realistic way. It poses this down-to-earth question: how far are you willing to go to achieve your dreams? Ariel's certainty that she was meant to be a human being flies in the face of everything her father has taught her. And, just like lots of adolescents in real life, she has to choose between the life she was born to and the one she yearns to join. And along the way, like we all must, she is forced to make sacrifices to achieve her ultimate goal.

In his 1989 review of the film, Roger Ebert called Ariel, "a fully realized female character who thinks and acts independently, even rebelliously, instead of hanging around passively while the fates decide her destiny." This wasn't some damsel in distress. This was a true-to-life young woman, Ebert implies, with a mind of her own, and the ability to shape her own destiny. It was a sentiment echoed in other major publications at the time. *The New York Times* called Ariel a

81

"rebellious heroine, a spunky, flirty little nymph who defies her father's wishes" and says she's "even capable of wit, which is more than could ever be said of Snow White or Sleeping Beauty or Cinderella." And the *New York Daily News* called her a "rebellious redhead."

Many reviewers pointed to the fact that Ariel actually saves Eric (rather than the other way around) and that she takes control of her own destiny by making a deal with the sea witch when no one will help her, as evidence of her feminist leanings. It was as if she was directly answering the princess critics, who were beginning to say that Disney princesses were too passive, waiting for their prince to come and solve all their problems. This came, in large part, from the filmmakers' conscious effort to model her after a rebellious teenager. Director Ron Clements said of Ariel, "We wanted her to feel like a real teenager, so we looked at movies about teenage girls." In short, critics and parents signed off. *The Little Mermaid* was a-okay for little girls to watch.

And watch it we did. In the theater, and in our homes, at birthday parties, and at sleepovers. Over and over again, as we grew from seven-year-olds into girls on the verge of adolescence. "I'm sixteen years old," Ariel tells her father. "I'm not a child anymore." Boy did we ever identify with that! Even at seven years old, we were already beginning to separate from our parents, yearning for identities of our own. (Of course, from my adult vantage point, it's easy to roll my eyes and smile knowingly but, back then, that's exactly what it felt like.) We didn't want to be kids anymore. We wanted to grow up!

The Little Mermaid tackles themes specific to teenagers (like rebelling against strict parents, breaking away from the values of your family, and experiencing intense romantic attachments) in a way that the other princess movies hadn't before. The other princesses *were* teenagers, but that was much more a symbol of their being on the cusp of adulthood, than an actual way of being. In real life, rebellion is a huge part of being a teenager. And, often, it takes the form of dangerous (at worst) or ill-advised (at best) behavior, as adolescents look for a way to differentiate from their parents. Without a strong connection to a stable family, it's possible for teenagers to really go off the rails. But *The Little Mermaid* lays these themes of adolescent rebellion atop a foundation of morality, good values, and strong principles. Which is why Ariel doesn't end up like a lot of teenage girls today who *haven't* learned those things.

Ariel feels restricted by the life she's living. She loves her father and her sisters, but she's chafing against the constraints of her life with them. She longs to learn more about the human world, but her father is adamant. He calls all humans "barbarians" and refuses to even allow her to go to the surface, let alone actually talk to a human. So there she is, like a lot of teenagers, stuck between her own independent interests and desires, and those of her father who is still her provider and protector.

Pretty much every teenage girl (and boy too, for that matter) feels that there's something about her that doesn't fit in with her family. *I* sure did. While my parents and my brother all found pleasure in intellectual pursuits like learning new languages for fun, and discussing classic literature around the dinner table, I was struggling to understand my history textbook and reading *The Babysitter's Club*. Did I need to understand Shakespeare in order to fit in in the world? Or could my less erudite (a word I had to look up just now to make sure I was using it correctly) interests lead to success?

Luckily for me, my parents have always embraced me for who I am, and never made me feel inadequate simply for not fitting in with the family norms. But not everyone is so lucky. And, even for those of us who are, that feeling of yearning for something different, something that fits with the picture of who we're meant to be, is all too familiar.

But the ability to follow your dreams, and live as your authentic self rests on the strength of your character. Fear of messing with the status quo, or offending your parents, or just plain failing can hold you back. Ingratitude and anger might cause you to cut off ties with people who love you because you can't see that they had your best interests at heart. It takes courage and strength to forge your own path, which is a lesson that teenagers (often looking for a quick fix, and immersed in their own egos) could stand to learn.

Which is why Ariel is who she is. Reviewers of the movie describe her most often as "rebellious" — which is true, since she's rebelling against her father's wishes — but the image of a "rebellious teenager" is one who is breaking rules that are made for her own good. Rules like sticking to a curfew, not consuming illegal substances, doing homework before watching TV, that kind of thing. Ariel is "rebelling" against her father's limited worldview. Against his prejudice and fear. In this case, I think her rebellion is warranted and, more than anything else, brave. She is a rebellious teenager overlaid on top of the fairy tale princess journey of growing up, separating from her family, and becoming who she truly is.

Ariel's love of all things human bumps up against her father's fear of the unknown. His belief that all humans are dangerous leads him to refuse, in no uncertain terms, to listen to Ariel's side of the story. And this, in turn, forces her to make a choice: submit to her father's rules, or pursue other means to get what she wants. Of course, as adults, we tend not to think of breaking your parents' rules as brave. But what if the rules are wrong? Then, I think, it's one of the bravest things a young girl can do.

Ariel opts to fend for herself, giving up something of great importance (her voice) in exchange for a shot at her dream of becoming human. And, ultimately, it's this courage and determination that convince her father that she was right and he was wrong. What pre-teen girl wouldn't love a story like that? *I* sure loved it. And so did my friends. And lots and lots of girls all across the country, and the world.

But then we grew up. The little girls who'd watched the movie and longed to be as brave as Ariel, passed through their own teenage years and on into adulthood. And while, for me, Ariel remained a symbol of courage and fortitude in the face of adversity, something happened to my peers. Those same girls who'd tied those bedsheets around their waists, and warbled out Ariel's signature melody with the best of them, turned their backs on her. If they'd passed her in the street they would have pretended they didn't even know her. Something had happened to these women. They'd succumbed to the rhetoric of the princess critics.

In an article for *feministing.com* Chloe Angyal describes rewatching *The Little Mermaid* as a nineteen-year-old college student and being horrified. Like me, (like lots of us) she'd loved the movie as a child. She writes, "I used to – and I can't believe I'm about to reveal this publicly – sit in the bathtub wearing swimming flippers, combing my hair and singing like Ariel." (Is this embarrassing? Sounds like fun to me.) But then she had her "feminist 'click' moment."

I personally find the whole idea of a "feminist click moment" incredibly pretentious and off-putting, but it's exactly what happened to lots of lots of women from my generation. They became "feminists" and suddenly loathed the things they'd loved. This movie that Angyal had loved so much — this character she'd wanted to *be* — was no longer acceptable. Worse, she was *anti-feminist*. The movie, she writes, is about "the triumph of 'good' women – young, slender, silent and lovesick – over 'bad' women – old, voluptuous, outspoken and sexual." In this comparison, Ariel is the "good" woman, and Ursula the sea witch is the "bad" one. But have you *seen* the movie. Ursula obviously *is* evil. It's not just that she's "sexual," it's that she advocates using your sexuality as a means to entrap men. Are we in favor of this now? Apparently, if you believe Angyal, we are. (Also, if you find Ursula sexy you're into some really weird stuff. But let's move on.)

But Angyal is not alone. In the early nineties, Ariel had been seen as "rebellious," "spunky," and "a fully realized female character." But twenty or so years later, women who had loved her unconditionally, suddenly began distrusting their own instincts, deciding they'd been brainwashed by some sort of evil Disney patriarchal conspiracy. In fact, according to polls on both *Bustle.com* and *Nerve.com*, Ariel is currently considered the least feminist of the three renaissance Disney princesses (Ariel, Belle, and Jasmine). They weren't simply outgrowing something from their childhood, their organic opinions were being swayed by the princess critics' false narrative.

So, what is it that everyone's objecting to? The criticism centers around superficiality. The characters, the plot, and the ultimate message of the movie, princess critics complain, promote a way of looking at the world that's only skin deep. Ariel and Eric, the critique goes, fall in love at first sight (which, as we've already seen, princess critics misinterpret as meaning they are only attracted to each other physically). Ariel's love for Eric motivates her to make a deal with the sea witch (thus jeopardizing her own safety and that of her family) which is unacceptable given that she barely knows the guy. To make matters worse, Ariel spends a large part of the movie without a voice, meaning she is forced to use "body language" (Ursula's words, not mine) to snare her man. It all seems pretty damning.

The only problem is that none of it's true. None of it is actually borne out by the plot of the film. Ariel and Eric *aren't* only attracted to each other physically. In fact, I think the movie is pretty clear that it's exactly the opposite. Additionally, Ariel's triumph is that she *doesn't* win Eric's love through physical seduction, but through her personality instead. Yes, love is a motivating factor for both of them. But it's a motivating factor for most of us. And I definitely don't think it's their only goal in life, though I do think that finding love is an important part of the story's culmination. (Don't forget Disney's message about the connection between love and the divine.)

Currently, the feminist critiques of *The Little Mermaid,* are considered accurate by most people who care one way or the other. People who continue to love the movie do so *in the face* of those criticisms (as in "I know, I know, it's really anti-feminist but I just still love it anyway. I'm sorry"), rather than disagreeing with them outright.

But the evidence actually proves that the princess critics' assertions aren't true at all. So let's *look* at that evidence, and prove the princess critics wrong.

*

Let's begin with the idea that love is Ariel's sole motivation for becoming human. In an article for *mommyish.com* called "I Regret The Day I Let My Daughter Watch *The Little Mermaid*," Sarah Bregel scoffs, "She morphs herself into a human at the age of 16 to go be with some dude she saw on a boat?" In other words, jeez Ariel, chill. Going to such great lengths, Bregel and others complain, to be with a *man* is anti-feminist to the *n*th degree. A man ought never to be a woman's motivating factor in any life choice.

I, of course, actually think that love *is* a motivating factor in the lives of all human beings. And that love can lead us to new heights, and wonderful experiences we would never have achieved alone, but let's put that aside for a moment (and come back to it later). Let's just look, now, at whether it actually *is* love that compels Ariel to trade her tail for legs.

When we first meet Ariel, she (and her fish friend Flounder) are exploring a sunken ship, looking for human artifacts. She acts like she's won the lottery when she finds a fork and a tobacco pipe inside. Later, a shark attacks the two friends and sends them swimming for their lives, but Ariel risks being eaten in order to rescue her bag full of treasures which has fallen to the ocean floor.

Then, after Flounder lets slip to King Triton that he and Ariel were looking for human treasures and that they had recently gone to the surface, we learn that Ariel's constant interest in the human world is a source of contention between her and her father. We learn, too, that Ariel's visits to the surface are frequent and that she makes them even in the face of her father's disapproval.

The portrait of Ariel as a mermaid in love with the human world is complete when, upset at her father's rebuke, Ariel and Flounder retreat to her grotto and we see the extent of her obsession.

87

Ariel's cave is filled from floor to ceiling with human artifacts. And it's here that she sings the now-famous ballad *Part of That World*. "Up where they walk / Up where they run / Up where they stay all day in the sun / Wandering free / Wish I could be / Part of that world." It's more than just an interest. She's obsessed with becoming human.

All this happens *before* she even lays eyes on Eric. "I wanna be where the people are," she sings. It's who she is. A human stuck in a mermaid's body. But, before Ursula gets her tentacles on her, dreaming is all she can really do about it. She has no way to become human. Enter Ursula who, motivated by her desire to entrap King Triton so that *she* can become ruler of the ocean instead of him, sends her eel henchmen to offer Ariel the possibility of legs.

"Can you *do* that?" Ariel asks, when Ursula says she'll turn her into a human. Ariel didn't know that was even possible. If it was something she *had* seen as possible, chances are she would have been lobbying her father to let her go for it. He would have said no, of course, but she would have pushed hard for it. Except she didn't know it could be done. When Ursula tells her it can (at a price) she's hooked.

Ursula's offer is to make Ariel human, not to let her be with Eric. Yes, Eric is a part of the deal (in that he needs to kiss Ariel in order for her to remain human), but he's not the prize. Legs are. When Ursula conjures a magic image of Ariel transforming into a human, Ariel stares at it mesmerized. It's the legs that are captivating her attention in that moment. Not Eric.

Eric is the catalyst, not the motivation. Ariel's love for him (and her father's refusal to allow her to see him anymore) forces her to take drastic measures. After falling for Eric, Ariel wants to be human *and* to be with Eric. And since one basically necessitates the other, her needs have reached a crisis point that force her into a dangerous situation. So, first she wants to be human. *Then* she falls for a human man. Not the other way around.

Okay, fine, but what about the fact that she falls in love with someone she's never even spoken to? It's true, she does. And we're far enough out of the world of fairy tale shorthand to question why that happens. But let's look a little deeper. Ariel sees Eric on board his ship and is immediately drawn to him. This is definitely a thing that happens in real life. Regardless of how you feel about romantic love, you have to admit that there's usually an element of physical attraction involved. And physical attraction often comes before any other kind of attraction. Tons of relationships begin because two people were attracted to each other physically and then took the time to get to know each other. This is a thing. You know it is.

But, calm down, there's more. Because she's attracted to him, she watches him. And, during the course of her observation, a series of events occurs which perfectly illuminate Eric's character and personality. There's a storm at sea. The boat that Eric and his crew are on begins to founder. Eric is immediately concerned with the safety of everyone on board. Even though he's a prince, he jumps right in with the work of trying to secure the ship, pulling on ropes and even grabbing the steering wheel to try to muscle the ship back on course. He calls out to crew members who would have been hit by a falling beam, and saves his manservant, Grimsby, by getting him safely to a lifeboat. When the ship bursts into flames, Eric leaps back out of the lifeboat and climbs back to the ship to save his dog Max who's been left behind. He throws Max overboard because his own leg is stuck and he knows the ship is going to explode. He's still on board when it does.

So, yeah, in real life if you saw a guy and thought he was pretty cute, chances are you wouldn't then get to witness a display of bravery and selflessness to let you know what kind of guy he really is. But, this isn't real life. It's a movie that — while it's more realistic than the original princess movies — is still drawing on fairy tale shorthand. We are witnessing what Ariel (the princess) sees when she looks into the soul of Eric (the prince). Cinderella looks at her prince and sees his inner soul. Ariel looks at Eric and sees *his* inner soul — and this time *we* get to see it too. By the time Ariel drags Eric safely back to shore, she's got a good idea of who this guy is. And she's fallen in love.

We could debate whether what she's feeling is actually love, or just the intense crush of a romantic sixteen year old. But it doesn't really matter. She's witnessed enough to know something about Eric's personality, and she's felt the spark of physical attraction. (Plenty of marriages begin in much the same way.) Couple that with her already intense desire to become human and it's enough to send her straight to Ursula's doorstep.

So, what about Eric? *He* doesn't witness a convenient display of Ariel's personality. In fact, he doesn't witness much of Ariel at all. How could he feel certain, after such a brief encounter, that the mysterious woman who rescued him from the shipwreck was destined to be his wife? The answer to this is also rooted in fairy tale shorthand and is, in fact, one of the central metaphors of the movie: he heard *her voice.*

When Eric regains consciousness on the beach, he is looking straight into the face of an unknown woman and she's singing to him. By the time he's completely alert, she's gone. That's it. So, yeah, not much to go on. But it's a moment that exists in the context of a movie that uses "voice" as a stand-in for identity. (Not to mention the fact that, if you thought you were going to die and instead woke up on a beach staring into the face of a beautiful stranger who sings a haunting melody and then promptly disappears, you might feel like fate was somehow involved and that you were meant to be together. Just saying.)

Anyway, to understand Eric's feelings (and a whole bunch of other things about the movie), we have to explore this idea of Ariel's voice. The fact that Ariel spends a large portion of the movie *without* her voice has prompted critics to determine that the point of the movie is that all a man cares about (and therefore all a woman should aspire to) is a pretty face.

In an article for *The Huffington Post* called *Why My Kids Will Not Be Watching The Little Mermaid*, Hilary Sheinbaum writes that the movie "portrays men as physically judgmental, only caring about the way a woman looks, bats her eyes and smiles — that they do not consider any thoughts, feelings or concerns in one's pretty little head." The idea being, that if Eric can fall for Ariel without ever hearing anything she has to say, he must be totally superficial. And that *would* be true, if Eric did that. Which he doesn't.

Ariel's voice is important — just as Aurora's was in *Sleeping Beauty*. When you think about the ways in which we talk about someone's "voice" in everyday life it's often used as shorthand for their ideas, or their intellectual contribution. We say things like, "let your voice be heard," and "speak up," and "give voice to your opinions." In *The Little Mermaid*, Ariel's voice is a metaphor for her identity. The *her* of her. It's what Ursula asks for in exchange for giving Ariel legs because she knows it's the thing that's most important to her. The thing that makes her who she is.

Ursula doesn't want Ariel to be successful. She's banking on Ariel being unable to get Eric to kiss her in the three day window, so that Ariel can become her slave and Ursula will be that much closer to her ultimate goal of becoming ruler of all the ocean. So, she's going to take as her payment the thing she thinks will make it most difficult for Ariel to snare Eric. Ursula could have asked for her *looks*. But she asks for her *voice*. Ariel's voice (her identity), the movie is telling us, is her most precious possession. It's not that, without it, she stops being herself. But, rather, that, when it's gone, she lacks the ability to accurately convey who she is. It's the key to understanding her essential self.

So, back to Eric on the beach. What he remembers, upon waking from unconsciousness, is not how beautiful Ariel was, but how wonderful her *voice* sounded to him. ("She had the most beautiful voice," he tells Grimsby.) And it's the sound of that voice that tells him he's got to find this girl and that, when he does, he's going to

91

marry her. Because, in her voice, he's recognized something about who she truly is. Just like, in watching his actions, Ariel recognizes something about who *Eric* truly is. The prince and the princess meeting.

Ariel immediately sees that losing her voice will be a huge problem if she wants Eric to fall in love with her. But Ursula tries to convince her otherwise. "You'll have your looks, your pretty face. And don't underestimate the importance of body language!" she says, swaying her enormous hips seductively. This speech is often quoted as proof that the movie promotes snaring a man with your body instead of your mind. But, consider who's saying this. Ursula is the *bad guy*. She's not to be trusted. And Ariel never once, throughout the whole movie, uses her body seductively. In fact, even when her friend Sebastian the crab tries to get her to flirt with Eric she doesn't listen. Literally. "You've got to bat your eyes like this. You've got to pucker up your lips like this," Sebastian instructs her. But it's been a long day for a little mermaid, and Ariel is fast asleep.

When Eric finds Ariel on the beach, after she's become human, he thinks at first that she must be the woman who saved him. But, upon realizing that she can't speak, he decides it can't possibly be her. The woman he fell for had *a voice*. Without her voice, Eric doesn't recognize her for who she truly is. And, even though he does find her physically attractive, he's not falling head over heels in love with her just because she's got a pretty face.

Eric does eventually develop feelings for Ariel, which adds fodder to the critique that he's only attracted to her physically, but it's not her looks that bring him around. Sheinbaum complains, "Eric falls in love with Ariel, who has never spoken a single word in his presence. Forget politics, religion and issues of the world — these two do not discuss anything." This is factual per se but doesn't really tell the whole story.

Although Ariel refuses to use her body to inspire Eric's lust, she *is* able to convey her personality to him through her actions (albeit not nearly as fully as she could when she has her voice). In the first act of the movie (when Ariel still has her voice) we learn that she is brave, passionate, and eager to learn. As Eric and Ariel spend time together, she shows him these things about herself. She is passionate and excited about all the new things she sees in the village square. She's curious about how the Punch and Judy puppets work, and eager to learn how to dance. And, when Eric hands her the reins of the horse pulling their carriage, she bravely spurs the horse over a jump. In the same way that Ariel witnessed a display of Eric's character earlier on, Eric witnesses Ariel's here.

But even this isn't enough to convince him to abandon all hope of the girl with the beautiful voice. And he continues to express qualms about starting a relationship with someone who he can't speak to. In the famous *Kiss the Girl* sequence, in which Sebastian tries to get Eric to kiss Ariel by singing a romantic song, Eric (overcome by the music) leans in for a kiss but then pulls back. The very next thing he does is try to figure out her *name* (another metaphor for a person's identity). He can't kiss her. He doesn't *know* her.

It's true that, eventually, Eric begins to think that maybe he should marry Ariel instead of his mysterious rescuer. But he now has a lot more information about her than he did when he found her on the beach. And he's starting to believe Grimsby, who keeps telling him that the other girl isn't real. (Which would make it difficult to marry her.) And even Grimsby isn't saying Eric should marry Ariel because she's pretty. He says she's "warm and caring." Which she is.

Of course, Eric's plan to settle for this nice (if mute) girl is foiled by Ursula's intervention. Realizing that Ariel might actually succeed after all, Ursula steps in (unwilling to accept defeat). She casts a spell to turn herself into a beautiful maiden, who calls herself Vanessa, and uses Ariel's voice to hypnotize Eric into saying he's going to marry *her* instead.

"What a lovely little bride I'll make. My dear I'll look divine," Ursula/Vanessa sings as she gets ready for the wedding. She's concerned with how she'll *look*. She's the bad guy, remember. If she says it, it's probably not a good thing. So her little song in front of the mirror is just another reminder that in *this* movie, it's not looks but personality that warrant true love.

There's one last thing about Ariel's voice. The most important thing, really. It's only when Ariel's *voice* is returned to her that Eric finally recognizes her as the girl who saved him on the beach. The one he's been waiting for. In the moment before the sun sets on the third day, Ariel's friends succeed in breaking the shell necklace containing Ariel's voice that Ursula/Vanessa has been wearing around her neck. Ariel's voice flows out of the shell and straight to its rightful owner. And it's in *that* moment, that Eric sees her for who she truly is: the love of his life.

In the final sequence of the movie, King Triton finally comes around and sees what everyone else has always seen: that Ariel will only be happy if she's allowed to be human. So he uses his magic trident to give her legs. Now she can be her true self. A human being with a voice.

The Little Mermaid features a brave and self-motivated heroine, who takes her destiny into her own hands and achieves success. Its central metaphor focuses on choosing personality over beauty. And it stresses the importance of being who you truly are, even if others tell you you can't. What's not to like?

If you've stayed with me this far, then there's really only one more hurdle to cross. Because, now that we've proven that it's not just that we *disagree* with the main body of criticism of the movie, but rather that it's actually *wrong*, there's only one critique of the movie left. Marriage. The movie ends with a wedding. And love is a part of the story.

Here, I'm willing to concede the point. The movie *does* end with a wedding. And love *is* a motivating factor for both Ariel and Eric throughout the movie. But there's no way you can convince me that this is a bad thing.

Look, if Ariel had been a perfectly happy mermaid, content to swim around the ocean all her life until she saw Eric once on a boat, I might feel like she should think things over pretty carefully before going in for the full tail-ectomy. But she wasn't. She already wanted to be human, and then she fell in love with one.

What, pray tell, is so wrong with love? I mean, really, honestly, what? And if you find yourself in love, what's wrong with getting married? It sure beats the alternative, doesn't it? Apparently not. Sarah Bregl literally can't handle it when she sees her two-year-old daughter acting out the wedding scene from *The Little Mermaid*. "A 2-year-old talking about marriage and imitating marriage?" she writes. "I'm just not into it. It doesn't seem healthy and it kind of freaks me out."

If her two-year-old actually *got* married, *that* would freak *me* out. But pretending is what little kids do. They pretend to be grown-ups. I'd much rather my daughter pretended to get married than pretended that she was a prostitute, or that she was living alone with eight hundred cats. Marriage is the natural next step in a relationship between two adults who love each other and feel pretty confident that they're going to *keep* loving each other for the rest of their lives. It cements their relationship and their intentions in a way that *not* getting married doesn't. It's a good thing. (Not to mention all the fairy tale shorthand of true love between princes and princesses and what that represents.)

So, when Ariel and Eric find that they love each other and feel certain they're going to *keep* loving each other, they get married. Simple. But I think, for princess critics, the problem is that they love each other at all. That, even though Ariel did love the human world before she met Eric, her love for him motivated her to follow her dreams with new intensity. The princess critic critique of this movie reveals that it isn't *only* love at first sight they object to, but love as a motivating factor at all. But isn't that what love does?

95

I mean, sure, Ariel might have been fine on her own. She might have gotten to become human, or learned to live as a mermaid, or become an advocate for better mermaid-human relations, or whatever. But she might not have. Because love — true love — makes us want to be the best versions of ourselves. It forces us not to settle for mediocrity, or live in fear. Because, in order to be worthy of someone else, you have to be worthy of yourself. Or, as Disney would have wanted us to understand, it taps us in to the divine. Ariel's love for Eric gives her the incentive she needs to follow the dream she already had. It doesn't make her less of her own person to love someone and feel love's motivating power in her life. People need other people. They just do.

This is what we were learning all those years ago, sitting immobilized on our floors, wrapped in our mothers' bedsheets. That when you find yourself trapped in a situation that doesn't allow you to be who you truly are, you need to find a way out of it. And that the love of a good man can be the lodestar with which you guide yourself home to your truest self.

The thing is, *The Little Mermaid* (like all good Disney princess movies) is a coming-of-age story. It's the story of a girl making the journey from childhood into adulthood. But, much more than the original princess movies, this movie is much more firmly planted in the real (rather than the symbolic) world. Which means that, before we're ready to leave her at the end of the movie, we need to know that she's going to be okay. In *all* areas of her life. And finding a romantic partner (whoever that might be), is definitely part of a fulfilling and full life. I'm sorry, but it just is. So we need to know, before we leave her, that Ariel has found that. Just like we need to know that she's found a way to become human. And that she and her father are still on good terms. That she's come through her teenage angsty-phase in which she hates her father, and emerged with a new respect for him and all he's done for her. You know, that she's happy. That she's going to be alright.

96

My point is simply this: It's okay to love *The Little Mermaid*. Not apologetically, or with an eye-roll, or air quotes around "love." But proudly. Unashamedly. And it's okay to show it to your daughter. To hand her the bed sheet when she asks for it, with a proud heart and a sense of nostalgia. And a feeling of gladness that Ariel is teaching another generation of girls to find their voices. To follow their dreams. To be wholeheartedly, and unabashedly themselves.

We loved Ariel when we were little girls because she was worthy of our love. We saw it then, through eyes unclouded by political correctness, and misguided feminist criticism. And we've loved her still, in secret, because something about her still spoke to us. Her voice sang out to us somehow through all the irrelevant chatter. If you love Ariel, don't hide anymore. Be proud. Be who Ariel taught you to be all those years ago. Be you.

Chapter Five: Belle

I was nine years old when I first saw *Beauty and the Beast*. We'd just moved from New York City to London, England and that feeling of being out of place couldn't have been more present for me. My little, homesick psyche grasped on to Belle's certainty that there was something else out there for her and held on for dear life. How many other little girls watched Belle grapple with feelings of being out of place and took courage from her resilience and mental strength? I know I sure did. Alone in my room I would fling my arms wide, as Belle did in the movie, and warble "I want adventure in the great wide somewhere / I want it more than I can tell!" And when Belle, gushing about the books she loves so much, is written off with a distracted "that's nice" from the town baker it felt so familiar. So often children's insecurities, heartaches, and fears are viewed as insignificant — adults know they'll be okay so they don't always validate their children's feelings. To the little girls of the world — even girls like me with kind and caring parents — this felt so familiar. *Belle!* we called out across the void *We know how you feel!*

To me, *Beauty and the Beast* — which came out in 1991 — is the epitome of the Disney princess movie. It holds within it everything that the Disney princesses had taught us up to this point, and adds to the Disney princess blueprint in a way that elevates it to its highest point. It's not that there are no good Disney princess movies after this one — there are — it's just that *Beauty and the Beast* does it best. Its characters are realistic — and realistically flawed — in a way that we hadn't yet seen in a Disney princess movie. But, at the center of their story, is fairytale symbolism at its finest. The movie perfectly blends characters who have realistic personalities and motives with the symbolism that only a fairytale can provide. In a way that *Sleeping Beauty* couldn't, *Beauty and the Beast* is able to blend fairytale symbolism with realistic characters, and the result is perfection.

"Disney films are about growing up," said Disney producer Don Hahn. "They're about that day in your life when you have to accept responsibility." In *Beauty and the Beast* we see that play out in what, I would argue, is the most interesting, most sophisticated, and most meaningful way yet.

*

Buoyed by the success of *The Little Mermaid* two years earlier, Disney upped the ante. *Beauty and the Beast* is a technical masterpiece — combining traditional hand-drawn artwork with cutting edge (for the time) computer animation in the famous ballroom sequence. The crisp, clean animation throughout has, in my opinion, never been matched, before or since. The musical duo of Howard Ashman and Alan Menken had hit their stride and created a cartoon worthy of the Broadway stage. And the story — based on the traditional fairytale but with a uniquely modern twist — was Disney's most complex yet.

In essence, what *Beauty and the Beast* does is zoom in on the inner workings of true love. The meeting of two compatible souls, which was represented symbolically in *Snow White* and *Cinderella*, is slowed down and cracked open so we can see what's really going on in there. Instead of true love's kiss (although that's in there too), or love at first sight standing in for the moment of falling in love, *Beauty and the Beast* shows us what's actually happening in that moment. Falling in love — how that happens, what it means, and what it does to your life

— is basically the entire plot of this movie. But, far from boiling a princess's dreams down to husband hunting, it illuminates the qualities a prince and princess need in order to lead fulfilling lives. Lives that allow them to live as their truest selves. In *Cinderella,* Walt Disney taught us the importance of true love. In *Beauty and the Beast* we learn what true love actually looks like, and how to find it.

Princess critics tend to grudgingly acknowledge that Belle is the most feminist of the Renaissance princesses. Of course, for them, that's not saying much. They still have a ton of problems with this princess and her story. But even *they* see that Belle is special. In many ways, she's a new kind of Disney princess. Unlike all the princesses before her, Belle is not an ingénue. Her journey from child to adult is not one of ignorance to knowledge. She doesn't need — like Snow White — to learn about her burgeoning sexuality and womanhood. Nor does she need — like Ariel — to assert her own individuality. She already knows exactly who she is, and she's willing to be completely herself in a place where no one "gets" her. No, what Belle is after is acceptance. Acceptance of the woman she already is. Which is another facet of adulthood. The next step, if you will. Belle is a more mature heroine, whose needs are more complex and less easily attainable. And that was intentional.

Beauty and the Beast screenwriter Linda Woolverton called Belle "a feminist." "I wasn't on a soapbox," she told *The LA Times,* "But it just wasn't in me to write a throwback. I wanted a woman of the '90s, someone who wanted to do something other than wait for her prince to come." Now, I obviously disagree that that's what the older princesses were doing, but it's important to note that Woolverton was intentionally creating a different kind of Disney princess, and that the story she was telling was *not* a simple boy-meets-girl. It's a love story — and its central theme revolves around love — but it would be hard to argue that it's about a passive damsel in distress, given that the actual screenwriter intentionally created Belle to be the opposite of that. "She was captured, but she transformed him," Woolverton said of Belle's relationship with the Beast. "She didn't become, you know, an object." She knew who she was all along. And *she* transformed *him*. She's not looking for her own transformation, she already *is* who she wants to be. Belle is a princess looking for acceptance. And she finds it through love.

*

This idea of acceptance is established in the very first sequence of the movie. Through a prologue animated in stained glass — which harkens back to the original Disney princess movies which opened with prologues told through an open storybook — we find out about the Beast's curse. An enchantress, disguised as an old beggar woman, comes to the castle offering a rose in exchange for shelter from the cold. But the prince, we learn, is "spoiled, selfish, and unkind." He sneers at the woman's "haggard appearance" and turns her away. The enchantress gives him one more chance, telling him: "Do not be deceived by appearances, for beauty is found within." But the prince refuses a second time and learns his fatal error. The ugly crone is really a beautiful enchantress. She turns him into a beast and his servants into objects. Because there was "no love in his heart," he will remain a beast until he can fall in love and earn love in return. He has until the last petal of the rose she had offered him falls. If he can't do it, he'll remain a beast forever.

The interplay between inner and outer beauty is the way *Beauty and the Beast* explores acceptance. In fairytale shorthand, remember, a person's outer beauty symbolizes his inner goodness. But the prince, who was beautiful on the outside, wasn't living up to his fairytale form. To him, physical appearance mattered more than personality. And that was his undoing. His outer self was beautiful, but his internal self was ugly. So the enchantress' curse matched his outer appearance to his inner self. The theme of inner and outer beauty is woven throughout the plot of the film. We must not be "deceived by appearances," because, in order to find acceptance, a Disney princess must stay true to her inner beauty, and find a prince who's worthy of it.

"But who could ever learn to love a Beast?" the narrator asks. Cut to Belle. The very first thing we learn about our heroine is this: she can learn to love a Beast. Not, as the princess critics want us to believe, that she's got a weird beast fetish (more on that later), but that she can *learn* to love one. As in, she sees the good in people — and the bad. She is someone who can see into people's secret hearts, and judges them accordingly. This is one of the central ideas of the movie — seeing and being seen for who you really are, seeing beyond the external to the soul within. Belle is someone who will come to see the Beast as a man worthy of love, and who sees Gaston (her heartthrob suitor) as the narcissistic villain he is.

Next, in the kind of choreographed musical number we'd expect from a stage musical, not an animated movie, we are introduced to Belle's "provincial town" and her place within it. "Little town, full of little people," Belle sings, and suddenly the town comes to life — people popping out of windows, carts rattling down the street, merchants selling their wares, and women haggling for the best price. Belle's initial statement about her neighbors makes many princess critics argue that Belle is an elitist snob. Mathew Guiver, of *Buzzfeed* says, "Belle is pretty much walking through the village throwing shade at everyone," and Roisin Lanigan, of *Babe*, says, "You definitely don't stand in the middle of your town centre in the morning shouting at the top of your lungs THERE MUST BE MORE THAN THIS PROVINCIAL LIFE . . . THESE PEOPLE ARE SMALLMINDED IDIOTS WHO AREN'T AS SMART AS ME, BELLE, THE GREATEST, SMARTEST PERSON EVER." But that's not the point here at all. It's not even close.

The genius of this first musical number is that it clearly and concisely develops the movie's themes while making us think we're just watching a super fun dance number. By the end of the five-minute sequence, we know everything we need to know about who Belle is, the world she lives in, and why she needs to escape it. "Every day like the one before," Belle sings. Far from saying that these people are "small-minded idiots," Belle is saying that the people in this town are happy exactly as they are. They are content to live in this little town, following their same routines, day after day. It's not about whether this is inherently good or bad, it's about the fact that *Belle* doesn't want to be like them. She has ambitions, dreams, and desires that go beyond the life the town can offer her. She's different and, in this town — as in many high-schools in America — different equals weird and unacceptable.

"Now it's no wonder that her name means beauty," the townspeople sing. "But behind that fair facade / I'm afraid she's rather odd." In this town, Belle's intellect and ambition is seen as a deficit. To them, Belle's internal self doesn't match her external one. According to the rules of the town, someone who is beautiful inside would be more like them — content with the life the village can offer. They *want* her to fit in. But she doesn't. And so, in spite of her beauty — which the townspeople obviously value — almost no one likes or understands her. "Very different from the rest of us / She's nothing like the rest of us / Yes, different from the rest of us is Belle!" Talk about throwing shade! The townspeople (with the exception of the kindly bookseller) cannot embrace Belle's difference, and Belle knows that she can't stay here forever. Because she *knows* who she is, and this isn't the place for her.

I am not who you think I am. I am not a child. I'm not yours to mold to your will. I am *myself*. Or, as Belle puts it, "I want so much more than they've got planned." If that's not a teen anthem, I don't know what is. My own personal version of this was to wail inarticulately, stomp loudly to my room, slam the door hard, and fling myself onto the bed yelling "Nobody understands me!" (I was a sensitive child.) But, however it's expressed, this longing for independence is the anthem of every Disney princess. Whether it's Snow White symbolically emerging from childhood to womanhood, or Ariel explicitly stating, "I'm not a child anymore," a Disney princess's mission is to find her way from childhood to adulthood, staying true to herself, and following her dreams.

Enter Gaston. The final — and perhaps most important — thing we learn about Belle in this magnificent initial sequence, is what she's looking for in a man. Gaston is the town heartthrob. His square jaw, deep voice, huge muscles, and confident swagger ooze masculinity and mark him as the hero. But of course, he isn't. In reality, he's a shallow cad who doesn't care at all who Belle is *inside* as long as she's beautiful on the *outside*. "She's the most beautiful girl in town. And *that* makes her the best," Gaston tells his sidekick, LeFou. "Here in town there's only she / who is beautiful as me / so I'm making plans to woo and marry Belle." It doesn't matter to Gaston that Belle is "odd" — not because he accepts her for who she is, but because her beauty is all that matters to him. And he assumes that she'll immediately fall for him because his external beauty matches her own.

This has been Gaston's experience all his life because, in this little town, Gaston's superior outer appearance signals an internal superiority — even if he doesn't actually posses it. And they have elevated him to leadership — he's the popular guy, the football player, the jock. And the girls are falling all over him: "Be still my heart, I'm hardly breathing! / He's such a tall, dark, strong and handsome brute!" sing the three silly girls who love him in the way *he* loves Belle — for his good looks, and the external trappings of masculinity. But Belle is having none of it. Belle sees Gaston's true *internal* self and finds him lacking. His outer beauty means nothing to her because his inner self isn't beautiful to her at all. He's a guy who finds *thinking* to be "a dangerous pastime." And he doesn't even come close to accepting her for who she is — "How can you read this? There's no pictures!" Gaston complains, looking at Belle's book. No, he's not the one for her.

Beauty and the Beast does something really original and interesting: it *separates* the external qualities of a fairytale prince, from the internal ones. In fairytale shorthand, remember, the prince's external handsomeness signals his internal goodness. When you see a handsome prince in a fairytale, you are being told that he's the one whose internal qualities match the princess's. Not because his handsomeness *makes* him good, but because his handsomeness *symbolizes* his goodness. But here, the handsome man is not the prince. We're still *looking* for the fairytale prince — the perfect man — but he doesn't look the part. The essence of the perfect man no longer resides inside its symbol. Gaston is the external shell of perfection, but the important part — the *internal* prince-ness — is somewhere else. So Belle — who is already a "princess" on the outside *and* the inside — has to go looking for the person whose internal qualities *make* him a prince, regardless of what he looks like on the outside.

Belle wants "adventure in the great wide somewhere." As if she was speaking directly to princess critics (which, in a way, she is) Belle is signaling that she wants to do more than just settle down. She wants something to *happen*. Of course, *all* Disney princesses up to this point had adventures (think of Snow White having to run from a wicked stepmother and survive hiding out in the woods, or Ariel going off on a quest to become her true self) but   the princess critics don't see that. Belle spells it out for them. And, if her wish for adventure wasn't enough, the movie throws in a proposal scene between Belle and Gaston that is practically an exegesis on Disney princess motivations.

"Picture this:" Gaston tells Belle, resting his muddy boots on her favorite book. "A rustic hunting lodge. My latest kill roasting over the fire. My little wife, massaging my feet." Belle is horrified by this picture of domesticity. Not necessarily, I think, because of the particulars but because of who is suggesting them. "Madame Gaston, his little wife. Ugh!" Belle sings, before reiterating: "I want much more than this provincial life!" It isn't that Belle doesn't want to settle down or start a family — she tells her father that Gaston's "not the one," implying that she hopes to find her perfect match — it's that she doesn't want to do it with someone like Gaston. Someone who doesn't value her intellect, and wants her to be his "angel in the house." Belle is well-versed in the feminine arts (later on, we see that she knows how to tend to the sick, believes in good table manners, is kind to animals, and knows how to dance) so it isn't necessarily that she doesn't want to be a traditional wife. It's that her perfect match will be her intellectual equal. And well . . . that ain't Gaston.

But, to say that the Beast is immediately recognizable as Belle's true love wouldn't be true either. In fact, he seems like even more of a bad guy, initially, than Gaston! Not to mention the fact that Belle meets him under particularly unfavorable circumstances given that he's just locked up her father for trespassing. In the movie's prologue, the Beast is described as "spoiled, selfish, and unkind." Gaston, had he encountered the Enchantress, could easily have been transformed into a Beast himself — he's also "spoiled, selfish and unkind!" So the Beast isn't exactly a fairytale prince in disguise. And he doesn't seem like a very likely candidate for Belle's affection when we first meet him.

Belle's first encounters the Beast as the snarling monster who has imprisoned her father. Unlike Gaston, the Beast's internal and external self initially match. He *acts* like a beast, and he *looks* like one too. That's the whole reason he was turned into a beast in the first place. Of course, there *is* a "prince" in there, but — just as Cinderella needs magic to reveal her true "princess-ness" — the Beast needs a kind of magic to enact his transformation as well.

But Belle is always herself. She immediately offers to take her father's place. As Anna E. Altmann and Gail De Vos write, in their book *Tales, Then and Now: More Folktales as Literary Fictions for Young Adults*, Belle has "courage, independence, spirit, and integrity," — she's a Disney princess. And the Beast, who we know is "selfish," sees Belle as someone who could potentially break the spell, and agrees to the trade. "Come into the light," she tells the Beast. She sees him, in all his external beastliness, and she agrees to stay. We know that Belle has the power to see beyond the external and into the internal, so we know that, in seeing the Beast's external ugliness, she sees his *internal* ugliness as well. He is who he says he is, she knows what she's getting, she knows the sacrifice she's making, and she makes it anyway. She takes her father's place.

The "magic" that will ultimately transform the Beast is love. "If he could learn to love another and earn her love in return by the time the last petal fell, then the spell would be broken. If not, he would be doomed to remain a beast for all time." Those are the terms of the Beast's curse. He must fall in love, but he must also *earn* another's love. And he's got until the last petal of the enchanted rose falls. But how will a "spoiled, selfish, and unkind" person earn the love of a "princess"? Here is the fascinating paradox of *Beauty and the Beast*: by loving Belle, the Beast will make himself worthy of Belle's love. Altmann and De Vos say "there is nothing in the Beast for her to see until she puts it there." But that's not quite right. Belle doesn't have the power to *insert* traits into the Beast's character. Instead, she *draws them out* by being someone the Beast can love. Remember that the Beast was, initially, a prince. An unkind one, yes, but don't forget the symbolism of the fairytale prince. There's good in there somewhere, we know it, because we know he's a prince — and because the enchantress chose him, and not Gaston, to turn into a monster. So we know there's *something* in there to be drawn out. And love is the way to do it. Love is the symbolic force of transformation in every other Disney princess movie, and this film is no different. But, *Beauty and the Beast* shows us how it *works*. And this is how: if a man has a "prince" within him, the love of a good woman can draw it out. And, in return, the woman gets a man worthy of her love. "In the end," says Linda Woolverton, "Belle gets a great guy."

The Beast's transformation begins immediately. "You would . . . take his place?" he asks Belle. It is a truly selfless thing that Belle is proposing. She is willing to give up all her dreams in order to save her father's life. The Beast has never heard of such a thing. It touches him — you can hear it in his voice. But he makes the deal nonetheless, throwing Belle into the tower room and Maurice into an enchanted carriage that takes him back to the village. "You didn't even let me say goodbye!" Belle admonishes. "I'll never see him again, and you didn't even let me say goodbye." The Beast is speechless. He didn't know he *should* have let her say goodbye. She's changing him already, showing him there's a different way for people to relate to one another — showing him what love looks like.

So now all the key elements are in place. We, the audience, know what is going to happen. We've been given all the pieces — a girl looking for her intellectual equal, a man looking for redemption, a curse that can only be broken by love. So we are watching and waiting to see how it will all take place. And the princess critics, as *they* watch and wait, complain. The princess critics' fatal flaw, as we know, is that they take everything too literally. And, when it comes to symbolism, that can only lead to misunderstanding. In *Beauty and the Beast*, the Beast's journey back to humanity is a symbolic one. As opposed to *Sleeping Beauty*, where the symbolic character never finds a way into the realistic world, *Beauty and the Beast* seamlessly integrates the two. The Beast is both a man, *and* a symbol of manhood. His relationship with Belle is both a realistic meeting of minds, *and* a symbolic representation of the transformative power of love. It's *both*. We can see that. *Children* can see that. Princess critics cannot.

See, to princess critics, *Beauty and the Beast* is about bestiality. Yup, you read that right. But that's what happens when you take things too literally. "Beauty and the Beast is about a bookish fish-out-of-water named Belle who shacks up with a hulking animal resembling an upright water buffalo with dreadlocks," proclaims Thelma Adams in *The Observer*. "He's a beast! La la la. She's a girl! La la la. She could be his guest—as an entrée! Anything that happens between these two that isn't verbal jousting is bestiality." But this implies that Belle falls in love with the Beast *because* he's a beast. As in, she looks at him and she's like, "Finally! A talking animal! I'm *so* into animals, but I couldn't find one I could discuss literature with. This is perfect!" That's ridiculous. The whole *point* of this movie is that she sees the *man* within the beast. She looks *beyond* his ugliness and sees his inner beauty. Jeez.

But there *is* a point to the Beast's beastliness. And it *is* wrapped up with sexuality. There's a reason the enchantress turned the prince into a *beast* instead of, say, a frog, or an object like his servants. He's a *beast* because beasts are aggressive, strong, stubborn, powerful, and selfish — a beast holds within himself all the basest urges of men. The Beast has been transformed into what the prince was to begin with — a man, without a woman's touch. Or, to put it another way, a man without a woman worth channeling those urges towards protecting, loving, and supporting. So, it's true that one of those urges is sexual. There's a sort of raw sexuality that emanates from the Beast, but it isn't his *beastliness* that is sexual. His sexual urges are *represented* by his beastly form.

I mean, think about it. Gaston *also* emanates sexuality. That's kind of all he is. "Every last inch of me's covered in hair!" he sings, ripping his shirt open. (You know who else is covered in hair? The Beast!) Gaston brawls, he spits, he shoots, he's square-jawed and deep-voiced, and he's got "biceps to spare." All this signals his masculine sexual energy. But the prince, when he's revealed as a prince, is *more* than that, in a way that Gaston is not. "The half-buried truth about Disney's "Beauty and the Beast" is that, in the end, the prince is a letdown," writes Jia Tolentino in *The New Yorker*. And there's some truth to that. Nine-year-old me certainly found him kind of weird-looking, when I first saw him as a prince, without really being able to say why. But it isn't because we want him to go back to being a beast. It's because there's something appealing to women about the raw sexuality of men. But in real life, a man can't be *just* his sexual urges — the way Gaston is — he's got to be more than that. So, when the Beast turns back into a man, we know that that sexual energy is still there within him, but it's been tempered by the love he feels for Belle such that he won't hurt her the way Gaston would.

So, the Beast's beastliness is a symbol for the way in which, as a man, he had allowed his base urges to take him over. And Belle's first clue that, perhaps, the Beast is more than what he seems is when, later in the movie, he uses those same urges to protect her, not hurt her. But, to the princess critics, this means that Belle's relationship with the Beast is not *just* bestial, it's also a product of Stockholm Syndrome — the psychological term for when a hostage falls in love with her captor. Yup, that's right, the princess critics are psychologists now.

"Belle gets pretty familiar with the Beast's moods and what will set him off, which may seem like she's getting to know him as a friend, but is really just an innate survival instinct telling her to tread lightly around his monstrous ass so he doesn't rip her in half in a fit of spectacular rage," write Simone Bower and Megan B. on *Cracked*. But, according to a *real* psychologist, Frank Ochberg, victims of Stockholm Syndrome "can't talk. They can't eat. They can't move. They can't use a toilet without permission," and they go through "a period of feeling that they are going to die." For all the Beast's yelling and stomping around, he never threatens Belle's life in any way. With *Beauty and the Beast*, more than, perhaps, any other Disney princess movie, the princess critics are grasping at straws.

So, what *does* happen? The Beast wants very much for Belle to like him — his life depends on it — but he has no idea where to start. "She's so beautiful and I'm . . . well, look at me!" the Beast rages. He can't imagine anyone being able to see past his ugly exterior. *He* couldn't see past the enchantress' ugliness when she was dressed as a crone, why should Belle see through his ugliness now? "You must help her to see past all that," his servants tell him. "I don't know how," the Beast responds. This is the Beast's problem: he doesn't know how to control his urges, he's never tried — never had a *reason* to try. But his servants try to counsel him. And, in doing so, they lay out the qualities of a real man — not a man ruled by his urges — a man in control of them, and able to use them to care for and protect the woman he loves. He must be *a gentleman.* "Give her a debonaire smile." "Impress her with your rapier wit." "But don't frighten the girl." "Be gentle" "Shower her with compliments." "But be sincere." "And above all: you must control your temper." So now we've got a clear alternative to Gaston's version of masculinity. A man versus a gentleman.

So the Beast, trying to act like a gentleman, asks Belle to join him for dinner. But Belle refuses (not the behavior of a frightened captive). She wants nothing to do with him. So the Beast, to save his own life, must woo her. And he does his best, regulating the tone of his voice, and even saying "please." But Belle continues to refuse, and the Beast — still a creature of his basest impulses — ends up yelling at her and storming out. "She'll never see me as anything but a monster," he moans in despair. To him, Belle is reacting to his external form. But, really, its his *internal* self she finds beastly. So, on the one hand, the Beast doesn't seem like a particularly nice guy. On the other hand, he was trying to be polite — which, it's clear, is contrary to his nature. Yes, he's doing all this out of a selfish desire to save himself. But it's a start.

Then Belle tries to escape. Out of curiosity, Belle enters the forbidden West Wing — the Beast's lair — and finds the enchanted rose. Mesmerized, she removes the protective glass cover and reaches out to touch the glowing flower. But, just before she touches it, the Beast swoops in and grabs the glass cover. "Do you know what you could have done?!" he screams at her. It's frightening, yes, but the Beast has a point. When the last petal of the enchanted rose falls, the Beast's curse becomes permanent. What if Belle had knocked off another petal? Or all the petals? The Beast is, understandably, concerned. But his gruff demeanor and inability to control his feelings, frighten Belle and convince her to break her promise. She runs from the castle, leaps onto her horse, and rides off into the forest. The Beast immediately sees that he's let his temper run away with him again and is ashamed. He's starting to see that there's another way to be.

The forest is full of wolves. Now, we have no way of knowing for sure what the Beast's motives are in following Belle into the forest. Presumably, one of them is the fact that Belle is his only chance of becoming human again and she's getting away — his selfishness again. But we can also assume that he knows the forest around his castle is full of bloodthirsty wolves and he doesn't want Belle to be eaten alive. Whatever his motives, the Beast follows her and finds her losing a battle with the pack of wolves. And it is in this moment that the Beast uses his brute force and animal aggression in service of protecting someone else for the first time. The Beast's own life is in danger. But he leaps at the wolves — biting, tearing, scratching — and frightens them off. But not before being injured himself. So injured that he can't get up — would die, if no one helped him.

And so we come to a pivotal moment in the narrative. Belle sees the Beast, lying helpless in the snow, and is initially prepared to leave him there. He's a beast, he imprisoned her, she's free to go. But she chooses to stay. She knows that he saved her life — without him the wolves would surely have killed her — and she know she owes him *his* life in return. So she brings him back to the castle and tends his wounds. It's worth noting here that, from this point on, Belle is basically there of her own free will. The wolves were gone, she could have run. Or she could have brought the Beast back to the castle and *then* run. But she stays, and takes care of him. Yes, technically she is still his prisoner, because those are the terms of his deal. But it's important that she has made a choice here. She isn't a helpless damsel in distress, imprisoned by a ruthless monster, doing whatever she can to survive. She has chosen to stay — she's willing to give him a second chance.

The moment that changes Belle and the Beast from enemies to friends happens as she tends to his wounds. *He* wants to act like a beast, licking at the gashes on his arms. *She* wants to act like a human, pouring hot water into a bowl and soaking a cloth to clean his wound. And as they struggle over whose method will win — beast or human — they begin to argue. She presses the cloth to the Beasts arm and he roars in pain, making the household objects cower. "That hurts!" he yells at her. But Belle isn't cowering. "If you'd hold still it wouldn't hurt as much!" Belle yells back. "If you hadn't run away, this wouldn't have happened," the Beast counters. "If you hadn't frightened me, I wouldn't have run away!" she shoots back. "Well *you* shouldn't have been in the West Wing!" "Well *you* should learn to control your temper!"

And there it is: learn to *control* your temper. Belle is the first person in the Beast's entire life who has given as good as she got. Belle is not cowering in fear, she's the same Belle she was in the village — a girl who knows exactly who she is. She knows the Beast was in the wrong, and she holds him to it. And, as they bicker back and forth, the one thing the Beast has no answer for is this: learn to control your temper. It's not, you see, that the Beast must change completely into someone else. It's only that he has to learn to control his urges. When he was fighting the wolves, the Beast's temper was an asset. In dealing with Belle, it's a hindrance. Belle is telling him he can exert control over his urges and best them. "This might sting a little," she tells him as she applies the damp cloth. And the Beast who, a moment earlier, might have yelled out in pain, simply closes his eyes, grunts, and bears it. He *can* reign himself in. He *can* get himself in check.

In this moment, suddenly, he is learning how to be a man. "Thank you," Belle says, "for saving my life." The Beast's startled expression says it all. He is being *treated*, for the first time, like a man. And being treated like one, he *acts* like one. "You're welcome," he tells her, his voice quiet and calm.

"I've never felt this way about anyone," the Beast — who is suddenly wearing clothes and walking on two legs instead of four — says as he watches Belle walk in the snow. In recognizing him as a man instead of a beast, Belle has awakened the Beast's humanity.

Suddenly he is capable of love — of tenderness. And the object of his love is the woman who saw him for what he was *inside*. And Belle, for her part, is coming to realize that "there's something in him that I simply didn't see." Belle, who is able to see inside the hearts of the people she meets, is surprised to find the Beast is different than she originally thought. But he's different because she *inspired* him to be different. And she reaches out to him, actively teaching him now how to be a man. She shows him how to be gentle — feeding the birds without frightening them. She shows him how to be civilized — sipping his soup instead of devouring it with his face in the bowl. She reads to him. She teaches him to dance. She's civilizing him. Giving him a reason to be a man instead of a beast.

And the Beast, who is eagerly learning all these lessons, feels that he wants to do something for Belle. This "selfish" beast, who couldn't understand why Belle would want to take her father's place, suddenly wants to do something for someone else. And what does he choose to do for her? He gives her a *library*. Belle, who's been seeking acceptance all her life, who was seen as odd in her village because of her love of *reading,* is given a library. It's the perfect gift and it shows that Belle has found what she was looking for: someone who accepts her for who she is. The Beast's desire to give her a library, — and his delight in her joyful reaction to receiving it — show that the Beast, more than anyone else in Belle's life, sees her for who she truly is. "It's yours," the Beast tells her. Not, you can come here whenever you want, or, you can read any of these books. It's *yours*. He has given something away to someone he loves. By being truly herself, Belle has inspired the Beast to find *his* true self. And, in becoming his true self, he is becoming someone who can give Belle what she needs: acceptance as a thinking person, not simply a domestic object.

To the princess critics, though, all of this means that *Beauty in the Beast* sends the message that a woman can *change* a man. Meet a jerk, love him enough, and he'll become a prince. That's what the princess critics think this movie is about. It promotes "the idea that the right woman can 'tame' a beastly, abusive, troubled man and turn him into a prince," says Peggy Orenstein in *Huffington Post*. "The love story in this one is one of the most disturbing ones in the princess lineup and rather regressive," writes Mari Rogers of the Feminist Disney Tumblr. But that's not it. It's too simplistic — as usual. The idea is actually this: if a man is truly a good man (like we know the Beast is, because he is a prince and because he was chosen for this curse) but he's allowed himself to be ruled by his urges, a woman's love can cause him to channel those urges and use them in service of the woman he loves. Had Belle tried to civilize Gaston, it wouldn't have worked. His beautiful exterior concealed a warped and evil soul. Belle doesn't try to teach the Beast anything until she sees — after he rescues her — that glimmer of humanity and goodness inside him.

So then we come to the Beast's most important moment in the movie. After a night of dinner and dancing, in which it seems clear that Belle and the Beast are falling in love, the Beast asks Belle, "Are you happy here with me?" Are you happy here . . . with *me*. The Beast wants to know if he has made Belle as happy as she has made him. Her happiness matters to him. And Belle says "yes." She *is* happy. She wouldn't say she was if she wasn't, we know that about her. She's found acceptance in the unlikeliest of places, but she's found it and she's happy.

But there is one more thing she needs for her happiness to be complete: to see her father, to know if he's okay. And the Beast immediately grants her wish with his magic mirror. But Maurice, determined to find Belle and rescue her, is lost in the woods, sick and alone. The animation in this sequence is brilliant. Somehow, the Disney artists suddenly make the Beast look like a man. He's still the Beast, nothing has changed, but his facial expression and something about his eyes render him human. "I release you. You're no longer my prisoner," he tells her. He believes he has sealed his doom. She won't come back. She can't possibly love him enough to stay if she doesn't have to. But he does it anyway. He condemns himself to

115

eternal life as a beast. And he does it for love. "I had to," he says afterwards. "I love her." His transformation is complete.

Upon rescuing her father and returning home, Belle finds that Gaston has put into motion a diabolical plot. He is going to lock Maurice up in an insane asylum if Belle doesn't agree to marry him. One man is willing to give Belle up out of love for her, another is wiling to commit a crime in order to force her to be his. Which one is the real man? "*He's* not the monster, Gaston, *you* are!" Belle tells him, after showing the townspeople that the Beast is real. It has become abundantly clear who is the monster and who is the man. But the monster looks like a man and the man looks like a monster. Both Gaston and the Beast have acted on their feelings for Belle, and each have become more themselves. Gaston has become a true villain, willing to risk innocent lives to claim his prize. The Beast has become a true hero, willing to give up his own happiness in order to ensure the happiness of the woman he loves. The contrast couldn't be clearer. True love, the movie tells us, is a meeting of hearts and minds — a union in which both people accept one another as the individuals they are and are willing to make sacrifices for the happiness of the other. It's not just implied through symbolism this time. We've seen it develop and grow, and play itself out within the plot of the movie. The moment of true love, writ large.

Now that Gaston knows about the Beast — and about Belle's feelings for him — he's got to kill him. He locks Belle and Maurice in a cellar and leads a mob of angry villagers to the Beast's castle. Gaston is a hunter looking for a trophy — a trophy that is just as much Belle herself, as it is the Beast's head. Initially the Beast is content to die. He thinks he'll never see Belle again and knows his life is essentially over. While the household objects mobilize to defend the castle, the Beast remains locked in his tower, resigned to his fate. But Belle is able to break out of the cellar and follows hot on Gaston's heels, intent on saving the Beast from the murderous mob. When the Beast sees Belle riding into danger, he rallies.

Both Gaston and the Beast are fighting for Belle. But Gaston wants to possess her and the Beast wants to keep her safe. "Did you honestly think she'd want *you*, when she had someone like *me*?" Gaston taunts the Beast. But he's got it wrong. The Beast *doesn't* think Belle wants him. He just loves her and wants to protect her. Still, even though he could have killed Gaston, he shows compassion. His internal transformation is complete. He is a *gentleman*. He doesn't kill Gaston, but tells him to leave and never come back. And Gaston, who a moment earlier had been sobbing and pleading for his life, leaps up and stabs the Beast in the back. *He's* decidedly *not* a gentleman.

The Beast, mortally wounded, looks up into Belle's tear-stained face. "At least I got to see you one last time," he tells her. I got to *see* you. Belle and the Beast are the only two people in the movie who, when they look into each other's eyes, see each other's true selves. "Please don't leave me!" Belle sobs. "I love you!" The Beast had been willing to die for Belle, Belle has returned to him. The Beast has become a man worth loving, and Belle has found acceptance from the man she loves. Belle's words enact the magical transformation to mirror the internal one that has already taken place. In a shower of sparkling rain the Beast is lifted into the air and changed into a man. He turns around, a completely different-looking person. "It's me!" he tells Belle, in a completely different voice. She looks into his eyes — the windows to his soul — and sees the man she loves. "It *is* you!" she cries in delight. And their kiss — true love's kiss — wields the power it always does: the power to transform. In a sparkling burst of fireworks, the castle and the servants are returned to their original selves.

*

With the Disney princess canon from Snow White to Belle, little girls have everything they need to know in order to be "princesses" in their own lives. They understand the deep and powerful meaning of true love. They know how to figure out if a potential love interest is worthy of them. And they've learned how to stay true to themselves, even in the face of adversity. They've seen grit and determination, kindness and empathy, resourcefulness and resilience. It's a perfect blueprint for how to grow up into a woman of integrity and courage without sacrificing femininity and grace.

If Disney had simply gone on creating heroines like Cinderella, Ariel, and Belle, little girls growing up into women would have been well-served for years to come. But that isn't what happened.

Even though Ariel and Belle were seen by most contemporary *viewers* as feminist heroines, the *princess critics* just couldn't leave well enough alone. By the time *Aladdin* came out in 1992, the effects of the princess critics' complaints were beginning to show. Not to the point of ruining the movie — not yet — but enough to foreshadow what was to come. That — among other things — is why *Beauty and the Beast* is the high point of Disney princess movies. In Belle, all the attributes of a Disney princess are personified — she is kind, brave, loyal, and true. And in the prince the Beast becomes, we see the kind of man we hope to find — a gentleman. The princess critics want us to believe that these traits are signs of weakness, and that a man — any man — is extraneous. But the princess critics are wrong. Girls, and women, who love this movie — or any of the Disney princess movies that came before — should know the truth: a woman is strong *and* graceful, and love is a force that enriches our lives.

Chapter Six: Jasmine

By the time *Aladdin* came out in 1992 Disney's Renaissance was in full swing. The enormous success of *The Little Mermaid* and *Beauty and the Beast* had made Disney animated features the gold standard for family-friendly entertainment. Audiences lined up in droves to see what the studio would produced next, and 10-year-old me was no exception. *Beauty and the Beast* had literally changed my life the year before, and I was primed and ready for another epic movie-going experience. With a giant box of Raisinettes (still my movie theater candy of choice) in hand, I waited with bated breath to see what world I'd be transported to next.

Disney delivered. The story of the scrappy street rat who follows his heart and uses his wits to save the day and win the girl was just what this pre-adolescent romantic was hoping for. It wasn't *Beauty and the Beast* level good — what film could be? — but it *was* good. And I — like so many others that summer in 1992 — left the movie theater satisfied. But, this time, it wasn't the princess we were interested in. Young princess-lovers like myself weren't seeking to emulate Princess Jasmine, we were falling in love with Aladdin. *Who cares about Jasmine?* we would have said. *The movie's about Aladdin!*

Jasmine may be a secondary character in *Aladdin*, but she's an "official" princess. She embodies the signature Disney princess

119

mindset, but she's also the first to negatively show the effects of the princess critics' complaints about Disney princesses. As such, she's a study in contradictions — stuck between two worlds. In some ways, she's a true Disney princess — loving, emotionally strong, and true to her principles — in other ways she's a spoiled brat — whining when things don't go her way and gloating over her pet tiger's bad behavior. In some ways she's forward-thinking and ahead of her time — insisting that her country's laws are wrong, and longing to live like the common people — in other ways she's more of an ingénue than any of the princesses who came before — having literally never left the castle walls. The hardship and adversity that honed the princess characteristics of the heroines that came before haven't touched Jasmine at all. The worst thing that's ever happened to her is that the law says she must get married by her next birthday. But, like the princesses before her, she is fighting against a true injustice — being forced to marry before she's found her love match. At every turn she is both a traditional Disney princess, and a product of the confused and misguided ideology of the princess critics. But she was destined to cement that ideology into our minds forever as truth.

The idea that Disney princesses needed a feminist reboot was well established by the time *Aladdin* came out in 1992. When all those film critics called Ariel "rebellious," "fully realized," and "spunky" back in 1989, they were alluding to the idea that there was now a notion that the original princesses of Walt Disney's day *weren't* those things — that they were passive, two-dimensional, and demure. And, by the time *Beauty and the Beast* came out in 1991, there was an active push to make Belle "a feminist" and a "woman of the '90s" — as *Beauty and the Beast* screenwriter Linda Woolverton put it. If you look at the Disney princess cannon as a spectrum moving from the traditional, on one end, to the radically feminist, on the other, *Beauty and the Beast* holds the perfect center. Disney's Renaissance provided a necessary update to the Disney princess narrative — drawing it out of the antiquated fairytale shorthand and into a more vibrant and modern present — and offered us characters that upheld the traditional fairytale ideals in a format we could understand. But, with *Aladdin*, Disney began to cross the line.

Contemporary film critics hailed Jasmine as a new kind of princess. *The LA Times* called her "unusually headstrong." Brian Lowry, of *Variety*, called her "defiant" and "anachronistically liberated." *Entertainment Weekly* called her "a spark plug" and said she was "the most full-bodied (in every sense) of the new Disney heroines." That reputation has only continued to grow. Modern princess critics *love* her. Candice Darden, of *Buzzfeed* writes that Jasmine "stubbornly defended herself against the patriarchy" and made Aladdin "WORK for her forgiveness." And Chelsea Mize, of *Bustle* says "All in all, Jazzy is a pretty strong woman with a solid feminist streak." She appears close to the top of every feminist ranking of Disney princesses on the internet. But is Jasmine really so different from the princesses who came before her? Do the traits that make her so "liberated" stand in direct opposition to the traits of the other princesses? The movie sure wants us to think so!

In presenting Jasmine as a new kind of princess, *Aladdin* implicitly compares her to the princesses that came before. Jasmine's penchant for speaking her mind, her unwillingness to compromise her core beliefs, and her insistence on finding a romantic partner who is her intellectual equal are all meant to signal that she's a "strong" woman. These traits tell us that she's not a "damsel in distress" waiting around for some random guy to save her. She's her own woman — capable of standing up for herself, and unwilling to fall in love with the first guy who comes along to claim her. But, as we've already established, *none* of the princesses who came before were simply damsels in distress. Internal strength, integrity, courage, and heart are qualities that could just as easily describe Snow White or Cinderella as they could Jasmine. The problem is: by telling us that all of these traits were *new* traits, Disney solidified the princess critic narrative about the old princesses. If Jasmine — and all her strength, courage, independence, etc. — was a *new* princess, then the *old* princesses must not have had those things.

Aladdin — and the way it sets up this distinction between the "new" and "old" princesses — was a turning point for Disney princesses. Forever afterward, an "old" Disney princess would be seen as a passive, husband-hunting damsel in distress. And, with Disney's new focus on actively imbuing their princesses with "feminist" qualities, Disney's princesses were doomed to become the man-hating, shallow, virtue-signaling puppets they eventually became. See, Jasmine actually *is* a traditional princess, but she presents her traditional princess characteristics like a true feminist would: by yelling, stomping around, and belittling anyone who disagrees with her. *Aladdin*, through Jasmine, was the beginning of the end.

*

Because the movie isn't really about Jasmine, much of her narrative plays out on the sidelines. So, before we begin talking about Jasmine, here's a quick refresher on the plot of *Aladdin*:

Aladdin is an orphan who lives by his wits on the streets of Agrabah with his pet monkey, Abu. But he is also "the diamond in the rough" — the only person worthy enough to enter the cave of wonders and retrieve the magic lamp. Jasmine is a sheltered princess who is railing against a law that says she must marry a prince by her next birthday. Refusing to follow the law, Jasmine runs away dressed as a commoner into the marketplace. There, she meets Aladdin. The two fall in love but are immediately separated by the palace guards who have been sent by Jafar, the Sultan's evil advisor. Jafar tells Jasmine that Aladdin has been executed.

Meanwhile, Aladdin discovers a magic lamp containing a genie (voiced by the brilliant Robin Williams). He uses his first wish to become a prince, thinking that Jasmine will only love him if he's royalty too. But when he shows up as Prince Ali Ababwa, intent on winning Jasmine's hand, she wants nothing to do with him, saying he's just like all the other vain suitors. Aladdin wins Jasmine over by acting more like himself (though not revealing his true identity) and taking her for a magic carpet ride.

Jasmine tells her father that she wants to marry Prince Ali, but Jafar intervenes, stealing the lamp and wishing to become Sultan himself. He banishes Aladdin to a frozen wasteland and makes Jasmine his slave. Aladdin tricks Jafar into using his last wish to become a Genie himself, then traps him in a lamp. The Sultan allows Jasmine to marry her true love and Aladdin uses his final wish to set the Genie free. Happy endings all around.

In many ways it's a typical Disney movie, full of daring heroes, dastardly villains, sacrifice, romance, and — of course — a happy ending. And that's how we watched it at the time, rooting for Aladdin to figure out that who he *is* is more important than what he *has,* and for the love story to reach its inevitable happy conclusion. But, underneath all that, were the first, small rumblings of the princess critics' hold on the Disney princess narrative — of the revision of the traditional narrative, and the statement of who the new "feminist" princess would be. It plays out under the surface of the main narrative, within the arc of a character who really ought to be a secondary player in the narrative: Princess Jasmine.

The princess critic version of the traditional princess narrative is spelled out in Jasmine's first scene. We find her arguing with her father about a law that says she must marry a prince before her next birthday. "I just want to make sure you're taken care of. Provided for," the Sultan whines at Jasmine. He doesn't say he wants her to be happy, to find her equal — the traditional princess happy ending. Instead, he uses the language of the patriarchy: "Taken care of," "Provided for." *This* the movie is saying, is what the *other* princesses were searching for. "The law is wrong!" Jasmine insists. "If I do marry, I want it to be for love." Jasmine's defiance is meant to signal her modernity. Linda Larkin, who voiced Jasmine in the movie, said, "She's not a victim . . . She's got spirit. And she has power." She's not, in other words, an "traditional" Disney princess. In *Aladdin,* traditional princesses waited around for a random, powerful men to come and take care of all their problems, but Jasmine is *different* because she refuses that fate by insisting on marrying for love.

There's only one problem: *all* Disney princesses marry for love. Alright, sure, the idea that a Disney princess wouldn't marry *at all* is a new one, but nothing else about this is. And almost all of them marry men that their caregivers are — at least initially — unhappy with. For those of us who love the traditional princesses, Jasmine's desire to stand up to the unfair law marks her as one of our own — not somebody new.

The idea that we would first meet our princess fighting back against injustice is nothing new either. All princesses face hardship and have to overcome it. When Jasmine's father insists that this is the law and that time is running out for her to pick someone to marry, Jasmine shoots back, "Maybe I don't want to be a princess anymore!" We're supposed to reel in horror (while princess critics jump for joy). Darden compares Jasmine favorably to other princesses saying that she doesn't care about "status" and "thwarted the restrictions" placed on her. *A princess who doesn't want to be a princess?!*, we're meant to cry. *Who ever heard of such a thing?!* Actually, everyone. Everyone has heard of this. Aurora said pretty much the same thing when she found out that being a princess meant she couldn't be with her mystery woodland lover. Belle has no idea the Beast is really a prince. Cinderella has no idea the man she's dancing with at the ball is really Prince Charming. Ariel is willing to give up being a mer-princess to become human. Princess-ness is actually totally unimportant to Disney princesses. Princess, remember, is merely a symbol. It's not the goal. But, since princess critics don't get that, here's princess Jasmine yelling about how she doesn't want to be a princess. Join the club, sweetheart.

We also learn that Jasmine has never left the palace walls. She longs to go out and see the world, meet new people, and have adventures (you know, in the great wide somewhere, or whatever). She's a princess, trapped in a situation she longs to escape. *That* sounds pretty familiar too. Actually, it's true about every other princess before her. Aside from the fact that we're being hit over the head with it, we relate to Jasmine the way we relate to every other Disney princess. And we love her, as we loved them.

Jasmine may not be the new kind of princess the princess critics hold her up to be, but there is a group of people in this movie who *are* distinctly different: the men. Until Gaston, from *Beauty and the Beast*, the villains in Disney princess movies were female, in keeping with the traditional fairytale symbolism of the blossoming woman pitted against the spent old crone. But a feminist princess isn't concerned with fairytale symbolism. She's fighting the patriarchy. So the villains become male — and remain male ever after, with one exception. And it's not just the villains that are different in *Aladdin*. With the exception of the Genie, the men in this film are either evil, infantile, or in need of instruction in the feminist worldview. The Sultan is a childish pushover (at one point we even see him alone in his room playing with toys!) who struggles to assert his will. The villain, Jafar, is two-faced and "toxic." And the hero, Aladdin, needs Jasmine to give him a stern talking to before he figures out how to be a hero. This, the movie seems to be saying, is the state of manhood.

"Good luck marrying *her* off!" rages the latest suitor as he stomps out of Jasmine's room, his underwear exposed where Jasmine's tiger, Raja, has bitten off his pants. Here is the traditional heroic suitor, his pants around his ankles, a laughingstock. *Ugh!* we're supposed to collectively sigh. *Men!* But, I mean, her tiger *bit* his *pants!* Who knows what kind of guy he normally is? And even if he actually *is* a jerk, as we learn later that he is, — he's just one guy! But, that's the problem. These men — these suitors — are here to own her, and she wants to own herself. And fair enough. But does that mean *all* men will feel that way? Debatable.

Faced with these dilemmas, Jasmine does what any Disney princess in her situation would do: she runs away. This is her moment of growing up, of asserting her will. Like Ariel realizing she must take her destiny into her own hands and visit the sea witch. Like Cinderella insisting that she go to the ball. Like Belle taking her father's place in the Beast's dungeon. Jasmine sees a future unfolding for herself in which she remains as sheltered as she has always been — passed from her father to her husband — and she rejects it. As she should. As any Disney princess would.

Kayleigh Dray, of *Stylist*, who ranks Jasmine fifth most feminist out of fifteen Disney princesses, says "she rejects the idea of an arranged marriage." But Aurora, who does the same thing, is ranked number fifteen. And Belle, whose marriage to Gaston isn't arranged, but is pretty much expected by everyone in the town including her own father, is number eleven. Jasmine, who makes a pretty reckless and fairly stupid decision to run away from home with no money, no change of clothes, no idea what's even out there, is the "feminist" one.

The first thing Jasmine does when she gets out in the world is get rescued by a man. "She's not sheltered," Linda Larkin proclaimed of the character she voiced. And that's the prevailing narrative about Jasmine, if all the "feminist rankings" are to be believed. But that's completely untrue. Jasmine has literally never left the palace walls. She's so sheltered she's never even heard of money. Which is how she gets in trouble and needs Aladdin to rescue her.

In true Disney form, the minute Aladdin sees Jasmine — even dressed as a commoner — he is drawn to her (like Snow White's prince at the wishing well). When he sees that she's in trouble, he leaps down from his perch on one of the other stalls and pretends that Jasmine is his half-wit sister. Jasmine, catching his drift, plays along, and the pair escape through the marketplace to Aladdin's "home" on a rooftop above the city.

This girl who, moments before, had been railing against the idea of being "taken care of" and "provided for" is promptly in need of that very thing, and accepts it readily. Not only does she accept Aladdin's help, but she allows herself to be seen as a total dunderhead in order to do it. The fact that she *needs* Aladdin's help is obvious —

she's completely out of her depth — and I, personally, take no issue with a woman being helped by a man. It's a sweet boy-meets-girl moment. I point it out only to illustrate that, for all her big talk, Jasmine is perfectly willing to accept a man's help. In a sense, the filmmakers make Jasmine *talk* a big feminist game, but, when reality hits, she sees that radical feminism doesn't actually come in handy.

In the very next moment, though, Jasmine is at it again, trying to show that she's a different kind of princess. On their way to Aladdin's rooftop home, Aladdin assumes that Jasmine won't be able to pole vault from one rooftop to the next — which *I* would assume too given that Jasmine has never left the palace walls and pole vaulting probably wasn't part of her princess training. So Aladdin lays a plank of wood down for her to walk across — a pretty gentlemanly act if you ask me. But Jasmine, a smirk on her face, grabs a pole of her own and vaults over Aladdin's head to the next rooftop. Aladdin's openmouthed stare could easily be translated as *"What a woman!"* But, really, who *cares* if a princess is able to pole vault? What does it say about her inner strength, her courage, her true heart? Nothing at all. But this is the first instance of a trend that would begin to emerge in the princesses that come after Jasmine — this emphasis on physical achievements rather than internal ones. In the same way that the Dream Big, Princess campaign tried to rebrand the princesses as athletes and prodigies, Jasmine's pole vaulting skills make her, somehow, more attractive to Aladdin, even though they say absolutely nothing about her inner character.

In Aladdin's hideout, we learn something important about *Aladdin*: he wants money. It makes sense — he's a penniless orphan who has to steal in order to eat — of *course* he wishes he was wealthy. But, as the hero of our story, his dreams seem a little superficial. He seems to believe that material things will solve all his problems. Who better to instruct him on the error of his ways than Jasmine!

Like the Beast, who has something in him Belle "simply didn't see" at first, Aladdin has a fairytale *something* that makes him more than just a homeless street urchin — he's the "diamond in the rough." But instead of drawing the gentleman out of the "spoiled, selfish, and unkind" exterior by being a woman worthy of a gentleman's love, Jasmine beats this realization out of him by flouncing around and delivering tongue-lashings. Poor, unenlightened Aladdin, must succumb to the will of Jasmine who knows better. It's true that Aladdin has a lesson to learn — he's the hero of the story, he's got to undergo some kind of change — but it's also true that Jasmine's methods reek of the contrived feminist manifesto that they are.

"Your Majesty, I am Prince Ali Ababwa," Aladdin tells the Sultan in a fake deep voice, arriving at the palace after the Genie turns him into a prince. "Just let her meet me. I will win your daughter." Which is when Jasmine, who's been listening behind the door, bursts in and delivers the line that endears her to the princess critics forever. "How dare you? All of you! Standing around deciding my future? I am not a prize to be won!" "She refuses to let people talk about her future as if she isn't there," writes Dray. "She's more than willing to call people out on their bulls**t." She "refuses to be objectified by her suitors," writes Mize. Okay fine, but *how* is this different from the other princesses?

The whole idea here is supposed to be that Jasmine is calling Aladdin and the Sultan out on something that the men in other Disney princesses movies do without being questioned. But which other prince has behaved as Aladdin does in this scene? Which other father has decided his daughter's life for her as Jasmine accuses the Sultan of doing? Jasmine *is* right to call Aladdin and the Sultan out on their behavior. Aladdin is acting like a pompous ass, and the Sultan is impressed with him because he has a flying rug. But they're acting this way because the filmmakers *made* them — they're straw men, meant to represent the suitors and fathers in the other movies. But they resemble none of them.

An article for *In Style* that identifies six "feminist" Disney princesses says that Jasmine "wears the trousers, both literally and metaphorically." *She's* the one in charge. Aladdin is her supplicant, and she holds the power to grant his wish or deny it. We're supposed to think this is one heck of a gender bender. Oh how the tables have turned! But no Disney princess has ever asked for her prince to use his wealth and power to save her.

None of the princesses who grew up poor (Snow White, Cinderella, Aurora) come to their princes begging to get married. The dynamic isn't "Oh how lowly and sad am I, please rescue me!" it's "I am good enough just the way I am." The whole *point* of the princes in the early Disney princess movies is that they recognize their princesses as fairytale princesses even when they're in rags. And the princesses fall for their princes not because they are princes in the literal sense, but because they are *fairy tale* princes, and worthy of their love. Snow White, Cinderella, and Aurora are confident in who they are, and completely at ease with being seen in rags by their princes. The prince and princess-ness of it all (as we've seen again and again) isn't about literal royalty. It's about internal goodness. So Jasmine's ability to hold her power over Aladdin's head is a refutation of nothing. Which means that, while it works in the context of the story — since Aladdin *does* need to chill out about the whole prince thing — it does nothing as a "gotcha" to princess traditionalists.

Aladdin's suggestion that "We could get out of the palace, see the world," is exactly what Jasmine has been longing for — what all Disney princesses long for — to escape and be free in the world. Aladdin already *is* the kind of person Jasmine wants. He's someone who can take her away from this sheltered life and show her everything she's been missing. Prince Ali is just more of the same. "I can show you the world / Shining, shimmering, splendid / Tell me, princess, now when did you last let your heart decide?" Aladdin sings.

It's seriously unfortunate that the lyrics of *Aladdin's* love ballad are written by Tim Rice instead of Howard Ashman. As Lowry writes, "Ashman's wickedly clever lyrics are easily told from Rice's bland, saccharine ones, and the comparison makes the void Ashman's death left in American musical theater seem even larger." Howard Ashman, who wrote the lyrics for *The Little Mermaid, Beauty and the Beast*, and some of the songs in *Aladdin* died of AIDS in 1991, mere months before the release of *Beauty and the Beast*. His genius is one of the main reasons for the success of Disney's renaissance. But "A Whole New World," which Jasmine and Aladdin sing as they fly through (somewhat improbably) the entire world on the magic carpet is Rice's, not Ashman's. And, as such, it doesn't pack the emotional punch it should, as the moment of Jasmine and Aladdin's affection for each other deepening into true love. But it gets the point across. Aladdin can give Jasmine exactly what she wants — to see the world, and to be allowed to choose her own destiny. And Jasmine, for her part, realizes that — no matter what the law says — she can't go back. Like Ariel, this freedom to be truly herself is what she *must* have. "I'm like a shooting star / I've come so far / I can't go back to where I used to be."

This is — almost beat for beat — the traditional Disney princess moment of the love between two equals providing the motivating force for the princess to accomplish her dreams. For all the princess critics' insistence that Jasmine is a new kind of princess — one who doesn't care about marriage or love — here she is caring deeply about both. Personally, I take no issue with this. Having the love of someone who values you for who you are, and allowing that love to take you to new heights, is one of the great joys of life as far as I'm concerned. But, if Jasmine is supposed to be this new kind of "feminist" princess, what's she doing following the traditional princess script? From a traditional princess perspective, she's doing everything right. It's what she *says* that's wrong. "Why did you lie to me? Did you think I was stupid? That I wouldn't figure it out?" she yells at Aladdin, when she realizes he's the boy from the marketplace. Even though she's right that Aladdin needs to stop being dishonest with her, *that's* not what a traditional princess would say. A traditional princess would be much more patient with the man she loved, and trust that her own moral core and strength of character would bring him around.

Arguably the most problematic scene in any Disney princess movie is a scene that can only be described as "the Jasmine-as-sex-slave" scene. It comes after Jafar has taken the lamp for himself and made himself Sultan. He's dressed Jasmine in red — the color of sex — and makes her feed him an apple — the fruit that represents sexual awakening (as we've already seen in *Snow White*). "A desert boom such as yourself should be on the arm of the most powerful man in the world," he tells her, pulling the chain attached to her handcuffs so she has no choice but to come close to him.

On the one hand, it's pretty straightforward — Jafar is the bad guy and he's doing something really bad. (Jasmine would have every right to claim #MeToo.) But, it's also another misguided feminist statement. Jafar (having made himself the Sultan) is now, essentially, the prince. And he's literally handcuffed the princess and is forcing her to marry him against her will. It's like some nightmare version of the Disney princess narrative. But that's the point. To princess critics, Disney princesses run off with the first guy they meet, because he's royalty and lives in a big castle, and because he's the man and that's what *he* wants. By throwing wine in Jafar's face and screaming "Never!" at the prospect of marrying him, the filmmakers are saying a Disney princess will never again marry the prince simply because he's the prince. But that's completely fine, princess critics, because she never *did* do that. Calm down.

It's what happens next — and the princess critics' reaction to it — that is truly bizarre. When Jasmine catches sight of Aladdin coming to rescue her, she tries to distract Jafar so Aladdin can make his move. But what she *uses* to distract him is sex. In one moment, the movie seems to be saying (correctly) that a man demanding sex from a woman is wrong. In the next, Jasmine is using sex to entrap the man. "I never realized how incredibly handsome you are," she purrs at Jafar, running her hand down her body and swinging her hips as she walks towards him. "You're tall, dark, well-dressed, and I love those eyebrows, they're so angular, and the gaps between your teeth . . ." she begins complimenting his appearance — the thing that doesn't matter. And yes, it's funny to listen to her try to compliment this completely un-compliment-worthy guy, but it's also really creepy and gross. And, when she finally resorts to *kissing* Jafar, everyone in the room — including Jafar's own pet, Iago — utters a collective "Eew!" And so do we, the audience. It's truly cringe-worthy.

Shannon Larson, on *Huffington Post,* writes that, in this moment, Jasmine "takes control of her sexuality to trap a predator." To princess critics, this is a feminist moment. She's using her sexual power over a man to defeat him. But she's also kissing and rubbing herself against a man she finds repugnant. How is that a win for women?! Not to mention the fact that, by using her "feminine wiles" instead of engaging in hand-to-hand combat, Jasmine is also asserting that women and men fight differently. Yes, women can use their sexual power over men as a weapon, but it also acknowledges that a woman's strength is different than a man's. Particularly since, in the very next scene, Jasmine gets literally immobilized inside a giant hourglass while Aladdin does all the sword fighting, and comes up with the idea of how to vanquish Jafar. There's a contradiction here. If Jasmine is to be seen as a "new" kind of Disney princess — one whose looks and passivity aren't as important as her intellect and ability to speak her mind — then surely using her body as a sexual weapon is antithetical to that. And yet, for princess critics, this is a powerful feminist moment of taking control of the narrative.

For princess critics, Jasmine's great triumph is that she finds a way to marry the man *she* wants to marry, and not the person she was *forced* to marry. And yes, that *is* a good thing. But it's no different from any other princess who came before her. Ariel did almost exactly the same thing. Cinderella defied her stepmother to break free of the life she was being forced to lead. Snow White found her way back to the prince the Queen was willing to kill her for loving. What makes Jasmine any more "feminist" than them?

*

Princess Jasmine is proof that the princess critics' narrative had begun to take hold. Her overt virtue-signaling implies an understanding on the part of the filmmakers that the princesses' "anti-feminist" qualities needed to be addressed. But the movie essentially pulled the wool over the princess critics' eyes, convincing them that qualities inherent in *all* Disney princesses were "feminist," by having the princess state them emphatically and angrily at every turn. The problem, of course, is that, without the realization that all Disney princesses are *already* "feminist" in all the ways Jasmine is, the reputation of the old Disney princesses would be tarnished forever.

Disney had crossed the line from traditional to "feminist", and nothing was standing in its way. Jasmine was a "feminist" and princess critics rejoiced, praised her, and asked for more. The things that Jasmine said — rather than the things she did — became the new standard for Disney princess movies. And the preaching, man-hating, femininity-denying princesses that followed appeased the princess critics, but lost Disney its audience of little girls, looking to the princesses for how to grow into women. The age of the princess critic had arrived.

Part III

"I'll Make A Man Out Of You": Historical Heroines

Chapter Seven: Pocahontas

We didn't know, at first, that Disney's renaissance was over. When we went to see *Pocahontas,* in 1995, we were expecting another romantic, funny, tour de force. A year after *Aladdin* had come *The Lion King* — not a princess movie, but fantastic nonetheless — and we'd become spoiled. *Pocahontas* came out the year I turned 13 and I was deep into *Beauty and the Beast* for the second time, thanks to the Broadway production that came out when I was 12. I remember being a little wary of this new movie based, as it was, not on a fairy tale romance but an historical event. But the poster of the statuesque girl, her hair blowing in the wind, surrounded by magical swirling leaves gave me hope that this movie would be just as magical as the others. I — along with everyone else — was destined for disappointment. *Pocahontas* is a preachy, sanctimonious, ideology-driven disgrace. But, worst of all — and most telling, for our purposes — Pocahontas and John Smith do *not* live happily ever after. What on earth was going on? *I'll* tell you what: the princess critics — that radical but vocal minority — had swayed the studio. Pocahontas is not a princess, she's a puppet.

Disney studios purposely set out to tell a story that flew in the face of the "traditional" princess narrative. With *Aladdin* they had set up the revisionist notion that traditional princesses were husband-hunting damsels in distress, and now they were intent on following through. And they were sure this would translate into another major blockbuster. They set their A team to work on *Pocahontas*, relegating their B team to a film they thought would do less well: *The Lion King*. Jim Pentecost, the film's producer, said "Pocahontas is the strongest heroine we've ever had in a Disney film." Supervising animator, Glen Keane, said Pocahontas had more "depth" than Ariel, Jasmine, or Belle. "Pocahontas is more of a woman instead of a teenager," Keane continued. Eric Goldberg, the film's director, said, "We wanted her to be a very spiritual person, somebody who has a connection with nature all the time and whose thoughts run deeper than might seem on the surface." In other words: she isn't shallow, she's not only after a man, and she can hold her own against anyone — particularly a mansplaining capitalist like John Smith (Ugh!).

But, to the studio's confusion and dismay, the movie was not the smash they were expecting. Contemporary critics hated *Pocahontas*. "What's this?" wrote Peter Travers in his 1995 review in *Rolling Stone*. "A Disney musical with the usual first-rate animation and hummable tunes but without the big laughs, the cute talking animals, the magic props and the happy ending. It's practically un-American." Travers went on to complain that the movie's "preachiness" and the fact that it was "somber history instead of the typical sweet fable" were what did it in. Roger Ebert said the film was "less entertaining than it might have been" and said, "on a list including 'Mermaid,' 'Beauty,' 'Aladdin' and 'Lion King,' I'd rank it fifth." And, while the film did do fairly well at the box office — due, in large part, to the expectations the previous renaissance movies had raised — it made hundreds of millions of dollars less than *The Lion King* (the movie it was supposed to surpass), *Beauty and the Beast*, or *Aladdin*.

For contemporary audiences, *Pocahontas* had missed the mark. Viewers, it turned out, still wanted the princess to have dreams that led her to the truest version of herself, to stand up to injustice with inner courage, and find love along the way. They liked the traditional princesses because they knew, inherently, that Disney's revisionist version of them was wrong. They felt cheated by a love story that needlessly ended in separation, a narrative that focused on historical injustices rather than personal ones, and a princess whose preachiness made her difficult to love. *Pocahontas* was, if not a flop, a major setback.

But, in the same way that Disney revised the narrative about traditional princesses, princess critics have revised the narrative about *Pocahontas*. She is now considered, by modern commentators, to be a shining example of feminist princesshood. If you ask them, *Pocahontas* is the moment Disney finally started getting it right. It's truly maddening.

Sophie Gilbert, of *The Atlantic*, revisited the movie in 2015, twenty years after its release. Pocahontas, she says, is Disney's very first "independent and fearless heroine with a strong sense of self." (What?!) Not just that, she's also apparently the "first truly empowered Disney heroine." (Huh?!) In fact, according to Gilbert, the film is a "radical story about female agency and empathy." (Give me a break!) Chelsea Mize, of *Bustle*, ranks Pocahontas the fourth most feminist Disney princess of twelve princesses. Kayleigh Dray, of *Stylist*, ranks her the third of fifteen. She's a "straight-up badass," says Mize. She's a "feminist hero," says Dray. Because she forces a man to adopt her worldview, scoffs at technology and progress, and gives up on love, Pocahontas is the perfect Disney princess — to the princess critics anyway. To the rest of us? Not so much.

The thing is, though, that, while Pocahontas *is* preachy, sanctimonious, and hard-headed, she also has no dreams of her own, is completely focused on a man (instead of allowing the love of a man to motivate her independent dreams), and is totally closed off to the viewpoints of others. In many, many (many!) ways, Pocahontas is weaker, less independent, and less internally strong certainly than Ariel, Belle, or Jasmine, but even Cinderella or Snow White. This would happen again and again as Disney created "feminist" princesses, intent on smashing the "traditional" princess narrative in favor of a new "enlightened" one. In trying to create strong, empowered women, Disney created weak, shallow ones. Pocahontas is not a "badass," even in the feminist sense of the word. She's a weakling and a coward.

*

Pocahontas is essentially a "feminist" reboot of *The Little Mermaid*. It's the story of a girl who feels like she was meant for something different than the life she was born to who falls in love with a man from a completely different culture. Roger Ebert compared the two films in his 1995 review of *Pocahontas*, saying that Pocahontas, like Ariel, has a father who "disapproves of the man she loves, because he belongs to a different race." Entire images, events, and lines of dialogue are lifted directly from *The Little Mermaid* and inserted into *Pocahontas*. It was clearly an intentional parallel. We got it wrong with *The Little Mermaid*, the filmmakers seem to be saying, but we're putting it right with *Pocahontas*. But in every instance that Ariel is strong, Pocahontas is weak. In every instance that Ariel has dreams that go beyond romance, Pocahontas is stuck worrying about John Smith. In every moment that Ariel proves, through her actions and her unwavering faith, that her viewpoint is correct, Pocahontas is left beating us over the head with her message of environmentalism which has nothing to do with the movie's actual plot. And, when Ariel's quest for belonging culminates in partnership with the man who has spurred her onward, Pocahontas's journey leads her right back to where she started, minus the man she has come to love. Shocker: it's actually Ariel who's the feminist, not Pocahontas.

Pocahontas begins in exactly the same way as *The Little Mermaid*: with a man on a ship. John Smith, setting off from England with the Virginia Company, is hoping for adventure in the New World. But, instead of being simply out to enjoy the "salty sea air, the wind blowing in your face," like Eric, John Smith has been hired by the Virginia Company to protect the explorers from Indians as they look for gold. "For the new world is like heaven / And we'll all be rich and free / Or

140

so we have been told by the Virginia Company," sing the men aboard the ship. Very early on, the movie sets up the "unenlightened" European attitude and negatively juxtaposes it to the "enlightened" Indian way of life. "Remember what awaits us there," the evil Governor Ratcliffe tells his men. "Freedom, prosperity, the adventure of our lives!" These ideals — the inherently American ideals of freedom, prosperity, adventure — are wrong, the movie tells us. We know because the bad guy believes in them and couples them with killing Indians — whom he calls "bloodthirsty savages" — and amassing personal wealth. And the men, blindly following Governor Ratcliffe, believe in these things too.

The movie's ideology is solidified when the scene cuts away from the explorers and pans over the Indian village. Here are the happy Indians, unconcerned with wealth or power, working together, filled with peace and happiness. "Help us keep the ancient ways / Keep the sacred fire strong," the Indians sing as they work. The message is clear: evil, bad Europeans out for money and power vs. good, peaceful Indians who believe in working together and respecting the land. But what on earth is this ideology even doing in a Disney princess movie? What does the historical enmity between settlers and Native Americans have to do with a princess's inner struggle and ultimate fulfillment? How does convincing us that settling the New World (and thus giving birth to everything we hold dear) was wrong, allow a girl to grow into a woman? It doesn't. But it *does* give Pocahontas something to yell at John Smith about until he capitulates and sees the supposed error of his ways. The man must submit to the woman. *This* is the new Disney princess narrative.

John Smith is set up early on as a teachable male. He's different from the other men on the ship who are excited to kill Indians and find gold because what he's *really* after is adventure, not money. And, just like Eric, he encounters a storm at sea which allows him to show us his bravery and selflessness, letting us know that he's really a good guy. He just needs a little help from a woman who

141

knows better. He jumps overboard to save a young sailor named Thomas, showing us that he's a man worthy of Pocahontas' love. The only difference between John's display of character and Eric's is that the princess isn't there to witness it. Whereas Ariel gets to see what kind of man Eric is — which allows her to fall for him — Pocahontas knows nothing of John's character when she is immediately drawn to him later in the film. *We* know. But *she* doesn't. And she's really the important one here.

When we first meet Pocahontas, she has stolen away from her village to stand on a clifftop surrounded by magical swirling leaves (there's a lot of magical swirling leaves in this movie for some reason), and has missed her father's return. Just like Ariel, she's not doing what she's supposed to be doing, she's off on her own with her animal friends. But, unlike Ariel, she's not pursuing a specific and valid interest, she's just kind of communing with nature and thinking about a random dream she keeps having about a spinning arrow (which means nothing to her). Standing on a clifftop, Pocahontas leaps and dives neatly into the water below where her friend Nakoma is waiting for her in a canoe. Pocahontas playfully tips the canoe, dunking Nakoma. "Don't you think we're getting a little old for these games?" Nakoma asks, spluttering. In response, Pocahontas spits water in her face. So much for being "a woman instead of a teenager." Pocahontas is very clearly still a child (despite the very womanly body the animators gave her) and her dreams are amorphous, at best.

Pocahontas then learns what every "feminist" Disney princess must: that her father wants her to marry a man she doesn't love. Kocoum is a mighty warrior, but he's a bit of a bore. He's much too serious for the playful Pocahontas and she feels sure he's not the one for her. She tells her father of her random spinning arrow dream and he interprets it to mean that she's ready for marriage (because, honestly, it's so vague it could mean anything). "He will build you a good house with sturdy walls," her father tells her. "With him you will be safe from harm." This is almost exactly what the Sultan told

Jasmine. The man will protect you and keep you safe. One of the main obstacles a "feminist" Disney princess must overcome is marriage without love. And fair enough. But this ridiculously serious warrior guy is the creation of storytellers who want us to see him as the traditional Disney prince. Pocahontas, we're meant to infer, is a real, live woman — smart, funny, playful — she doesn't need some cardboard cutout of a man like Prince Charming. She needs a real man. (Or no man at all? We'll see.)

Pocahontas rushes off to talk to a tree — as you do. Grandmother Willow is Pocahontas' mystical fairy godmother, who offers vague platitudes in lieu of helpful advice. "Listen with your heart. You will understand," Grandmother Willow tells Pocahontas unhelpfully. This is just as vague as Pocahontas' dream of the spinning arrow. Over and over again princess critics use the same words to describe Pocahontas. She's "strong, noble, free spirited, and fiercely independent," says Dray. She's "fiercely independent," echoes Mize. She's "an independent and fearless heroine with a strong sense of self," says Gilbert. But is she really? Now that we've been introduced to her, what do we know about her? She has no specific dreams of her own. She likes to play childish games with her friends. She doesn't want to marry the boring guy her father picked, but she has no other ideas about what to do with her life. Compare that to Ariel who is actively pursing her passion for the human world. Or Belle or Cinderella who long to be seen as people of worth. Or Snow White who is earning her keep to save herself from a murderous witch. Or even Jasmine, who wants to change her country's laws. Of all these Disney princesses, I'd say Pocahontas is the least fiercely independent or free spirited of the bunch.

So then she meets John Smith. The British settlers have landed and Ratcliffe immediately orders them to begin randomly digging all over the place and chopping down trees for no reason. There's more talk of how the Indians are savages and there's a forced comparison between "mine" like mine for gold and "mine" like mine, all mine. So by now we get that the Europeans are really the savages and the Indians are super great. But John Smith — who's different remember — goes off on his own and informs us that what *he's* really after isn't gold but "A land I can claim, a land I can tame." Still bad, in the world of this film, but not *as* bad as wanting money. Pocahontas encounters him as he's exploring and follows him. But, unlike Ariel, she witnesses nothing of his brave display of heroism from the beginning of the film, she basically just watches him wandering around and learns nothing about him except that he's blond and handsome.

When finally John realizes he's being followed and sees Pocahontas, he's struck immediately by her beauty. John and Pocahontas are literally the first couple in a Disney princess movie to fall in love based on looks. The fairytale shorthand of lovers recognizing each other's inner worth doesn't apply here — this isn't a fairytale. They've witnessed nothing of each other's character — John hasn't even heard Pocahontas' voice the way Eric heard Ariel's. They haven't worked together to solve a problem like Jasmine and Aladdin do. Nothing. Literally nothing at all has prompted their attraction for each other except physicality. "Pocahontas has a remarkable amount of acuity when it comes to choosing a romantic partner," writes Gilbert. Sure, if what you're looking for is a hunky British guy. But, seriously, their initial attraction is based on nothing other than the fact that they're both hot and the fact that the magic swirly leaves show up again and randomly teach Pocahontas to speak English. Thanks, magic swirly leaves!

Now that Pocahontas magically speaks English, the pair sit down to talk. So, naturally, John starts mansplaining. (Because that's how men talk to women, right?) He tells her about all the wonderful things they have in Europe — like buildings, roads, the wheel, you know, stupid stuff like that — and Pocahontas is interested until he tells her that he wants to bring that stuff here. Pocahontas tells him they're fine just the way they are thank you very much. But John, unaware of what movie he's in, tells her "You think that only because you don't know any better." So, the very first thing they do after falling for each other's good looks is have an argument. John says that Indians are savages but that he knows how to help them become civilized. Pocahontas takes issue with being called a savage and says she has everything she needs and doesn't want his technology. So then, to signal which one of them is right (according to the ideology of the film) and which one's wrong, John Smith falls out of the tree they're sitting in and looks like a total idiot.

But I mean, overlooking the violent methods the Europeans used in dealing with the Native Americans, John's got a point. A point that has no business being addressed in a Disney princess movie, but a point nonetheless. Pocahontas' people are — if not savages — backward. They haven't invented the wheel, they've been living the same way for thousands of years, progress is unknown to them. If you really think that way of life is better than ours, please immediately move out of your home, get rid of your car, and live off the land. We are living the life that people like John Smith claimed for us. Quarrel with their methods if you want, but not their lifestyle. But, in this movie, John is completely and utterly, hopelessly and dangerously wrong, so there, nah nah nah nah boo boo.

Pocahontas sets out to teach John the error of his ways. "What you mean is," Pocahontas preaches at him, Indians are "not like *you*." And then she proceeds to sing the most sanctimonious song ever written for a Disney movie. "You think I'm an ignorant savage / And you've been so many places I guess it must be so / But still I cannot see / If the savage one is me / How can there be so much that you don't know?" she begins. Then she lays out her worldview: "I know every rock and tree and creature has a life, has a spirit, has a name." Which, I guess, is fair enough given that she literally knows a talking tree. "The heron and the otter are my friends," she explains, even though she presumably eats them when she's hungry. "How high will the sycamore grow? / If you cut it down, then you'll never know," though presumably she does cut them down when she needs firewood so she doesn't die of frostbite during the winter. "You can own the Earth and still / All you'll own is Earth until / You can paint with all the colors of the wind," she concludes, whatever that means.

As she sings, she and John romp through the forest, roll around in each other's arms on the ground, and generally have a grand old time. And, by the end of it, John's sold. He's seen the error of his ways. Technology is bad, the British are evil, and Pocahontas is really, really hot. It's every feminist's dream come true. Take a hot but mansplain-y guy, sing a super sanctimonious song at him about everything you think he's wrong about, have him admit that you're totally right and lie down like a puppy dog at your feet. It's a match made in feminist heaven. "She then proceeds to list off all the things that John Smith knows zilch about, calling him out on his racist misogynist bulls**t as she does so – and forces him to acknowledge that he's wrong," writes Dray. Swoon!

In *The Little Mermaid*, this is the scene where Eric shows Ariel his kingdom — the world she has longed to explore for as along as she can remember. She's delighted with the town square, the Punch and Judy show, the food, and the carriage ride. She's finally where she has always wanted to be. The man she's with is an added bonus, but these are things she wanted long before she met Eric. In *Pocahontas*, our heroine is showing John Smith her world (and her worldview) but this isn't John's dream come true. He was looking for adventure and freedom, not Native American culture. This isn't the fulfillment of John's lifelong dream, and it's certainly not Pocahontas' dream come true either. Her dreams were amorphous, at best — and certainly didn't previously include a man whose ideology she finds repugnant. Pocahontas isn't "independent," she doesn't have a "strong sense of self!" She forges her dreams on a chance encounter with a man she finds sexually appealing but morally repulsive. That's *exactly* what princess critics complain that "traditional" princesses do. The only difference is that Pocahontas gets her guy by yelling at him and forcing him to admit that he's wrong (even when he's not) which, to princess critics, is just *so* romantic.

After this one meeting — in which Pocahontas berates John Smith, and John falls out of a tree, looks like an idiot, and admits everything he ever believed about everything is wrong — John and Pocahontas are in love. And yes, Cinderella fell for Prince Charming after one dance, Snow White fell for The Prince after one song at the well, Aurora fell for Prince Philip after one walk in the woods, but (as we've seen again and again) these were all *fairy tale* encounters. They communicated by fairy tale shorthand the meeting of two compatible souls. In the more realistic mode of the Disney Renaissance, Ariel had to learn about Eric's character to fall in love with him, Belle had to slowly draw out the man within the beast, Jasmine had to break down Aladdin's inner walls to find the "diamond in the rough." *Pocahontas* isn't even a fairytale. It's a (highly fictionalized) account of an historical event. Pocahontas and John Smith should need to get to know each other *even more* than the Renaissance princes and princesses. But, instead, they learn that they abhor each other's worldview but like each other's physical appearance. How is this *more* feminist? (I'm serious, somebody *please* tell me!)

So then comes the moment of truth — the moment when we learn whether these two people from completely different worlds can find happiness together. In *The Little Mermaid*, this moment comes when Ariel's father, King Triton, finally sees what Ariel has been trying to tell him all along: that she wants to be human, that it's her *dream* and the expression of her true self. In *Pocahontas* it comes from the British settlers who have nothing to do with Pocahontas' story at all except as stereotypically evil villains intent on ruining her blissful (if uncivilized) existence. Pocahontas' suitor, Kocoum, witnesses John and Pocahontas kissing and becomes angry. Thinking Kocoum is about to kill John, Thomas (the sailor John saved at the beginning of the movie) shoots Kocoum and kills him. John heroically takes the blame and Pocahontas' father imprisons him, saying he'll be executed in the morning. Distraught, Pocahontas goes to Grandmother Willow where she finds John's compass — a spinning arrow! The fulfillment of her dream.

Pocahontas is a Disney princess whose entire dream for her life is literally a man. Cinderella and Snow White wait around for men to rescue them? Ariel falls for a guy she doesn't know? Aurora sleeps through the action of her movie? Belle's got Stockholm Syndrome? Cinderella wanted to express her true self! Snow White provided for herself! Aurora wanted to marry for love! Ariel wanted to be human! Belle wanted to be accepted for who she was! Pocahontas? This paragon of feminist virtue? This independent free spirit? What does she find out she wanted all along? A man. Literally *just* a man. She could have wanted to see the world. She could have wanted to be chief of her people in her own right. She could have wanted to unite the explorers and the Indians. Anything at all really! Any dream of her own that would lead her to the truest expression of herself — like every other Disney princess before her. But no. She just wants the hot British guy she met earlier today. But she's a feminist, okay? Don't argue.

Knowing, now, that John Smith is her destiny, Pocahontas rushes to stop his execution. She argues with her father, trying to convince him not to kill John, but her father is adamant, and furious with her for falling in love with John. Pocahontas' admission that "I love him father!" is almost identical to Ariel's "Daddy, I love him!" And both fathers respond with anger and an unwillingness to see their daughter's point of view. The difference is that Triton ultimately comes to see that Ariel isn't *just* in love with a human, she's in love with human culture. She wants to *be* a human. He comes around because he sees the validity of Ariel's dreams (because they go beyond love for a man). Powhatan sees nothing valid in Pocahontas' fervent pleas for a man she barely knows, and nothing beyond her love for John — because there *is* nothing beyond that. But, at the moment of

John Smith's execution, Pocahontas throws herself across John's body and saying, "If you kill him you'll have to kill me too."

For princess critics, this is a triumphant moment of the princess rescuing the prince, rather than the other way around. "Pocahontas is no damsel in distress. Rather, she saves John Smith's life," writes Mize. But this is less an act of bravery as it is an act of desperation. In finding out that her destiny (as prophesied by her dream) is literally John Smith, she must save him at all costs. Otherwise she has nothing to live for. And it's this act that causes Powhatan to recant and agree to a truce between the Europeans and the Indians. Whereas King Triton comes to see the broader scope of Ariel's dreams, Powhatan simply uses Pocahontas' narrowly focused dream to create a broader good. The truce wasn't Pocahontas' goal — it wasn't the dream she was trying to accomplish all along — she only cared about saving John's life.

Even though Powhatan agreed to a truce, Governor Ratcliffe — who has been looking for a reason to fight the Indians — sees his justification in John's execution and shoots at Powhatan from afar. But he misses and hits John instead. Critically injured, John realizes he must return to England where he can get medical treatment. Because in England they have the technology to help him because they're, you know, civilized. He asks Pocahontas to come with him. But this girl who has discovered that the one thing she's been dreaming of all her life is this man, who was longing to leave her village and find out what was waiting "just around the river bend," who showed no interest in marrying someone from her own tribe or ruling her people, says no. She won't go with him. She's going to let him go.

"Instead of sacrificing something for love (like Ariel giving up her voice, or Belle her freedom), Pocahontas puts her identity and heritage first," writes Gilbert. "Pocahontas is one of the few Disney films in which the heroine accepts that her destiny is bigger than any romance, and willingly chooses to forgo romantic happiness even though it's right in her grasp," writes Mize. "No man can tie her down," writes Dray. There's only one problem: being with John Smith is literally the only thing she's ever dreamed of. She was willing to die to preserve their love. But, "I'm needed here," Pocahontas tells John. Really?! Needed for what exactly? Sanctimoniously singing in the faces of every settler that comes to the New World? She's found her prince! She's overcome the odds to be with him! She put herself in harms way and stood up to her father for the right to be with him! But now, after all that, she's going to say "actually, never mind." It makes no narrative sense whatsoever. But oh! the feminism of it all. The beautiful, wonderful, feminism of totally screwing yourself over and giving up the one thing that will bring you happiness and fulfillment. You go girl.

So she lets him leave. And she stands on a clifftop and watches him go, surrounded by the magical leaves that taught her to speak English but can't teach her not to be a total dimwit and go to England with her boyfriend. For Ariel, leaving the only home she's ever known, and the family and friends who love her, is a sacrifice she's willing to make in order to follow her dreams. Pocahontas isn't making a bold statement, she's being a coward. But as long as she doesn't find love — even if love is the only thing she ever wanted — she's a feminist heroine. Hooray. (Hooray?!) And off John Smith goes into the sunset, never to be seen again. The end? Yes. The end.

*

The reason *Pocahontas* didn't do nearly as well as any of the Disney princess movies that came before is that it doesn't give the people what they want. Disney, blinded by the feminist preaching of a vocal few, thought they were making a masterpiece — a new kind of princess narrative. But the rest of us wanted more of the same. We wanted more fairytales. We wanted more romance. We wanted more girls growing into women and realizing their true potential. We wanted heroines we could model ourselves on, heroes we could look for in our own lives. And *Pocahontas* didn't deliver.

It shouldn't be feminist to give up on love. It shouldn't be feminist to yell at people and force them to believe what you believe. It shouldn't be feminist to give up on your dreams. It shouldn't be, but it is. Now that the narrative about "traditional" Disney princesses has been rewritten to be about damsels in distress who wait around for random men to rescue them, the "feminist" princesses can be feminist just by turning down their suitors — even if they love them. They can be feminist just by browbeating them into believing in something — anything!

Even though Pocahontas wasn't the people's princess, she was the new standard. The movie's poorer showing at the box office and luke warm response from critics should have turned Disney back toward the traditional. But it didn't. They doubled down. And *Mulan* — while narratively a better movie — upholds the same "feminist" values and makes just as little sense as *Pocahontas*. It was a good thing for me that I was already growing up — that the "traditional" message had still been part of my childhood — other kids wouldn't be so lucky.

Chapter Eight: Mulan

There's a meme I keep seeing on social media about *Mulan.* It goes like this:

"Me: *Watching Mulan.* *Awesome drumbeat starts.*

Me: I will not sing.

Me: I will not sing.

Me: I will n- LET'S GET DOWN TO BUSINESS."

It's a reference to the catchiest song from the movie — a song called "I'll Make A Man Out of You." ("Let's get down to business" is the first line.) It's the action song. The one where the princess decides to take control of her fate — to make the sacrifice, do the hard thing, be who she really is. It's "Whistle While You Work" for Snow White, "Part of That World" for Ariel, "Belle" for Belle — you get the idea. And the song *is* catchy, and it *is* hard not to sing along. And its message — which is meant to be a challenge which Mulan triumphantly accepts — sums up everything you need to know about *Mulan.* It's the perfect crystallization of how far Disney studios had fallen down the princess critic rabbit hole: "I'll make a *man* out of you."

By the time *Mulan* came out in 1998, the movie reviewers had gone full-on princess critic. The new narrative about who the traditional princesses were — which was first articulated in *Aladdin* and solidified in *Pocahontas* — was now the accepted truth. "It took long enough, but Disney has finally come up with an animated heroine who's a good role model and a funky, arresting personality at the same time," wrote Owen Gleiberman in his 1998 *Entertainment Weekly* review. Finally come up with a good role model?! (We'll talk about why Mulan is a distinctly problematic heroine in a minute, but the idea that Disney princesses aren't good role models is ridiculous — as we've seen again and again — and a direct product of the revisionism that Disney studios and the early princess critics had successfully inserted into their movies.) Michael O'Sullivan, of *The Washington Post*, called *Mulan* "a brazen departure from the traditional girl-centric cartoon fare about women whose chief heroic accomplishments involve falling in love." He goes on to compare the movie favorably to films like *The Little Mermaid*, *Pocahontas*, *Beauty and the Beast*, and *Snow White* saying *Mulan* "features a heroine whose strength, discipline, courage and self-sacrifice — instead of her beauty — win the honor of her family and country." Oh, as opposed to all the other princesses who came before? What a load of you-know-what!

The idea that Disney princesses before *Mulan* were passive victims waiting around for a man to come solve all their problems is categorically untrue. (As I hope I've proven by now!) And it wasn't always the accepted narrative. (Which I hope I've proven too!) But now, in the late '90s, it was the unquestioned truth. Which meant that each new princess movie had to outdo the next to conform to "feminist" values and eviscerate the "stereotype" of the earlier princesses. Which is how we end up with Mulan, a princess who literally has to become a man in order to prove her worth.

In his 1998 review of the film, Todd McCarthy wrote, in *Variety*, that "there is also a feeling here of how every last plot turn, line and gesture has been calculated and weighed for its full dramatic, ideological and cultural impact." In other words, this movie isn't just a story, it's a manifesto. But I, for one, am uncomfortable with what it tells little girls about being a girl. Because, surely, implying that, in order to be taken seriously, a girl must be able to successfully embody male traits, implies that male traits are the goal. Surely this, in turn, implies that male traits are better than female ones. Is that really what we want to tell little girls?

Modern princess critics *love* Mulan. She is almost always ranked in the top three in feminist rankings online. Princess critics's praise almost universally centers around Mulan's ability to do things a man can do. "Mulan was the first Disney heroine who proved a woman can be as courageous and strong as a man," wrote the staff of *ScreenCrush,* who ranked Mulan the second most feminist of the Disney princesses. But that isn't actually true. *All* the Disney princesses who came before (with the possible exception of Pocahontas) were *as* courageous and strong as a man. They just weren't courageous and strong *like* a man. And this difference — which princess critics completely fail to understand — is the reason why the message of *Mulan* is so harmful to little girls.

Refusing to acknowledge the feminine strength and courage of heroines like Cinderella, Ariel, and Belle implies that the only acceptable kind of strength is the masculine kind — physical strength, courage in battle, and feats of athleticism. But *this* kind of strength is accessible only to a talented few. Sure, some girls are great athletes, but some aren't — and frankly, who cares? The *internal* strength that Disney princesses traditionally embody is accessible to *everyone* and much more valuable when discovering how to be a successful adult living a life of integrity. But the course was set, the princess critics, movie critics, and Disney studios had aligned, and little girls got *Mulan*.

*

When we first meet Mulan, she seems like a regular Disney princess. She's stuck in a situation she doesn't feel she belongs in and she's chafing against its constraints. Of course, the situation she wants to escape is of the new, revisionist, kind — in that she is being asked to behave like a typical Chinese girl and impress the matchmaker so she can find a good husband — but it's still the Disney princess trope of needing to escape a difficult situation. We see that — unlike the other girls in her village — Mulan isn't graceful, or good at pouring tea, or interested in wearing fancy clothes and makeup. She'd much rather play board games, wear comfortable clothes, and chew with her mouth open. The specifics fit into the new mode of modern Disney princess rebelling against fake old princess tropes, but the general idea is the same: Snow White or Cinderella feeling they're not meant to be servants, Ariel feeling she wasn't meant to be a mermaid, Belle feeling she didn't belong in her small, unaccepting town. And Mulan's parents — as the parental figures always have in Disney princess movies — insist that she conform. They want her to "uphold the family honor" and they pray to the ancestors that she will impress the matchmaker.

Anna Breslaw, of *Cosmopolitan*, writes, "Mulan is a badass who's relatable and easy to like." Mulan isn't, Breslaw's comment implies, perfect. She behaves the way so many of us have — messing up important tasks, looking like an idiot, forgetting things — and that makes her "relatable." But, in making Mulan relatable in this way, Disney has completely removed all the symbolism of "princess" that was inherent in the fairy tale princess stories that came before. In fact, Mulan is the only official Disney "princess" who isn't actually a princess. So her story isn't even symbolic in the ways that princess stories necessarily are. Which means that, later in the film, we have to take at face value Mulan's ability to fight seasoned warriors three times her size and infer that this is a literal depiction of what a girl must do in order to be successful.

The matchmaker lays out the criteria for being a good woman — the qualities now accepted as being of extreme importance to the traditional princesses. "Men want girls / With good taste / Calm, obedient, who work fast paced / With good breeding and a tiny waist." If any Disney man before John Smith wanted these things I'll eat my tiara. The film doesn't mince words: "A girl can bring her family great honor in one way: by striking a good match." (Wait, what's that sound? Oh, it's Walt Disney turning over in his grave!) When Mulan — who we've already seen stand up for the girls in her village by getting a girl's doll back from a boy who's taken it — totally screws up her interview with the matchmaker, the matchmaker proclaims, "You will never bring your family honor." Disney filmmakers have set up a situation in which there are only two choices for being "honorable": follow a very specific feminine path, or act like a boy. By making the movie specifically *about* gender norms, Disney has pulled something that once was deep and meaningful into the realm of the superficial. We *know* — because she's a Disney princess — that Mulan will break free from her situation and find her own path (like Cinderella, like Ariel, like Belle, blah blah blah). But making it about whether she's acting like a girl or a boy makes it about her physical abilities, not her internal ones. And *that's* superficial.

After Mulan fails her interview with the matchmaker, she is upset. She knows she doesn't want to be like the other girls, but she doesn't want to dishonor her family either. "If I were truly to be myself I would break my family's heart," she sings. Looking in the mirror she asks, "When will my reflection show who I am inside?" This is the first time we bump up against the movie's central contradiction. It isn't clear — or rather it seems to be different from one moment to the next — whether Mulan wants to be a girl who's allowed to do boy things, or whether she actually wants to be a boy.

If Mulan's reflection in the mirror were somehow able to show who she actually was, then surely there's something physical about her that she wishes were different. If Ariel had said the same thing we'd understand that she wished her tail was legs instead. Does Mulan want her femininity to shift to masculinity? Some princess critics thinks so: "If this movie isn't a giant transgender metaphor, I don't know what is," writes *Screencrush*. But others think its power lies in its depiction of a *girl* defying strict gender norms. "Who isn't a sucker for the old 'girl dresses up like boy to do something girls aren't allowed to do' story?" writes Breslaw. So, which is it? I mean, it has to be one or the other, right? If it's a transgender empowerment story then Mulan necessarily must be a girl who yearns to be a boy. If it's a female empowerment story in which a girl proves that girls can be warriors too, then Mulan necessarily must be a girl. But no one seems to know which it is. Even the princess critics who love it.

When the Huns — led by the evil Shan Yu — invade China, each family is ordered to send one male member to serve in the army. Since Mulan's aging and injured father is the only man in their family, he is told he must go. In order to save his life, Mulan secretly takes his armor, his sword, and his conscription notice, chops off her hair, and joins up — as a man. Now, of course, this *is* brave. Her father would surely have died, the army doesn't accept women, so she did what she had to do to save him. But, instead of the traditional princess moment of action in which she finds a way to become her true self, Mulan is doing this for someone else. So we don't actually know if becoming a soldier is something she aspired to do — something that makes her truly herself — or if it's just something she feels so *must* do in order to protect her family. In his 1998 review of the film, Roger Ebert wrote, "The message here is standard feminist empowerment: Defy the matchmaker, dress as a boy, and choose your own career." But is it? Is Mulan finally doing what she's always wanted to do? Or would she have preferred to become a board game designer, or a chef, or a motivational speaker, or something, instead? We don't actually know, which makes the message even more garbled and problematic.

Aided by a weird-looking dragon creature named Mushu (voiced by Eddie Murphy doing a bad Robin Williams impression) Mulan heads to basic training. Here — as opposed to in the earlier scene in front of the mirror — Mulan seems to be very much a girl. The habits of the other soldiers prompt her to assert that men are "disgusting." She bathes in the river saying, "Just because I look like a man doesn't mean I have to smell like one." When Mulan sees the hunky Captain Li Shang with his shirt off she is very obviously attracted to him. And when the other soldiers sing about "a girl worth fighting for" Mulan suggests that that girl might be someone "who's got a brain and always speaks her mind," obviously referring to herself. (The men, of course, don't seem to find that idea so appealing.)

The concept of a "girl worth fighting for" is very much a trope of traditional fairy tales. It's one of the major themes of *Beauty and the Beast,* for example, in which Belle's internal goodness sparks the Beast's ability to channel his masculine urges. But in *Mulan* it's held up as a prime example of misogyny. The idea that the men are out fighting while the women are sitting around at home serving no other purpose than to be there for the men when they get back is held up as yet another reason that the traditional narrative is bad. But who's to say that the woman back home doesn't have "a brain" or "speak her mind"? I mean, obviously within the confines of this movie she wouldn't, but this movie is set up to make us think that that's what it's always like. Who's to say the woman back home isn't content to be there, bravely keeping house and raising the children while her husband is away? Sure, the men in *this* movie turn up their noses at the idea of a smart girl, but the rest of the Disney men don't. Look at the Beast: he gives Belle a *library* for goodness sake!

The movie is very clear about what it means to be man. A man is "swift as the coursing river," has "the force of a great typhoon," has "the strength of a raging fire," and is "mysterious as the dark side of the moon." Aside from "mysterious," these are all physical attributes. In order to fit in with the guys, Mulan has to learn to be swift, forceful, and strong. These are qualities that, in real life, a girl (or a boy for that matter) may or may not be able to master. They aren't internal traits like courage, hope, or determination that anyone could muster, they are specific skills that may or may not be possible. What if Mulan had been in a wheelchair, or physically impaired in some other way? It might then be impossible for her to be swift, forceful, or physically strong. She could still be *internally* strong, though. *That's* why the insistence that the new princesses showcase their athletic abilities over their internal qualities is so superficial. But this movie holds up these external abilities as the goals that determine Mulan's success. So, not only are they achievements that a man would —randomly and inherently — be better at than a woman, they are also totally superficial.

As Li Shang trains the soldiers, he compares them to women for their lack of ability. "Did they send me daughters when I asked for sons?" We're meant to take this as sexist narrow-mindedness. But honestly, could a girl really fight as well as a trained soldier? Could a trained female soldier do all the physical feats a trained male soldier could? Calling a man a "daughter" because he's acting cowardly is one thing — women are more than capable of courage equaling or surpassing a man's. But commenting on the differences between men's and women's physical abilities isn't necessarily sexist. When Mulan finally proves herself by completing a challenge of climbing a tall vertical pole — which the other soldiers weren't able to do — she earns Li Shang's respect and friendship. She even bests Li Shang in hand to hand combat which is so unrealistic as to be laughable — Li Shang is a career soldier and Mulan is a woman who has been training for a number of days. These feats of physical achievement mark Mulan's acceptance into the ranks of the men. She is one of them now. So, is she a girl who proved that girls can do anything men can do? Or is she embodying her male identity? Nobody knows.

But it matters. Particularly in the relationship that begins to develop between Mulan and Li Shang. Soren Hough writes, on *RogerEbert.com*, that Yi Shang is "someone who found himself attracted to someone who presented as a man for part of the film." Hough takes Li Shang's interest in Mulan — which seems to be simply friendship or respect — to be something more. "Instead of a woman meeting man, we have a man meeting a man," Hough continues. Is Mulan actually a man? Sure, Li Shang thinks she is, but is that what the movie is actually saying — that, in acting like a man Mulan becomes one? Or is she a woman who acts like a man? Or is she a woman showing that "male" things aren't really just for men? It's a problem that's never really resolved. But, as Hough points out, "If all Shang has seen of Mulan is her saving the emperor, then he's known her as a woman for approximately a few hours. In any good romance story, that wouldn't precipitate a marriage proposal." And he's right. The romance tacked on at the end of *Mulan* feels ridiculously forced and shallow. But, if Li Shang is actually gay — or maybe bisexual? — then the romance has been building all along and makes more sense. But I think it's fairly clear from watching the film that romance was *not* on Li Shang's mind until Mulan turned out to be a woman. Mulan — who knew she was a woman all along — *did* have feelings for Li Shang. Which implies she feels she's a woman. Or maybe she's a man and she's gay? Or . . . who knows?

     Mulan and the other soldiers go into battle. They are outnumbered by the Hun army, led by the evil Shan Yu — a gargantuan warrior with glowing yellow eyes — and all seems lost. But Mulan uses a cannon to fire at a mound of snow that turns into an avalanche and buries the Hun army. Because of this, some princess critics say Mulan uses brains, not brawn, to win the day. This would imply that Mulan is, in fact, a woman who can't compete with the men in masculine tasks but can still hold her own in battle because she can use her wits. "Far more than *Beauty and the Beast* or the stolidly virtuous Pocahontas, Mulan showcases a girl who gets to use her wits," writes Gleiberman. And it's true, in this act Mulan is using strategy and not brute force. So, after all those scenes of training, and working hard to prove she can compete physically with the men, Mulan's first moment to prove herself as a valuable soldier culminates in the "feminine" act of using brains instead of brawn. So, which is it? Is she just as capable as the men? Or is her skillset different? In this scene it's different, but a minute later we see her physically pulling Yi Shang — a man much larger than her — out of the flow of the avalanche. Is a woman's success the same as a man's? Or is it different? The movie doesn't seem to know.

During the fighting, Mulan is injured and, in the course of her treatment, her female identity is discovered. The law dictates that she should be executed for impersonating a man to join the army. Because she saved his life, Li Shang doesn't kill her, but he says she can no longer fight and leaves her alone in the snow. On her way home, Mulan realizes that the Hun army is back and tries to warn Li Shang and the Chinese troops, but they don't listen to her and the Emperor ends up being kidnapped by the Huns who barricade themselves inside the palace. Mulan again uses her brains to devise a plan to get into the palace.

Mulan dresses some of the Chinese soldiers up as concubines — their costumes reminiscent of what Mulan had to wear to the matchmaker at the beginning of the film. The presence of the "women" distracts the Hun guards who are too busy ogling them to notice that the Chinese army is getting into the palace. The message, again, is a confusing one. On the one hand, we can infer that a woman's power lies in her sex appeal — which doesn't seem like a very feminist statement. But we can also infer that some situations call for something other than brawn and that a woman is the best person to orchestrate those situations — which *does* seem like a feminist idea. The fact that the men are willing to dress as women implies that they accept that women can serve a purpose in battle (just not the same one as men). But their willingness to leave Mulan alone in the snow for being a women a few moments before implies that they *don't* accept that. In this moment, the movie seems to be saying that women and men are different but both are valuable — a worthwhile message. But, in the next moment, the movie is promoting male abilities again.

When Mulan finds herself trapped on the palace roof with Shan Yu, Mulan is able to best him in hand-to-hand combat. The idea that Mulan would be able to topple this military juggernaut — even with the distraction of a fan that she opens to confuse Shan Yu — is utterly ridiculous. By offering it as part of Mulan's final victory over the Hun army the movie implies that her physical abilities are a vital part of her success. This, in turn, sends the message that the ability to compete with men in tasks that men are naturally able to do more easily is an important part of being a girl. Mulan explains that she wanted to prove that she could do "something right" — that she was "worthwhile." If military combat is the way that a girl must prove her worth, then masculinity must be better than femininity. Is this what we want to teach our daughters?

O'Sullivan wrote that *Mulan* "may do for the sword what *Cinderella* did for the glass slipper — create a symbol of female transformation-except in this case one that has less to do with physical appearance than personal accomplishment." But, of course, Cinderella's glass slipper wasn't about looking pretty at the ball. It was a symbol of Cinderella's inner attributes — her strength, her determination, her optimism, and her grace — made manifest for others to see and acknowledge. Mulan's sword, on the other hand, is not a symbol. It's a tool which allows her to take part in an activity — combat — which other girls may or may not ever be able to accomplish. In order for Mulan's sword to be comparable to Cinderella's slipper, the sword would have to represent something about Mulan's inner self. Instead, it represents only her outer self — her ability to fight. In terms of Mulan's journey of self-discovery, we still don't know if she's found her true self.

When the Emperor tries to reward Mulan for saving China by offering her a position on his counsel, Mulan declines. This implies that she *hasn't* found her true self. She opts, instead, to go back home where, surely, her future is the same as it was when she left — marriage and housewifery. Mulan's refusal to stay with the Emperor tells us that entering the realms of men — fighting and advising — is not what she truly wants. But we've just watched her go through this whole journey to achieve that. Yes, she saved her father (and China) which is good in the context of the story, but what about the journey of a Disney princess from child to adult, becoming her true self along the way? This, it seems, has been lost in the attempt to depict a girl acting like a boy.

When Mulan arrives home, her parents accept what she has done and express their pride. The implication is that they now see her for who she truly is and accept that she doesn't want to be like the other girls. But who *is* she? What is it that they're accepting? She doesn't seem to want them to understand that she's a boy. She doesn't seem to want them to understand that she's a soldier, or an advisor to the Emperor, or an adventurer. Here she is back at home. What is it that they're meant to now accept? Alright, they're not going to marry her off to someone random, but — given that the matchmaker said she was hopeless — they probably weren't going to do that anyway. For all her heroism, we still don't know what Mulan actually wants.

When Li Shang shows up at Mulan's house to awkwardly imply that he kind of has a crush on her now — "You fight good," he tells her — we have no idea why he likes her. He thought she was a dude like ten minutes ago. Shouldn't a "princess" who is trying to subvert the trope of love at first sight have a love interest with whom affection has built up over time? I mean, sure, they were friends but Li Shang doesn't seem to like women who act like men. He left her alone in the snow because she was a woman who said she was a man! Why would his admiration for her as a solider translate into romantic feeling? We know that Mulan has had a crush on *him* for a while — due, in large part, to his hot body — but his romantic feelings for her seem shallow and tacked on, which is exactly the complaint that princess critics make about the traditional princes.

At the end of the film, Mulan is living at home, being pursued romantically by a man she will probably end up marrying. Yes, the man now knows that she's not a "typical" girl and seems to be okay with that, but this situation isn't really all that different than the one we found her in at the beginning of the movie. Since she's given up being the Emperor's advisor, or being in the military — and since she hasn't expressed any other interests — it looks like she'll probably end up being a wife and mother (which is what her parents wanted for her in the first place). I, of course, see no problem with her becoming a wife and mother (it's been working out great for *me*!) but for all the princess critics' rhapsodizing about how Mulan is a "feminist icon" and a "strong, empowered" princess (Chelsea Mize of *Bustle*), her fate seems a lot like the other princesses' who the princess critics dislike. Mulan's great achievement in the film is that — for a few days — she was able to hold her own with the men.

*

Mulan performed even worse at the box office than *Pocahontas*. But the critics loved it. The divide between the fans and the princess critics was now firmly established. And Disney, stuck between wanting to make money and buying into the feminist misunderstanding of the princess films, gave up on princesses. There wouldn't be another Disney princess for eleven years. Part of this was the new direction Disney was going with Pixar films like *Toy Story*, *Cars*, and *The Incredibles*. But it was also clear — based on the box office numbers — that these new, "feminist" princesses weren't working with the fans. And little girls, suddenly princess-less, turned to the classics — Snow White and Cinderella — and the Renaissance princesses — Ariel and Belle — to get their princess fix. Because little girls — as Disney would soon discover — aren't willing to give up on princesses. Nor are they willing to accept the message of *Mulan* — that boys are better than girls.

When Disney princesses made their comeback — first in 2000 with the introduction of the Disney princess franchise, and then in 2009 with *The Princess and the Frog* — little girls were ready and waiting. They put on their Cinderella costumes, their Snow White headbands, and their mermaid tails and stood up tall. They begged their mommies — who were now indoctrinated to believe that all these princesses were harmful — to take them to the first new Disney princess movie

164

to come out in their lifetimes. And their mommies, horrified but powerless to fight the princess passion, took them to the theater. Where these little girls banded together, raised their warbly little voices, and — against all odds — gave Disney princesses one last hurrah.

Part IV

"Almost There": Return To The Traditional

Chapter Nine: Tiana

The little girl in the Snow White costume peeped over the back of her theater seat to stare at me. Her confusion was valid. What was this grown woman doing at the special opening-weekend showing of Disney's *The Princess and the Frog?* (Where was my kid?) How could I explain that I *was* the kid? Or at least, that the kid was still a part of me and I was taking her to the movies. Luckily, I didn't need to explain. A particularly hilarious game of peekaboo sufficed. But, honestly, tiny Snow White was right — heartbreakingly right. I was too old for this. My time had passed. I was turning twenty-seven, an adult — for better or worse. And yet, here I was, hoping with all my might that Disney had finally come to its senses — that the eleven years since *Mulan* had woken Disney up to the reality that little girls (and some big girls, ahem) still love traditional princesses. Even the fact of tiny Snow White's presence gave me hope. The fact that she — and her equally princess-clad compatriots filling up the theater — could even get her hands on a Disney princess costume was a new and potentially positive development.

In the year 2000, Disney's new chairman of Consumer Products Worldwide, Andy Mooney, was attending a Disney on Ice show in Arizona when he noticed something. The theater was packed full of little girls dressed in lovingly-created homemade facsimiles of their favorite Disney princess dresses. This gave him a goldmine of an idea: if *Disney* made the dresses, little girls (or their parents anyway) would turn up in droves to buy them. Not only that, in addition to costumes, Disney could sell bedsheets, hairbrushes, shoes, lampshades . . . everything a little girl might want to make her bedroom princess-tastic. Mooney branded the princesses together under a single franchise and got to work. By the time *The Princess and the Frog* came out, nine years later, little girls who hadn't seen a new princess movie come out in their lifetimes were making the Disney princess franchise a multi-billion dollar enterprise. The stage was set for another princess.

But what kind of princess would she be — "feminist" or traditional? In the years since *Mulan*, Disney had entered a bit of a slump. Pixar was stealing the limelight with computer-animated mega-hits like *Toy Story 2*, *Monster's Inc.*, and *The Incredibles,* while Disney Animation Studios was making actual flops like *Treasure Planet* and *Brother Bear.* When Disney bought Pixar in 2006, it looked like Pixar's signature male-centered, computer animated movies would become Disney's standard fare. And, for a while, it did, with films like *Cars*, *Ratatouille*, *Wall-E*, and *Up*. But when Disney CEO Michael Eisner — who had instituted a no-more-hand-drawn-animation mandate — was replaced by Bob Iger, there was a sea change. Couple that with the roaring success of the princess merchandise, and the stage was set for another Disney fairy tale in the traditional, hand-drawn style.

Fans and reviewers alike were entranced by the look of *The Princess and the Frog.* Roger Ebert called it "a cool shower after a long and sweaty day," rhapsodizing that "*This* is what classic animation once was like!" Justin Chang, of *Variety*, called it a "long-anticipated throwback." It *looked* like the old, traditional Disney princess movies and, even though princess critics were at pains to attack the plots of those movies, they had apparently been missing them — or the way they looked, at any rate. For my part, I emerged from the theater, hand-in-hand with my own prince charming, into the first gentle snowfall of the year, transported along with all the other little girls, by a movie that felt like a pathway back to Disney's Golden Age.

The Princess and the Frog pulled the wool over the princess critics' eyes. Tiana looked like a truly modern heroine, one the princess critics could be proud of. In many ways, she *is* a completely new kind of Disney heroine — as opposed to "new" princesses like Jasmine and Pocahontas who weren't actually new at all. Tiana worked for a living, dreamed of restaurant ownership, and actively turned up her nose at romance. Reviewers (who were largely all princess critics now) loved it, as do contemporary princess critics. Dan Kois, in his 2009 review for *Slate* said that the movie represented "a course-correction" for Disney, because it "attempts to celebrate the virtues of hard work and pluck." (This is obviously a ridiculous assertion given that Snow White and Cinderella exist in the Disney princess canon, but we'll leave that alone for the moment.) Beatriz Serrano, of *Buzzfeed*, called Tiana "an independent woman," and *ScreenCrush* called her "one of the more self-reliant heroines in Disney history."

But, while Tiana truly *does* embody all of those characteristics, her journey throughout the film is towards the realization that nothing matters if you don't have love — romantic love. Love, the movie wants us to know, makes working hard, and saving your money, and opening your restaurant all worthwhile. Without it, you might as well give up on your entrepreneurial dreams. So, even though Tiana begins the movie like a good "feminist" princess should, she ends it much closer to a traditional princess. Not only that, this film incorporates themes we haven't seen in earnest since Disney's Golden Age — themes of wishes, good and evil, and yes, even a little bit of Christianity. But, because Tiana's dreams are more realistic (and less symbolic) than those of the traditional princesses, princess critics embrace her. And, in embracing Tiana, princess critics must also embrace her ultimate realization that romantic love is part of a full and complete life — even if they don't know they're embracing it. And *that* is the genius of this movie. It slips the truth under the radar and gets the princess critics to adopt the very thing they'd spent years — and would continue to spend years — trying to get rid of. If Disney could have stayed the course, the princesses might have been saved for good.

*

The movie begins — startlingly, given the princess movies that had come immediately before — with the wishing star. Anything is possible, we're told, if you wish on the evening star. This plants us firmly in traditional princess territory — back in the domain of Snow White's wishing well, Cinderella's fairy godmother, and Aurora's magical gifts from the fairies. And if, in the very next moment, we seem to be faced with a princess who turns her back on all that, it would only be because we were watching the movie like princess critics and missing the movie's underlying message.

Much is made of the fact that Tiana is the first African-American princess. For some princess critics this is a major coup, for others it's a travesty that the first black princess spends the majority of the movie as a frog. Is it offensive that the first black princess is poor and her rich friend is white? Or is it laudable for its gritty realism? All of this is interesting to dissect, I'm sure, but, since Tiana's race isn't actually the focus of the story (nor should it be) it's not something we're going to tackle here. The much more interesting comparison between Tiana and her best friend Charlotte is not that one is black and one is white — or even that one is poor and one is rich — but that one is actively denying the traditional princess narrative and the other is comically embracing it. Let's be clear, though, when I say "the traditional princess narrative" I'm talking about the narrative the princess critics have now accepted as truth — the whole, waiting-around-for-a-man-to-solve-all-my-problems narrative. You know, the one that never existed.

We first meet Tiana and Charlotte as children. They are sitting in Charlotte's pink-tastic bedroom — a room quite reminiscent of the bedrooms of little girls whose parents have shopped for Disney princess merchandise — listening to Tiana's mother tell the story of The Frog Prince. Eudora (voiced by Oprah Winfrey) is a seamstress, employed by Charlotte's over-indulgent father to create as many princess dresses as Charlotte's little heart desires — and that's a *lot* of dresses. (It's worth noting that, while the black characters in this movie *are* poor, they aren't servants. They all work for themselves, choosing whom to work for and how to earn an income.) Charlotte rapturously says, "I would kiss a hundred frogs if I could marry a prince and be a princess." Tiana thinks that's disgusting and doesn't seem to care much about marrying royalty. Charlotte, we are meant to understand, is the "old" kind of Disney princess — she's sweet and nice, but shallow — obsessed with pink, and pretty dresses, and marrying a prince, no matter who he is or what he looks like. Tiana, on the other hand, is of the "new" variety — determined, hard working, and uninterested in romance.

When Tiana goes home with her mother at the end of the day we see how different Tiana's life is to Charlotte's. The New Orleans trolley takes them past the opulent mansions of Charlotte's part of town and on towards the broken down shacks of Tiana's. But there, on the wrong side of the tracks, Tiana is introduced the lesson that it will take her the entire movie to learn.

At first, it seems like Tiana's interactions with her beloved father all point toward the entrepreneurial dreams that will be Tiana's motivation for most of the film. Tiana's father, James, is determined to open his own restaurant — which he will call "Tiana's Place" — and is teaching Tiana how to make his famous gumbo. "That old star can only take you part of the way," James explains of the wishing star. "You gotta help it along with some hard work of your own." In a 2016 retrospective of the film, Mari Ness, of *Tor*, calls this a "genuinely shocking moment" in which "the film abruptly turns its back on about sixty years of Disney marketing and suddenly announces that, no matter who you are, when you wish upon a star, your dreams will only come true with a lot of hard work—and maybe not even then." But that's not true at all.

The Disney film that makes the most use of the wishing star is, of course, *Pinocchio*. In it, Pinocchio's father, Geppetto, wishes on the evening star that his wooden puppet will become a real boy. The puppet comes to life, but only *Pinocchio* can do the work that will turn him "real." He must prove his worth. The wishing star doesn't just deliver your heart's desire — it gives you what you need to achieve it yourself. Tiana's father doesn't tell her that the star doesn't work, he tells her that she's got to "help it along." This has always been true. So, even though Tiana's wish is more specific — and therefore, one could argue, more inconsequential — than Geppetto's wish for a real, live son, the fact that she is wishing on a star at all plants us squarely in traditional Disney territory.

Not only that, James has one other important bit of wisdom to impart to his daughter: "Never lose sight of what's really important." He means love. And he says it with his arm around Eudora. Romantic love. Family. Nothing matters without that. And since we learn that James dies shortly after this interaction, we know that this message is the key message of the film. Fight for your dreams, work hard, never give up, but remember what's *really* important — what it's all *for* — love.

In the next moment, we flash forward to Tiana as a young woman. We learn that she is working two waitressing jobs and saving up all her money to buy the restaurant her father always dreamed of but never achieved. She's exhausted and frazzled but she's working towards her goal. It's a brilliant new twist on the Cinderella narrative. Instead of doing menial chores because she has no choice Tiana does exactly the same kind of chores — cooking, cleaning, waiting on people — because she chooses to. It looks like the answer to the princess critics' prayers. She's Cinderella with agency! "She knows what she wants (her dream from the start is to open her own restaurant) and she works hard to get it (to achieve her dream, she juggles two jobs)," crows Serrano. She's "defined by her desire to open a restaurant instead of by her romantic prospects," swoons *ScreenCrush*. "She's obsessed with hard work," rhapsodizes Vanessa Golembewski, of *Refinery29*. It looked like Disney had finally done it. They'd dragged Cinderella into the modern age, given her a feminist sensibility, and slapped her down in New Orleans.

But it soon becomes clear that Tiana has forgotten her father's most important lesson. "All you ever do is work," a friend who comes into the restaurant tells her when she refuses to go out dancing. Her whole life is focused on restaurant ownership. As opposed to Charlotte whose whole life, we learn in the next moment, is focused on romance. Charlotte swoons into the restaurant to giddily announce that an actual prince — Prince Naveen of Maldonia — is coming to New Orleans and will be staying with her and her father. Charlotte hopes that Naveen will fall madly in love with her and make her a princess like she's always wanted. It's pretty obvious what's going on here. Charlotte is the "old" kind of Disney princess and she's played for comic relief. The message is clear: the "old" kind of princess is so ridiculous it's funny. But, obviously, Charlotte's single-minded focus on the title of "princess" has nothing to do with the traditional princesses of Disney's Golden Age. She *is* funny. And the movie also manages to make her likable which is an interesting choice in a movie which, on the surface at least, is presenting a feminist princess.

Tiana has no interest in meeting the prince. Her attention is laser-focused on opening her restaurant. And when Charlotte offers to pay her an enormous sum of money to make her famous beignets for the ball she's hosting for Prince Naveen, Tiana giddily realizes she's about to make her dream come true. She rushes to the property office, hands over her tin cans full of coins and dollar bills and purchases a ramshackle old building in an entrepreneurial ecstasy. "All the money she has, she's worked for," writes Golembewski. "All of Tiana's money belongs to her and only to her," says Serrano. And this is true. Tiana's hard work *is* admirable. Her ability to buy her own restaurant *is* impressive. That's what's so brilliant about this movie. She hasn't done anything that anyone would disagree with. She's not opening an abortion clinic or donating to the NRA or doing some other thing that lots of people would disagree with. She worked hard, she made money, she bought a restaurant. Good for her!

But then, while she and her mother are cleaning up the derelict building she's just bought, Eudora expresses her own wish that Tiana meet her "Prince Charming." "I want some grandkids!" she says. Tiana tells her she has no time for things like that, she's got to get the restaurant ready to open! Eudora tries again: "It's a shame you're working so hard." She even offers Tiana James' gumbo pot as a way to try to remind her of her father's parting message. But Tiana is single-minded. The restaurant is all that's important. In fact, Tiana sings her signature Disney princess ballad right there in the restaurant about how close she is to being a restaurant owner. "Her Broadway-style 'I Want' song, 'Almost There,' is all about how much closer she's gotten to saving up enough money to live out her dead father's dream as a restaurateur, far from the hapless romantic pining of Snow White or Aurora from Sleeping Beauty," writes *ScreenCrush*.

If *The Princess and the Frog* really was a "feminist" Disney movie, the movie would be over. Tiana has her restaurant, she avoided falling in love, what more could she want? But the movie isn't over at all — it's barely begun. So, obviously, the fulfillment of Tiana's dream to own a restaurant isn't actually her happy ending — or not all of it at least. There's something missing. The thing her father tried to get her to understand. The thing her mother is *still* trying to get her to understand. She doesn't have romantic love. And *that*, the movie is unequivocally saying, is *necessary*.

So then we cut to Prince Naveen. On first glance, he doesn't seem much like a Disney prince. He's lazy, fun-loving, irresponsible, and broke. He's come to New Orleans — with his uptight manservant Lawrence — to find a rich woman to marry because his parents have cut him off for being so carefree. He's hoping that Charlotte will be just the rich girl he's looking for — which seems great since Charlotte's hoping the same thing. But Naveen can't stay focused on his mission. He's delighted with the sights and sounds of New Orleans — the jazz, the women, the hustle and bustle of city life. He ends up in a voodoo parlor. So he's not a prince in the Prince Charming or even Prince Eric model. But he isn't so far off from the Beast. He's a man who's giving in to his impulses, shirking his responsibilities, and uninterested in love. Like the Beast, he needs an intervention. And, like the Beast, he finds it through magic, and a girl.

Dr. Facilier — the sinewy, waistcoated voodoo magician — is happy to provide the magic. In language that harkens back to the religious symbolism of *Cinderella*, Facilier (or The Shadow Man as he's called for most of the film) calls himself "a sinner." He appeals to his "friends on the other side" to do his bidding and grant the wishes of his hapless victims. He targets Naveen specifically because he wants Charlotte's father's fortune for himself, so he can rule New Orleans. "The real power in this world ain't magic, it's money," he explains. If we needed another indication that money alone wasn't the goal, here it is. If the bad guy says it, you know it's not good! Not to mention the fact that "Facilier" is a play on the French word "facile" which means "easy." Going to Dr. Facilier is taking the easy way out. And — as we all know — taking the easy way usually makes things a lot harder!

Playing off Lawrence's jealousy of Naveen, Facilier fills a talisman with some of Naveen's blood which lets Lawrence take Naveen's form while he's wearing it. (Naveen turns into frog . . . because . . . why not?) The plan is for Lawrence (as Naveen) to win Charlotte's hand and give the fortune to Facilier. Which is how Lawrence ends up attending Charlotte's ball as Naveen, Naveen attends as a frog, and Tiana is there serving beignets.

In a play on the imagery of the traditional princess movie, Charlotte enters her ball in a stunning ball gown, stands in a shaft of light, descends the stairs to the prince, and dances with him in the spotlight. But the prince isn't really the prince (he's Lawrence), the spark of true love has definitely not been kindled, and everything about this moment is superficial — the way princess critics think it always has been. But while Charlotte's "happy ending" seems to be playing out, Tiana's "happy ending" is crashing down around her. The landlords of her new restaurant come over to her beignet table to tell her that someone else made a higher offer on the building and it's not hers after all. They call her a "little woman" and tell her she's probably "better off where you are." On the one hand, you could read this as the patriarchy rearing its ugly head — and the landlords certainly are patronizing — but, on the other hand, it seems fairly clear that Tiana can't realize her dream yet. She hasn't yet achieved fairy tale princess-hood.

In an act of kindness one wouldn't really expect from a superficial husband-hunter, Charlotte leaves her prince at the party to comfort Tiana. When a plate of beignets falls on Tiana, ruining her outfit, Charlotte takes her up to her room to help her change her dress. And this is how Tiana, dressed as a princess, ends up on Charlotte's balcony wishing on a star once again for her restaurant. But what does she get instead? A prince. Well, a frog. But he's really a prince. (A beast, maybe?) Anyway, the star gives Tiana what she *needs* not what she wants. It gives her a chance at romantic love. The star is the divine force, Facilier and his voodoo friends are the opposite. One advocates for love, the other for money. Is this a "feminist" message? That remains to be seen.

Naveen, thinking Tiana is an actual princess, decides that, if they kiss, he'll turn back into a man. Tiana is completely unwilling to do this (not caring about getting a handsome prince in return) until Naveen lies and tells her he's very wealthy and that he'll buy her restaurant back if she turns him back into a man. She kisses him and — whoops! — she turns into a frog too because she isn't actually a princess. In the symbolism of fairy tales, neither Naveen nor Tiana are who they are meant to be. They haven't yet realized their true potential and become a "prince" and a "princess." Naveen is still shallowly obsessed with fun and frivolity, Tiana is still too hyper-focused on her restaurant — she *kissed* a *frog* for money! They have a lot to learn. And off they hop to figure it all out.

Tiana and Naveen initially clash — as we'd expect any good Beauty and Beast to do. But, unlike Belle, Tiana has a few things to learn from Naveen as well. "Life is short, when you're done you're done / We're on this earth to have some fun," Naveen sings. Neither Naveen nor Tiana believes in the transcendent power of true love. They both think that it's the superficial things that matter. For Naveen this means creature comforts. For Tiana it means her restaurant. Golembewski writes that Tiana "educates Prince Naveen about the importance of really earning what you want in life," and that may be true. But Naveen educates Tiana too — about the importance of fun, creativity, and openness. Tiana and Naveen need to learn those things, but it's only *together* that they can learn what they both lack: an understanding of the importance of emotional connection to another person.

In their initial moments as frogs, both Naveen's and Tiana's faults are on display. Finding themselves in the bayou, Naveen loafs around letting Tiana build a raft all by herself and formulate a plan to get back to New Orleans, find Facilier, and reverse the spell. He assumes Tiana will find them food to eat, and won't help row the raft. But Tiana is bossy and uptight, refusing to see the beauty of the New Orleans bayou, or appreciate the music that Naveen and a jazz-loving crocodile named Louis play together, or explore the fun of her new bug-catching abilities. "You do not know how to have fun," Naveen complains. "You're a no count, philandering, lazy bump on a log," Tiana counters. They are equals in their faults and in their need to be saved by one another. They each have something the other one needs — this is why they are *both* frogs (or beasts). For princess critics, Tiana "educates" the wayward Naveen in the joys of hard work. But Naveen has just as much to teach Tiana, because hard work is important but (like her father tried to tell her) it means nothing at all without romantic love.

Naveen and Tiana learn about a voodoo lady named Mama Odie, who lives in the bayou, who might be able to help them turn back into frogs. As they journey through the swamps, they come to see the strengths — not just the weaknesses — in one another. Their lives — which they had previously thought were complete — might be lacking. Naveen sees Tiana whip up a delicious gumbo using only the plants around her and realizes that he doesn't know how to do anything for himself. When Tiana teaches him how to mince the vegetables he finds that he's really proud of himself for learning a skill. A moment earlier, he would have scoffed at doing that kind of work himself. Naveen teaches Tiana to dance and she finds that she enjoys the feeling of cutting loose and having a little fun doing exactly the thing she avoided at home. As they each begin to see the merits in the strengths of the other, Naveen and Tiana begin to develop feelings for each other. Like the Beast, transformed by his recognition of Belle's inner beauty, Naveen and Tiana find that their appreciation of each other's inner qualities is transforming them into better people.

When they arrive at Mama Odie's treehouse and tell her that they want to be human again, the old blind woman explains that that's what they want, but it isn't what they *need*. Just like the evening star sent Tiana a chance at love, even though she asked for a restaurant, Mama Odie knows what both Tiana and Naveen are lacking. She tells them to "dig a little deeper" and "find out who you are." The important thing, you see, isn't what you want, it's who you *are*. That's the signature Disney princess message — the internal matters more than the external. Mamie Odie is trying to redirect Tiana — and Naveen too — back to the traditional Disney princess narrative. Kois calls the movie a "clever and careful recalibration of the princess archetype," meaning that it moves the princess away from husband-hunting and swooning, and towards entrepreneurship and independence. But that isn't actually true at all. Really, the movie is very subtly and quietly — so quietly the princess critics miss it — moving the princess archetype back to where it started.

As Mamie Odie sings, Tiana seems to finally cut loose — dancing and singing along to the song, agreeing to "dig a little deeper." This seals the deal for Naveen — he's head over webbed green heels in love with her. In the moment that Tiana seems to allow herself to acknowledge the things in her life that have been missing — to become truly herself — Naveen really "sees" her and falls for her. And, in allowing himself to feel the importance of romantic connection, he — like the Beast — realizes that he's got to change. He needs to get a job, take responsibility, and be the kind of man worthy of Tiana's love. In that moment, Naveen's side of the transformation is complete. He's ready to turn back into a man.

It's Tiana who isn't quite there yet. After all her singing and dancing, Tiana declares that she understands it all now: she has to work even harder to get her restaurant! But that isn't it at all and everyone around her knows it. Everyone in the *movie* that is. The princess critics are something else altogether. Ness writes that the movie's message is that "working, not magic, brings happiness." Serrano says the "moral of the story" is "work, work, work, work, work." Chelsea Mize, of *Bustle*, applauds Tiana for having "economic independence and stability" as her "chief aim in life." But, if all that was true, Tiana wouldn't have needed to turn into a frog. And she certainly would have been ready to turn back into a person after meeting Mama Odie and doubling down on the whole restaurant thing. But she isn't — and she doesn't. She stays a frog because, unlike Naveen, she still doesn't get that — even though her dream of opening a restaurant is a good one and the hard work she has done is laudable — none of it matters without love.

Since Mama Odie sees that Tiana isn't ready to understand any of that, she tells them that there is one other way for them to turn back: Naveen has to kiss a princess. Tiana and Naveen quickly realize that this means Charlotte, whose father has been crowned "King of

181

the Mardis Gras" which makes her a princess. But only for that night — the night of Mardi Gras. Tiana and Naveen jump aboard a riverboat back to New Orleans to find Charlotte. On the boat, Naveen decides that he's going to propose to Tiana. He doesn't care, anymore, that he'll be poor. He's going to get a job and pull his weight. He uses his new-found mincing skills to make Tiana a frog-sized meal and tries to tell her how he feels about her. But he can't quite get the words out and Tiana, unaware of what's going on, interrupts him when the boat glides past the building where she wants to open her restaurant.

"Belle, are you happy here with me?" the Beast asked before declaring his love. His love for her meant that her happiness was more important to him than his own. When Belle told him that her father was sick and needed her, the Beast realized he had to let Belle go to him, even though it meant he'd be doomed to remain a beast forever. When the objects asked him why he did it, he answered simply "I love her." When Tiana starts talking about her restaurant and how much it means to her, Naveen realizes that, if he doesn't have the money to buy it for her, Tiana won't ever be happy. He puts the ring away and resolves to marry Charlotte instead, so that he'll have enough money to keep his original promise to Tiana to give her the money she needs to buy the building. Like the Beast, Naveen believes that Tiana doesn't love him — couldn't possibly love someone like him — but his love for *her* means that he is willing to do whatever it takes to make her happy. He's willing to let her go.

When they arrive in New Orleans, unbeknownst to Tiana, Naveen is captured by Facilier's demonic minions who have been chasing him to get more of his blood to fill the talisman that keeps Lawrence looking like Naveen. While he's gone, Tiana learns that Naveen is in love with her and was going to propose. Like Belle, who realizes she loves the Beast when it seems like she might lose him to the angry mob, Tiana finally understands that she loves Naveen when it seems like she might lose him to Charlotte. She opens her heart and allows herself to acknowledge that she wants love in her life — she wants Naveen. Like Belle rushing back to the castle, Tiana rushes into the Mardis Gras parade to find Naveen. But, when she sees Charlotte standing next to Lawrence (who looks like Naveen) she thinks that he's already kissed Charlotte and is getting ready to marry her — and that Tiana somehow didn't turn back into a person. She runs away, crushed.

If the movie was really a "recalibration of the princess archetype," then surely this would be the happy ending — Tiana realizing that love isn't the answer to her happiness and refocusing herself on her career goals. She would pick herself up, dust herself off, and go get her restaurant, triumphantly opening it up with much fanfare and rave reviews. But that's not what happens. She's crushed. She *wants* to go back to believing that romance doesn't matter, but now she *knows* it does. She just needs one more little push.

Naveen, who's actually still a frog, escapes from his cage and jumps on Lawrence, knocking him to the ground and knocking the talisman loose. Without the talisman, Lawrence takes on his real form and reveals himself to be a fraud. Tiana ends up with the talisman so Facilier offers to make her a deal to get it back. If she gives over the talisman, he will turn her human and give her her restaurant. When she refuses, he shows her a vision of everything that has been sacrificed for the dream of the restaurant. He shows her all the hard work that she's done, the jobs she's worked, the disappointments she's suffered, and he shows her her father and all the hard work *he* put into the restaurant only to die with his dream unfulfilled. Tiana is tempted. But, in a flash, she has a realization. Her father didn't get what he *wanted*, but he always had what he *needed*: love. She smashes the talisman into a thousand pieces.

The moral of the story is "work, work, work, work, work"? No! One of Tiana's inner strengths is her ability to work hard for what she wants, to stick to her guns with determination and grit, and to fight for what she wants — like Cinderella, like Ariel, like Belle — but the moral of the story is love (love, love, love, love). Nothing else matters without love. Because love is the fairy tale force of true recognition. It brings out all your best qualities and allows the world to see you for who you truly are. *This* is the film's message.

When Tiana finally catches up with Naveen again, he's telling Charlotte that if she kisses him by midnight (which is fast approaching) he will turn into the real prince and he will marry her — as long as she promises to give Tiana the money for her restaurant. He tells Charlotte that, even though he'll marry her, he loves Tiana. Tiana understands that Naveen loves her truly, *sees* her truly, and is willing to give her up so that she can be happy. But Tiana is now *also* ready to become human again, because she has had her pivotal realization and she comes out of her hiding spot to tell Naveen that she loves him too and doesn't want to open her restaurant if she can't have him with her. Charlotte is so touched by Naveen and Tiana's love that she agrees to kiss Naveen with no strings attached. Charlotte, who, through the film has been the sort of comic relief version of a traditional Disney princess, finally reveals herself to have understood all along. It's *true love* that really matters. Yes, she was looking for it the wrong way (by going after a prince, instead of a "prince") but she understands that, because a Disney princess does. She kisses Naveen.

But midnight has struck. Charlotte isn't a princess anymore. The kiss doesn't work. It doesn't work because this movie has now definitively placed itself within the confines of traditional fairy tale. True love, princes, princesses, kisses, and transformation all live within the fairy tale domain. And, in a fairy tale, a kiss only holds transformative power if it's shared between two people who love each other truly — or who have come to a symbolic recognition of each other as their true selves. And Charlotte and Naveen do not.

The genius of this movie is that, even though it operates squarely within the fairy tale realm, it offers enough modernity to make the princess critics think they're watching a feminist retelling. When Naveen and Tiana realize the kiss didn't work they make a decision that seems, on the surface, shocking. They'll stay frogs. Their love is what's most important to them, so they are willing to stay in the form they've spent the whole movie trying to get rid of. As long as they are together, nothing else matters. This, of course, is the message of *all* fairy tales — that who you are *inside* is much more important than what you look like *outside*. But, in a traditional fairy tale, the kiss and the transformation is a representation of that understanding. The true selves of the lovers is made manifest in their transformation — their inner selves represented by their outer beauty. In *The Princess and the Frog*, that final realization is pulled out of the symbolic. They are content with who they are, and who they are to each other. Just as all other fairy tale princes and princesses are.

Tiana and Naveen head back to the bayou and get married — as frogs. But, when Mama Odie pronounces them man and wife (or frog and frog), the movie delivers its final twist. The kiss that Naveen and Tiana share transforms them back into people because, in marrying Naveen, Tiana is now a princess. And she's also a "princess." After allowing the final transformation to play out literally, the movie lets it play out symbolically as well. By the end, Tiana and Naveen are both a man and woman in love, and a fairy tale prince and princess — with all the symbolism that embodies. Their journeys have led them to themselves and, in being themselves, they found each other.

The pair return to New Orleans where their fearsome-looking friend Louis the crocodile scares the landlords into sticking to their original deal with Tiana. Naveen rolls up his sleeves and helps her finally open the restaurant of her dreams. In the final sequence, Naveen and Tiana dance together on the roof of the restaurant which is no longer called "Tiana's Place" but is, instead, "Tiana's Palace." Kois says that *The Princess and the Frog* "does away with" the notion that being a princess meant "wealth, beauty, and happily ever after," emphasizing that "Tiana's palace is a restaurant." But that misses the point entirely. Her palace is a restaurant because it houses her love —

as a princess's palace must. Her dream of a restaurant was a good one, but it meant nothing without love. Without love, it's just Tiana's Place. *With* love, it's her Palace.

*

The Princess and the Frog is quirky and different. It blends the old and the new ideas about princesses in a way that had never been seen before and wouldn't be seen again. Princess critics think it is radical because it offers a princess who wants to be a business owner. And, while that's certainly new, its *real* message is more shocking still. In a moment in which the Disney princess trajectory had been rocketing away from romance and fairy tale symbolism, *The Princess and the Frog* knocked that rocket right off course. It pulled together the feminist idea that the princess should have realistic agency, and the traditional idea that romance could be a force for transformation. It was a work of subtle genius.

Though the movie did fairly well at the box office, it didn't recapture the former glory of Disney's Renaissance. A few factors probably contributed to this, particularly the fact that it came out in the same week as the highly popular movie *Avatar*, and the fact that the Disney movies that had come before it were pretty bad so audiences stayed away. But another princess film was already in the works, and *that* movie was an enormous success — and as traditional as they come.

For little girls in Snow White costumes, sleeping under Cinderella bedspreads, and dreaming of the transformative power of true love, it suddenly seemed like Disney was going to give them what they wanted. I, for one, walked out of that movie theater into a sudden soft snowfall and felt, for the first time in a long time, the contentment that comes from the transformative power of a fairy tale. And, walking next to my husband, I knew (as I still know, now) that I'd found my own Prince Charming — not because he has a castle, or a crown, or even a white horse, but because he's the person who sees me for who I truly am, and I him. *Just hang in there*, I wanted to tell tiny

186

Snow White as she walked from the theater, hand in hand with her mother. *Hold onto the princess dream and, one day, it'll come true.* If only Disney had held on too. If only.

Chapter Ten: Rapunzel

In 2010, Disney made a startling announcement: no more fairy tales. Spooked by the somewhat lackluster showing for *The Princess and the Frog,* the executives at Disney were looking to lay blame. They settled on princesses. "Films and genres do run a course," Pixar Animation Studios chief Ed Catmull, who oversaw Disney Animation Studios, said in 2010. But Disney already had two other princess films already in the works. *Tangled,* Disney's retelling of Rapunzel, would come out in 2010, and the film that would become Pixar's *Brave* was set to come out a few years later, but after that, no more. "We don't have any other musicals or fairy tales lined up," Catmull said. We, of course, know that the studio went back on its word almost immediately — releasing *Frozen* just three years later — but, at the time, this was the word from on high. Disney was unwilling to lose the boy audience — and the revenue it generated — by making movies about princesses.

This, of course, was ridiculous. Disney's most lucrative and iconic movies had been about princesses. But the success of the male-driven Pixar movies had Disney Animation Studios second guessing itself. Not to mention the fact that the movie critics, having become *princess* critics, were likely to react negatively to a "traditional" princess. So, what to do about Rapunzel — a movie about a flaxen-haired princess rescued from a tower by a man? Could there *be* a more traditional damsel in distress story? The studio began by changing the film's title from *Rapunzel* to *Tangled* and playing up the role of the daring and irreverent love interest, Flynn Ryder. "We did not want to be put in a box," Catmull said of the name change. "Some people might assume it's a fairy tale for girls when it's not. We make movies to be appreciated and loved by everybody."

Another issue was the studio's perception of the changing interests of young girls. During the time in which Disney's heroines had been shifting more and more away from traditional fairy tale values and toward "feminist" sensibilities, little girls' interests had begun to shift as well. "With the advent of 'tween' TV, the tiara-wearing ideal of femininity has been supplanted by new adolescent role models such as the Disney Channel's Selena Gomez and Nickelodeon's Miranda Cosgrove," wrote Dawn C. Chmielewski and Claudia Eller in *The LA Times*. Was there a connection between the advent of the less symbolic, more jaded cartoon heroines and this shift in little girls' interests? I can't say for sure, but it seems likely! Dafna Lemish, chairwoman of the radio and TV department at Southern Illinois University, said, at the time, that by the time little girls are five or six, "they're not interested in being princesses." Instead, "they're interested in being hot, in being cool." Whereas, once, princesses had taught little girls far older than six the universal lessons of growing up into women of integrity and strength, they were now just shallow facsimiles — pushing athleticism, superficial dreams, and the evils of romance. No wonder little girls were turning away from them!

Disney has, of course, always had the bottom line in mind, but *Tangled,* in particular, was a film driven by the studio's fears of another lackluster turnout in a market dominated by Pixar. But here's the crazy (or not really that crazy) thing: Disney did everything it could to make a movie that people would love, and guess what happened. They made a fairy tale — and a princess — as traditional as they come. And know what? People *loved* it. The movie was a *huge* success. It grossed h̶ than any other Disney Animation Studios movie that had come out before, except *The Lion King*. Audiences turned up in droves and the critics couldn't help it — they loved it too. *Tangled* was "fun but not feminist," wrote KJ Antonia, on *Slate*. "*Tangled* is old, yet new," wrote Todd McCarthy in *The Hollywood Reporter*. "There are some hiccups along the way, but by the end there is success," wrote Kenneth Turan in *The LA Times*.

Movie critics and princess critics (who were basically the same at this point) didn't know what to do. They liked the movie — against their better judgment — and it was clear that audiences also loved it, which couldn't be ignored. Some, unable to help themselves, tried to point out all the "anti-feminist" things about the movie while still basically giving it a good review. Others tried to find ways that Rapunzel really *was* a "feminist" and add her to the ever-growing canon of princess-critic-approved Disney princesses. But no one said what we all know to be true: it was Rapunzel's very traditional-ness that *made* her feminist — or at least made her a good role model for girls. Because, in Rapunzel, girls found — for the first time in their lifetimes — a heroine who embodied the universal fairy tale shorthand, but spoke, reacted, and thought like a modern teenager. She was jut the princess little girls needed to reintroduce them to the role models they so desperately needed. If Disney hadn't already been veering away from princesses — and traditional princesses specifically — Disney could have entered another Golden Age.

*

When Disney began to shift away from the traditional and toward the "feminist," the princess movie villains shifted from female to male. The story was no longer about a girl who journeys from childhood to adulthood by pushing back against an evil mother-figure, now it was the journey of a woman taking her independent place in the world by pushing back against the patriarchy. But, with *Tangled*, we get a female villain who's as wicked as they come — the first since *The Little Mermaid*, over twenty years before. The inclusion of Mother

Gothel — a witch obsessed with staying young and beautiful forever — returns us squarely to the fairy tale shorthand of growing up, symbolized by an adolescent girl breaking away from a jealous crone. Gothel is Snow White's wicked stepmother yanked terrifyingly into the "real" world.

Mother Gothel kidnaps the infant Rapunzel from her royal parents because Rapunzel's hair holds the magical ability to heal wounds, and keep people young. But only when it's attached to her head. If it's cut, it stops being magic. So Gothel takes Rapunzel, locks her up in a tower, and convinces her that she (Gothel) is actually her mother. But, instead of the overt evil of The Evil Queen or Cinderella' Stepmother, Gothel is an emotionally abusive mother — the frighteningly realistic kind. She convinces Rapunzel that everything she does for her she does out of love — the world outside is scary and full of people who want to kill her, she's just keeping her beloved daughter safe. She makes derogatory comments about Rapunzel's weight, her looks, and her intellect and, in the same breath, tells her how much she loves her. And she refuses Rapunzel's greatest wish: to go outside and see the "floating lights" that appear every year on her birthday (a sign, unbeknownst to her, of her grieving parents' remembrance of the baby they lost).

So Rapunzel is a true ingénue — even more than princess Jasmine. Not only has she never been outside the walls of her tower, but the only other person she's ever met is her awful "mother." And she's primed and ready for the most traditional of all princess adventures: growing up. Her task — it's very clear from the moment we meet her — is to get out from under the thumb of Mother Gothel, assert her own independence, and get out there into the world. And, even though Gothel has convinced her that it's "not so bad in there," her heart cries out for the floating lights because they represent who she truly is — the life she should have had with her real parents, and the larger world which, in turn, represents her independence. So, her dream is more amorphous than the specificity of, say, Ariel's wish to be human. But it's much more specific than, for example, Pocahontas' random dream of a spinning arrow that means nothing to her for most of the movie. "When will my life begin?" Rapunzel asks in her very first scene. She knows there is more than this tower, she just isn't sure exactly what.

But, even though Rapunzel has literally never seen a male human being, she isn't a total airhead. She cooks and cleans like a traditional princess, but she also reads, paints, plays chess, and charts the stars. She's a bright, intellectually curious, talented teenager — the way Cinderella or Snow White would be if you pulled her into the real world and allowed her to be more realistic. And it is, in part, these accomplishments that allow some princess critics to find something to love about Rapunzel.

But the thing that really gets the princess critics' little hearts thumping with joy is what Rapunzel can do with her *hair*. Because Mother Gothel can't allow Rapunzel to cut it — lest it lose its magical properties — Rapunzel's hair is as long as her tower is tall. And, while it does its traditional job of acting as a rope for Mother Gothel to enter the tower window, in this version of the story it can do all kinds of other things as well — like be a lasso, a whip, and a grappling hook. She "LEARNS TO FIGHT WITH HER HAIR" crows Beatriz Serrano of *Buzzfeed*. She twirls her hair "like a lariat," said Tom Charity of *CNN*. "That mane is quite the force of nature, 70 feet long and capable of many things, including tying people up and batting them down," wrote Kenneth Turan, in *The LA Times*. But, while Rapunzel's hair does have a life of its own, it's hardly the traditional princess-critic-approved weapon with which to fight as well as a man. It is a definitively feminine attribute and, when used in a fight, wielded out of necessity not martial prowess.

Rapunzel's love interest (Flynn Ryder, real name: Eugene) is of the Aladdin/Beast variety. Much like Aladdin, he's a thief whose dreams initially revolve around money and luxury. When we first meet him, he's running over rooftops — like Aladdin — saying "I want a

192

castle." He steals a crown (which turns out to be Rapunzel's) from the castle and is running from the royal guards when he stumbles upon the clearing where Rapunzel's tower stands. He's smooth-talking, vain (a running gag in the film has him obsessing over the way his Wanted posters get his nose wrong), and convinced of his overwhelming appeal with women. So we've got the traditional ingénue princess paired up with the more modern Aladdin/Beast type prince. "What is it with Disney and good girls who reform bad boys?" complains Antonia. (Ooh! Ooh! Pick me! I know!) It's almost as if, in *Tangled*, the traditional princess has come back to undo the "feminist" storyline. Unlike Jasmine, who berates Aladdin into understanding that she's not a prize to be won, Rapunzel shows Flynn — by being authentically herself — that love, connection, and wonder are more important than money.

When Rapunzel (whose eighteenth birthday is coming up) works up the courage to ask Mother Gothel for permission to finally leave the tower and see the lights up close, Gothel refuses. "Mother knows best.," she sings, in a terrifyingly passive aggressive musical number. "It's a scary world out there," she explains, full of "ruffians and thugs, poison ivy, quicksand, cannibals and snakes, the plague," and, worst of all, "men with pointy teeth." After terrifying Rapunzel completely, Gothel holds her close, singing "Mother's right here / Mother will protect you / Darling, here's what I suggest: / Skip the drama / Stay with mama." And then she moves to the guilt: "Me, I'm just your mother, what do I know? I only bathed, and changed, and nursed you. Go ahead and leave me, I deserve it, let me die alone here, be my guest! When it's too late, you'll see, just wait." Rapunzel, Gothel explains, is "sloppy, underdressed, immature, clumsy," not to mention "gullible, naive, positively grubby, ditzy and a bit, well, hmm, vague." She'll never make it in the world. She also throws in "gettin' kinda chubby," which she says she's only telling her "'cause I love you." And, after all that, Gothel says: "Don't ever ask to leave this tower again."

It's an amazing reanimation of the traditional symbolism of the mother-figure holding the maiden back from doing what she must: separating. It's still the symbolic evil crone holding back the innocent maiden, but now she's in the almost too realistic shape of an abusive mother. Rapunzel's task won't be easy, but it must be done. In order to be a fully-functioning, happy, and fulfilled adult, Rapunzel must get away from Gothel — even as Gothel does everything she can to keep her a child. The world, Gothel tells Rapunzel, is scary and frightening, full of awful things — like men! She'd be much better off remaining a child forever. The filmmakers could have made Gothel much more overtly evil and dropped the charade she has created for Rapunzel that she loves her. But, the truth is, a girl must separate from even the most loving parents if she wants to find her way to adulthood. Obviously, most seemingly loving parents don't turn out to actually be evil witches who only want your magic hair, but placing Rapunzel in a situation where she believes she is loved and cared for and must fight back anyway is a much more realistic representation of this fairy tale trope.

When Mother Gothel leaves Rapunzel alone again, Flynn Ryder shows up. At first glance, his entrance looks like a nod to the princess critics — a feminist revision of the traditional fairy tale. Flynn doesn't climb Rapunzel's hair in order to rescue her and spirit her away. Instead, he's running away from the palace guards and sees the tower as a place to hide. His motives are purely about him — he doesn't even know Rapunzel is up there. And, when he makes it to Rapunzel's room — using arrows as handholds instead of Rapunzel's hair — Rapunzel is ready and waiting to do the thing that princess critics love her for: hit him over the head with a frying pan.

Serrano writes, "How cool is it for a Disney princess to grab a frying pan and use it as a weapon? Is there a more forceful way to reappropriate a symbol of feminine oppression than beating the s**t out of someone with it?" Okay so *now* the princess critics want to get symbolic? Are we really supposed to believe that every single other princess movie should be interpreted completely literally, but that this one gesture is symbolic of fighting back against the patriarchy? Seems pretty unlikely. How about this: Rapunzel is terrified of the outside world. Someone from the world is climbing up the side of her tower and into her room. She grabs the object she owns that is most likely to work as a weapon, and uses it. It's a frying pan because she's not a fighter — she's a woman — and, when she isn't being physically threatened, she likes to cook. And, once she's used it, she screams and runs away. Because she's terrified, and she's never seen a man before. It's believable that she's able to knock Flynn out because she took him completely by surprise, rather than besting him in combat. And it's believable, too, that she would be totally unsure what to do next. Essentially, she fights like a girl. And that's *good*.

The first thing Rapunzel does, when she's got Flynn knocked out on her floor, is check is teeth. Gothel told Rapunzel that the world was full of "men with pointy teeth." The fact that Flynn's teeth are normal-looking is the first crack in the narrative that Gothel has sold Rapunzel. Rapunzel has never seen a man before and, instead of being terrifying and monstrous the way she's been told they would be, this man is handsome and intriguing.

Using her hair to help her — and with much huffing and puffing — Rapunzel manages to lock Flynn, unconscious, into her wardrobe. Even as Rapunzel performs physical tasks, she does them realistically. We can tell that Flynn is heavier than her and that she's struggling with his weight. Without the help of her hair she wouldn't have been able to get him in the closet and, even then, it takes her multiple tries. Knocking someone out unawares and struggling to drag their body across the room is very different than fighting in a battle. It's true that she's protecting herself physically, but she isn't making any kind of assertion about how her physical achievements compare to a man's. This movie — as opposed to the princess movies that came directly before — is not about gender difference. It's about growing

SAVING CINDERELLA

up, becoming your true self. And Rapunzel, here, is engaged in her first truly independent undertaking.

With Flynn locked up, Rapunzel finds his satchel and the crown inside. Not knowing that the crown is actually hers, Rapunzel puts it on her head and looks in the mirror. In that moment, Rapunzel sees a glimmer of her true self. She doesn't know she's really a princess, or that Gothel isn't her real mother, but she recognizes that this crown *means* something for her. "When will my reflection show who I am inside?" Mulan asked meaninglessly. But, here, Rapunzel's reflection actually *is* showing who she is inside. She is a literal princess, and the crown shows that, but she's also a *symbolic* princess. Somewhere within — if she can only find it — is her true self, the ideal of perfection, the truly realized person.

When Gothel returns, Rapunzel is initially resolved to be a good daughter and tell her about the man locked up in her wardrobe. She's proud of herself for being brave and wants to use that as proof that she could make it in the world. She's still buying into Gothel's story about the world and wanting to please her. But when, in a moment of uncharacteristic honesty, Gothel tells her that she won't be leaving the tower "ever," Rapunzel has second thoughts. Rapunzel loves Gothel, but she's unwilling to remain a child forever. We meet her at the moment when her desire to break away has overcome her desire to remain safely a child. She finally sees that Gothel will never be wiling to let her go.

So she tells Gothel that she'll stay in the tower but that she wants something else for a birthday present: a special shell to make paint from that can only be found far away. To keep her happy, Gothel agrees, and off she goes. In this moment, Rapunzel reveals herself to be resourceful and determined — like her traditional princess sisters — and willing to do what it takes to accomplish her goal. Cinderella *will* go to the ball, Ariel *will* become human, Snow White *will* find a way to survive. It's the traditional princess narrative, unadulterated by complaints about gender roles. Her act of rebellion

196

— unlike Jasmine's, or Pocahontas', or Mulan's — isn't about fighting back against a made up version of Disney princess patriarchy. It has nothing to do with a man at all. It's simply about self-discovery, growing up, and becoming truly herself.

With Gothel gone, Rapunzel gets to work fulfilling her dream. She ties Flynn up with her hair and wakes him up. Flynn's first reaction to being tied up by a beautiful girl is to try to get away by turning on "the smolder." He tries to charm Rapunzel into swooning all over him and letting him go. Rapunzel, knowing nothing about the fake things that men and women do to try to attract each other, is totally unfazed. Here, again, is a princess whose complete inability to be anything other than who she truly is, allows the man to drop his guard and change for the better (like Belle). It looks, perhaps, like a princess-critic-approved moment, in which the woman has tied up the man and is in control and totally uninterested in his romantic overtures. But it isn't men that Rapunzel is uninterested in, it's artifice. She doesn't understand what Flynn is trying to do and so it doesn't work on her. Rapunzel is the first girl who doesn't fall all over Flynn and this unnerves Flynn.

Rapunzel is now totally dead set on getting out of the tower. Her realization that Mother Gothel wants to keep her there forever has pushed her one step closer to separation. She shows Flynn that she has the crown and tells him she'll only give it back if he agrees to take her to the floating lights. Like Snow White, Rapunzel uses her wits to find a way to get what she wants by making a deal. It's her first independent act. It has nothing to do with Flynn as a potential love-interest. It is simply Rapunzel's way of getting what she wants. Flynn agrees — because he has no other choice — and Rapunzel leaves her tower for the very first time.

Her reaction to leaving her tower is the realistic version of the fairy tale trope. "Rapunzel is stereotypically overly emotional, swinging from one end of a mood swing to another," writes Natalie Wilson in *Ms Magazine*. Which is true, but it isn't — as Wilson implies — a sign of her weakness. She *is* alternately elated and terrified. She runs around leaping and whooping with happiness and then starts crying in terror. She wants to go out on her adventure and then she wants to go back to her tower. She's an emotional mess. As well she should be! She's literally never been outside. She's just taken a huge step towards growing up. She's out in a world that she's been told all her life is full of horrible dangers she's unprepared to handle. It's Cinderella losing her belief, Snow White lying terrified in the woods, Ariel sobbing in her grotto. It's the moment when the princess isn't sure she can do it — isn't sure she can go it alone, forge her own path, and be her own person. But, ultimately, Rapunzel says "I can't believe *I* did this!" *She* made this happen and she's going to see it through. In response to Rapunzel's conflicting feelings, Flynn sardonically observes, "This is part of growing up. A little adventure, a little rebellion." He's right: Rapunzel *must* rebel in order to get away. There is no situation in which she can do what she has to do *and* maintain her relationship with Gothel.

Flynn takes Rapunzel to a pub full of tough-looking ruffians because, at this point, he is trying to dissuade Rapunzel from her plan so she'll go back to her tower and give him back the crown. But the thugs recognize Flynn from the Wanted posters and jump on him. Rapunzel — rather than jumping into the fray like a "feminist" princess might — uses her wits and her unimpeachable true-heartedness to stop them. She tells them she *needs* Flynn to help her achieve her dreams and asks the thugs if *they* have dreams. And, of course, it turns out they do.

It's funny to watch these pirate-looking ruffian guys dancing around singing about their dreams of piano playing, flower arranging, and miming. But it's also thematically relevant. On the one hand, one might say that it's emasculating that these tough guys have secret dreams that are more "feminine." But, on the other hand, within the trajectory that the princess narrative had been on since the '90s, the idea that the big, scary, men of the patriarchy turn out to want to help our princess on her way is important. They support Rapunzel in her dream and they berate Flynn for being so jaded. "I don't sing," Flynn tells them when they ask him to join in. And when they force him to he sings that his dream is to be alone "surrounded by enormous piles of money." The scary-looking men look down on Flynn for being superficial and cynical and praise Rapunzel for following her dream. It's as if, in this very silly musical number, Disney is recommitting to the traditional princess narrative. And even though we know that the studio was actually in the process of dismissing this type of story, this movie begs to differ. And so did the fans.

When the palace guards show up at the pub looking for Flynn, Rapunzel's new friends help them escape through a tunnel. But they end up trapped in a small cave that is rapidly filling with water. Thinking they are going to die, Rapunzel apologizes for getting Flynn involved in this mess and Flynn tells her that his real name is actually Eugene Fitzherbert. Flynn Ryder, the dashing, "smoldering" hero, is actually just a guy named Eugene. Again, on the one hand, you could read this as Flynn shedding his "toxic masculinity" and revealing that he's actually the far less "toxic" Eugene. But, on the other hand, Flynn is dropping the artifice. He's allowing Rapunzel to see his true self. He's not really a beast, or Prince Ali, he's a man. And he's allowing his guard to drop for a woman.

Rapunzel uses the glowing light of her magic hair to find a way out of the cave. She rescues them with her wits, not with physical might. In fact, it's Flynn who uses his strength to push aside the rocks that cover their exit. They are each what they are — a man and woman — with the resulting strengths and weaknesses.

Flynn is shocked to learn that Rapunzel's hair is magic. She tells him she can use it to heal his hand (which he cut in the cave) but "just don't freak out." She is sharing something secret and personal with Flynn — a secret Mother Gothel never let her share. And, in return, Flynn tells her more about himself. He reveals that he was an orphan who took the name of a dashing hero from a book and became a thief. He took on the name of a male role model, but became a criminal. Flynn's masculinity isn't "toxic," he just hasn't actually become a "man" in the fairy tale sense of the word. He's lost his way — doing things no fairy tale prince should — and needs to find it again. In admitting his lies to Rapunzel, he is finding his way back to himself. And, in revealing her secret to someone other than her mother, Rapunzel is finding her way to *her* independent self.

When Flynn goes to get firewood, Mother Gothel shows up. She's been tracking Rapunzel and tries to get her to come back to the tower by telling her that Flynn doesn't care about her, he only wants the crown that he stole back — once she gives it to him, he'll leave her. It's a moment of truth for Rapunzel — she can continue to believe the version of the world that Gothel has sold her her whole life, or she can assert her own. Whereas, before, Rapunzel got Gothel out of the way in order to begin to break free, now she must actually face her. It's Cinderella insisting she's invited to the ball, Ariel telling her father she loves Eric, Aurora telling the fairies she doesn't want to be a princess. And Rapunzel joins their ranks. She tells Gothel that Flynn *does* like her for herself, and that she'll prove it by giving the crown back now and seeing what Flynn does. Bested, Gothel retreats into the shadows.

Gothel must maintain the facade she has built for Rapunzel that she is her loving "mother." Otherwise, Rapunzel could just cut off her own hair and leave Gothel with no way of staying young. If Rapunzel begins to suspect Gothel's picture of the world isn't true, Gothel is in danger of losing what she wants most: her youth. It's the archetypical princess narrative — the old must cede power to the young, and they won't go quietly. Rapunzel is fighting a battle. But it's not with the Huns in military combat, it's a much more difficult kind of battle — the inner kind. *This* is the way a princess can fight, and this is the way she can win.

But, once Gothel is gone, Rapunzel has a change of heart and decides not to give Flynn the crown yet. Even though she's engaged in a symbolic battle, she's also a much more realistic character than Snow

White, Cinderella, or Aurora. She suffers from very human indecision. Growing up is hard. Even for those of us whose mothers aren't literal witches. It's hard to break away from the person who's cared for you all your life, whose view of the world has been passed on to you. It's hard to truly believe that your own path might be different from theirs — or different from the one they wanted you to follow. So Rapunzel continues onward in this intermediate state — not totally detached, but not completely joined either.

The next morning, Flynn and Rapunzel finally make it to the town square where, that night, the floating lanterns will be released. Like Ariel, experiencing human life for the first time in the town square with Eric, Rapunzel's joy and curiosity are on full display. And, like Eric, Flynn finds himself drawn to the purity of Rapunzel's expression of excitement and wonder. This jaded thief finds himself seeing the world around him through new eyes. By simply being herself, and experiencing the world *as* herself, Rapunzel begins to teach Flynn that there's more to life than material things. She doesn't berate him, or tell him to see the world as she does, she simply *is* herself.

"What if it's not everything I dreamed it would be?" Rapunzel asks about the lights. "And what if it is? What do I do then?" "You get to find a new dream," Flynn tells her. Rapunzel's very real fears about growing up are devastatingly relatable. And Flynn's response tells us both that Rapunzel is changing him — making him see the world differently — and also that growing up isn't just one fairy tale moment of realization, but a string of real-live moments. *We* can live like princesses in our own lives. It really can happen.

When night falls, and the lights finally appear, Flynn and Rapunzel realize that they are falling for each other. And this realization comes, for Rapunzel, simultaneously with the realization that the outside world is where she's meant to be. Like Ariel, Rapunzel's dream came before she met her man — she wanted to see the lights up close — but her emotional connection to someone else solidifies her understanding that her dream was worthwhile. "I'm where I'm meant to be," Rapunzel sings. "The world has somehow shifted," she continues, "now that I see you." In a traditional fairy tale, the love interest appears to the princess when she has realized her true self. The prince is a symbol of the princess's ability to project her inner self outwards so that it can be seen by others. The prince sees and recognizes her for who she truly is. Rapunzel finally understands how wrong Mother Gothel's vision of the world has been. She can't ever go back to the tower — can't ever be a child again. And in seeing this, she begins to build her adult world: life outside the tower, a place in the world, a man by her side.

And Flynn, as the fairy tale prince in this scenario, suddenly recognizes his feelings for Rapunzel in the moment when she *becomes* her true adult self. And he does his princely job of *seeing* her true self. "At last I see the light," Flynn sings. "If she's here / It's crystal clear / I'm where I'm meant to go." Flynn and Rapunzel have found where they belong. For Rapunzel, it's literally a *place* (outside the tower), and symbolically represented by a *person* (the one who sees her for who she truly is). For Flynn, Rapunzel's ability to be *her* true self has caused him to become *his* — like the Beast. And this has metaphorically changed his world — it's the same world, but it's different now because Rapunzel is in it. "The world has somehow shifted."

After having this realization, Rapunzel is ready to give Flynn back the crown. It's an act that signals her willingness to completely reject Mother Gothel and her lies and begin a new life that is completely her own. Flynn, for his part, takes the crown and promises he won't leave her. *He* has also rejected his cynical worldview and is willing to adopt a more emotionally vulnerable one, tied to Rapunzel.

But Rapunzel's acceptance of her new role is tested when Flynn is kidnapped by thugs hired by Mother Gothel, making Rapunzel think he actually *did* leave her the minute he got the crown. Gothel shows up, pretends she's saving Rapunzel, and offers to take her home. All the growing up Rapunzel has done comes crashing down around her. With Flynn gone, she thinks she's made a mistake — that Gothel was right all along. She agrees to go back to the tower.

It's a heartbreakingly realistic thing to happen to a symbolic princess. She's come to her traditional understanding of who she is, she's been seen by her prince as her true self, she's made the sacrifices, and symbolic gestures that prove she's ready to be a "princess" in the fairy tale sense and then, bam, she's right back where she started. "You were right about everything," she tells Gothel. Growing up is hard to do. It doesn't happen in a moment. Your mother holds a pull on you that no one else can, even if she's abusive — sometimes especially then. It's a perfect melding of symbolism and reality, because now Rapunzel has all the symbolic things she needs to break away for good. She's succumbed, in a very realistic way, to the pull of childhood. But she's now equipped to break the ties.

Her final separation is of the traditional kind. Seeing a symbol of a sun on a souvenir flag she got from the marketplace, she realizes she's been painting that symbol on the walls of her tower all her life. A fragment of a memory surfaces of seeing that same symbol on a mobile above her crib. She suddenly knows that *she's* the lost princess. The reason she's been so obsessed with the floating lights all her life is because they were for *her*. Her entire life with Gothel has been a lie. She's really a *princess*. In realizing that she's literally a princess, Rapunzel also becomes a symbolic one. A princess is who she truly is, just as being a "princess" means realizing who you truly are. She confronts Gothel, telling her, "You were wrong about the world and you were wrong about me!" Gothel tries to subdue her but she tells her "For the rest of my life I will fight! I will never stop trying to get away from you!" Her fight is a mental one. Rapunzel will fight in the way a princess fights — with her inner courage and her will.

But when Flynn finally escapes the thugs and comes back to the tower to find Rapunzel and explain what happened, he finds her bound and gagged by Gothel. The witch — as usual — isn't going down without a fight. She stabs Flynn and uses the same passive aggressive strategy with Rapunzel she's used all her life: "Now look what you've done Rapunzel." But Rapunzel isn't under her control anymore. She *sees* the truth of Gothel's manipulation now. And she's willing to do what a true princess must: she's going to make a sacrifice. "If you let me save him I will go with you." She will do what she must to preserve the world she has created for herself. Rapunzel will sacrifice her freedom in order to keep alive the man she loves — the "prince" who holds within him the symbolic world of her adult life.

Gothel says she can save Flynn's life if she comes with her and never asks to leave the tower again. Rapunzel agrees. "When Rapunzel gains strength, she doesn't use it to defy the witch and take her rightful place in the kingdom, but to offer herself as a sacrifice for the life of Flynn," moans Antonia. But that's not what's going on here. Rapunzel's life in the world isn't worth living if Flynn's not in it. Not because her dreams revolve solely around a man, but because the man is the symbolic representation of the life she longs to live. Their lives are symbolically entwined. She can't grow up without the symbol of her adulthood.

Flynn, though, has the same problem. He can't live in the world without Rapunzel either. And so, as she leans in to use her hair to heal him, he cuts it off. *He* makes a sacrifice too because, like the Beast, Rapunzel has drawn out *his* truest self too and he can't let Rapunzel return to her life with Gothel. But, in sacrificing himself by cutting off Rapunzel's hair, Flynn frees her from Gothel. He does his princely job — he solidifies her adulthood, cements her separation and makes it permanent. And, of course, when both the prince and the princess make a sacrifice to save each other they are almost at their happy ending.

Without Rapunzel's magic hair to keep her young, Gothel crumbles into dust. Rapunzel is free. But Flynn is dying. "You were my new dream." "And you were mine." They tell each other. Because, of course they were. Seeing floating lights isn't a life goal. But living as your truest self with the person who sees you for who you truly are — that *is*. And with that admission — like Belle's "I love you" — Rapunzel finds that her tears still hold the magic of her hair. They fall on Flynn and he is restored. The life Rapunzel has built for herself is saved. And, with Flynn by her side, she finally gets to meet her real parents, who love her for herself, not her magic hair. She enters into the life she was meant to have — as a true fairy tale princess does, once she grows into her womanhood.

It's worth noting that Rapunzel's magical hair — this "feminist" symbol of her abilities as a gymnast and a fighter — must be cut off in order for her to be her true self. Her hair is the thing that Mother Gothel covets, which tells us immediately that it isn't truly worthwhile. It's only when it's gone that Rapunzel is able to be herself. "To sum up," writes Wilson, "we have a film dominated by male characters that focuses on the magical golden hair of a white princess who must be saved from an evil dark witch." But, in fact, the focus on the magical golden hair is *not* to impress us with the wonderful loveliness of being blonde. It's telling us the exact opposite: it's not the hair (or the clothes, or the title) that make you a princess. It's the internal wonderfulness of *you*. Rapunzel's hair turns from blonde — the traditional princess hair color — to brunette at the moment of her transformation to "princess." She, like the traditional princesses before her, is telling us that it's what's on the inside that matters. Because, of *course* it is. If only we could get the princess critics to understand.

*

Disney's decision to give up on princesses turned out to be a miscalculation. Audiences loved *Tangled*. People *did* want a traditional princess story — a fairy tale musical — and the box office numbers reflected that. But the ship had already altered course. *Brave*, which was the only other princess movie that had already been in the works when Disney made the choice to shift away from princesses, was now a princess critic's dream come true. And, even though Disney musicals based on fairy tales would return to the silver screen almost as soon as

205

they'd left it, the damage was done. Because *Brave* is, by far, the worst Disney princess movie that's ever been made.

Part V

"A Bit Of A Fixer-Upper": Disney Princesses In The Modern Age

Chapter Eleven: Merida

One evening, in the spring of 2012, my husband sat patiently across from me at an all-night diner as I tried to rewrite the plot of *Brave*. "Maybe if the bear had really been a prince? Or if they cut the ancient bear subplot? Or maybe if *Merida* turned into a bear? Or . . ." I threw my hands up in disgust. "Why were there so many *bears*?!" I wailed. It was hopeless. I had been duped. Duped badly. And I was mad. After *The Princess and the Frog*, in 2009, and *Tangled*, in 2010, I'd been lulled into a false sense of security. The princesses were back. Traditional narratives and fairy tale symbolism was back. *Tangled* had been a huge success, surely Disney understood that we *wanted* princesses, and love stories, and happily ever afters. Surely I'd be safe if I went to see the latest princess movie. But I'd never been so wrong. *Brave* is a horrible feminist dumpster fire of a movie. Its plot makes no sense, its heroine is a childish brat, and — worst of all — it subverts the fairy tale symbolism to the point of corruption. It's a movie that actively promotes staying home with mom and dad instead of growing up. Not only that, it reimagines the transformative power of true love so that it occurs between mother and daughter instead of prince and princess. Yuck. It's a disaster.

Brave was Pixar's first attempt at a Disney princess. Disney had acquired Pixar in 2006 but, until *Brave*, Pixar's films had had exclusively male protagonists and steered away from fairy-tale-type stories. Much was being made of Merida — Pixar's first princess. The incredible innovation and success of Pixar movies meant that much was riding on this latest movie. And the expectation of the movie critics was that the way that Pixar's innovation would manifest in a *princess* movie would be to make the princess as radically feminist as possible.

It's a sign of how fully the movie critics had become princess critics that the general consensus was that *Brave* wasn't feminist *enough*. It was a movie about a princess who shoots arrows, rides horses, snorts when she laughs, and refuses to get married or fall in love at all. But it wasn't enough because she was still a princess, there were still suitors, and she didn't do battle with anyone to win the day.

"Parents will be disappointed if they're hoping for another Pixar groundbreaker," wrote Roger Ebert in his 2012 review. "*Brave* seems a wee bit conventional by comparison with, say, how radically *The Incredibles* reinvented the superhero genre," wrote Peter Debruge in *Variety*. Tom Watson, of *Forbes*, noted that the fact that Merida is a princess "met with some derision from the feminist commentariat." Princess — as an entity — had become anti-feminist. But, even though critics wished Pixar's first girl protagonist had been something other than a princess, they all seemed to agree that, as a princess, she had a lot to offer in terms of breaking up the "anti-feminist" tropes of the genre.

The filmmakers were overtly trying to create the most feminist princess Disney had ever offered. The film's creator, Brenda Chapman, said Merida is "not just a simpering pretty face waiting around for romance! She was created to turn that whole ideal on it's head!" Of course, "that whole ideal" was, itself, a creation of the early princess critics. It was the narrative about the traditional princesses that first appeared in *Aladdin* — and continued as the accepted truth in the rest of the princess movies — that a princess is just sitting around waiting to marry the man that someone else picks for her. So Chapman — and the rest of the team at Pixar — were fighting a straw man. But it was a straw man that, in the intervening decades, had grown a brain, put on regular clothes, and was masquerading as a real, live person. Hardly anyone, even people who loved the older movies, remembered that "that whole ideal" wasn't real — that it had never existed.

So Merida doesn't fit in (like every single other Disney princess), she doesn't want to marry someone she doesn't love (like every single other Disney princess), she clashes with her parents (like every single other Disney princess), and on and on, blah blah blah. The only thing she "turns on its head" is the fact that she doesn't grow up, she doesn't find love, and she has a fairly unhealthy relationship with her mother. Hooray! Feminism wins! Really?! (Also the movie makes absolutely no sense, is unnecessarily vulgar, and has a bunch of bears in it for ... some ... reason.) It also offers a depiction of men that is like a radical feminist's weird fantasy. They are emasculated, childish, and totally terrified of women. Okay, kids? Enjoy the show!

*

If you remove the incomprehensible subplot about an ancient prince who turned into an evil bear named Mor'du, which has literally nothing to do with anything at all, *Brave* is essentially *Beauty and the Beast*. It's a story about a person who's turned into a beast (okay, fine, a bear) and a princess who must use her love for that person — and that person's love for her — to turn the beast back into a person. Except, in this story, the beast isn't a man, it's the princess's *mom*.

Just in case we've been hanging out with too many princess critics, here's a refresher on the symbolism of *Beauty and the Beast*. The prince is transformed into a beast because he has allowed his base male instincts to take over. The princess, in her ability to be her true self and not take any of the beast's crap, causes the beast to see that he needs to channel his urges and act like a gentleman in order to be worthy of the princess's love. This, in turn, gives the princess a man *worthy* of her love. It's a fairy tale about the differences between men and women and the ways in which their separate strengths and

211

weaknesses fit together like a puzzle. By the end, the traditional symbolism of the prince as a representation of the princess's life apart from her family is at play, allowing her to begin an independent life with the person who sees her for her true, adult self — who she, in turn, sees as *his* true adult self. So, yeah, not really something you want to go through with your mom.

But Brenda Chapman — who created the story and shares directorial credit because she was fired midway through due to "creative differences" — has no idea that fairy tales are symbolic. "I went through many fairy tales looking for a mother-and-daughter story, and I just didn't find one," Chapman told *The Hollywood Reporter*. "I'd find some with a mother, but she would disappear for no apparent reason, and a prince would show up to save the day." Hmm, I wonder why that might be. Could it possibly be because the mother represents the childhood the princess must break away from? Maybe? Just perhaps? (Jeez!) Yes, in real life, it's good to maintain a healthy relationship with your mother, but it's much more important to break away from her and be your own, adult self. If that means you have to break some of the bond you share with her — perhaps because she is struggling to let you go — then that is something you *must* do, no matter how difficult. But Chapman has no idea that this is even a fairy tale idea. "So," she explains, "I decided to try to create my own story." Your own story would be fine. Your own *fairy tale*? Maybe take a literature class or something first. Ugh.

Merida's mother, Elinor, is, essentially, a female Beast. But, instead of letting her base male urges to take over (since she doesn't have any) she has allowed the outer trappings of princess-ness to overtake the internal goodness of the fairy tale princess. "She's a lady!" she shrieks at Merida's father, King Fergus, when he gives her a bow and arrow for her birthday. "A princess strives for perfection," she instructs. "This is what you've been preparing for your whole life," she says, when it's time for Merida to meet her suitors. But all this only serves to show the filmmaker's lack of understanding of fairy tale shorthand. A princess doesn't *strive* for perfection, she *is* perfect. There's a difference. You don't get to *be* a princess unless you embody the feminine ideal. That's what "princess" represents. The filmmakers think Elinor is trying to get Merida to act like a traditional princess and Merida is fighting back because she's, according to Chapman, "a better stronger role model." But, really, Elinor has forgotten that a princess isn't a set of actions, it's an inner attribute. She's not "spoiled, selfish, and unkind" like the Beast, she's "OCD, contrived, and unoriginal." For Elinor, becoming a beast makes no sense If she's going to transform, she has to turn into something that represents her problem — something that symbolizes her fixation with outward feminine appearance rather than inner goodness.

In a totally random, unnecessarily verbose, prologue, Merida explains that "some say our destiny is tied to the land, as much a part of us as we are of it. Others say fate is woven together like a cloth, so that one's destiny intertwines with many others. It's the one thing we search for, or fight to change. Some never find it. But there are some who are led." What does this mean? I have absolutely no idea. But the movie places a lot of stock in the idea of "fate." The movie's tagline is "change your fate." But, surely, the actual definition of fate (in, like, you know, a dictionary) would imply that this is literally impossible. Fate is defined as "something that unavoidably befalls a person." If you could change your fate, then it wouldn't actually be your fate. So . . . ugh, this movie makes no sense. The point is that this stupid prologue is trying to place us — albeit inexpertly — within the confines of a fairy tale. And it's trying to tell us that it's going to change the traditional fairy tale ending into something different. But, since the filmmakers seem to have no idea what an actual fairy tale ending *is* — let alone what the meanings of basic words are — it seems fairly inevitable that they're going to screw everything up.

Merida is faced with the regular "feminist" princess problem of needing to get married. In order for the four clans of DunBroch to remain united, Merida has to marry a prince from one of the other clans. And, in an extra twist of the feminist knife, they've got to compete for her hand and literally "win" it — as if she was "a prize to be won" (hi Jasmine). "It's a tale as old as time: A princess's parents arrange for her to marry a man for the good of the kingdom, forcing her to be a subservient pawn in a system that completely robs her of any agency," writes Chelsea Mize, of *Bustle*. "Merida is a princess with a very Disney problem: her mother has ordered her to enter an arranged marriage with one of the less than desirable idiots from the neighbouring Highland tribes," writes Kayleigh Dray of *Stylist*. So . . . when exactly did this happen in other Disney princess movies before *Aladdin*? (I'll concede that the arranged marriage thing happened in *Sleeping Beauty* but Prince Philip wasn't a "less than desirable idiot.")

Merida's suitors, on the other hand, are definitely "less than desirable" and they are certainly "idiots." One is fat and doltish and speaks some kind of dialect that no one understands. Another is egotistical, posturing, and prone to temper tantrums. The last is tiny, timid, and unsure. None of them is a "prince" in the fairy tale sense of the word and all of them are played for laughs. *This* is what men *are*, the movie is saying — stupid, preening, self-obsessed idiots, not worth a woman's time. "I can't applaud enough over the fact that Merida made clear she just wasn't interested in suitors," writes Caitlin Flynn, of *Bustle*. But who *would* be interested in these suitors? They're awful! There's a big difference between saying "No thanks, Mom and Dad I'm not going to marry a total weirdo just because you want me to," and saying "I totally renounce romance, love, starting a family of my own, or anything else that is part of a complete and fulfilling life." Why would anyone do that? What other random rules do princess critics make for themselves that detract from their lives?

The first thing these suitors and their fathers do is get into an enormous brawl. They do this because they can't help it — they're *men*. Even Merida's father, Fergus — who she loves and identifies with, who has accepted her much more than her mother has — can't help but join in. And Elinor, marching into the center of it, pulls these grown men (including her husband) by their ears up to the front of the room and scolds them. Like children. Men, you see, are no better than children — always fighting, breaking the rules, and being crude. And, most of all, men need *women* to keep them in check. Without a woman to reprimand, scold, and corral them, men would behave like spoiled children. The logic of modern feminism (if you can call it logic) is that men and women *aren't* different when it comes to what women want — which is to be like men. But they *are* different when it comes to who's *better*. See, women are wonderful beings who can succeed at any task — be it traditionally male, or traditionally female — but men are pigs and wouldn't it be better if they just went away?

Once Elinor has disciplined everyone, including her own husband, she explains the rules of the competition for Merida's hand in marriage. The firstborn of each clan may compete for the princess's hand, and the princess may choose the event. Hooray! *Merida* is the firstborn, she's great at archery, she'll compete to win her own hand!

"As far as Merida is concerned," writes Debruge, "she doesn't need a man to live happily ever after — a novel concept in the relatively narrow world of cartoon logic, and one that allows the movie to do without a lowly stable boy or other replacement love interest." But this is not a "novel concept" at all. A Disney princess doesn't *need* a man. In the case of the traditional fairy tale movies, she *gets* a man as a representation of her transition to adulthood. In the case of the Renaissance movies, her dreams are fully formed before she ever meets a man. A princess — a woman — *wants* a man because she wants love in her life, a family of her own, and the children that proceed from that love. A woman who rejects the prospect of romantic love entirely rejects her adulthood. Which is exactly what Merida does.

Merida steps up to the archery butts, pulls off her hood to reveal her wild red hair, rips her dress so she can move better, and wins the archery competition. She rejects the external trapping of princess — the dress, the headdress, the composure — and reveals her true self. But that's so *backwards*. The external trappings of "princess"

215

represent the princess's true self. Her *inner* self. In this movie, Merida has been forced to accept the outer representations of princess-ness without embodying the internal attributes. We're supposed to feel, as Flynn writes, that Merida is refusing "to conform to any stereotype that doesn't suit her." But it isn't a stereotype that's at stake here. It's Merida's ability to become a woman. And if, after winning her own hand, she went off into the world to find her way — or achieve a goal, like the other princesses — and, along the way, found a man who saw her for *her*, then we could all be like yay go Merida! But that's not what happens at all. That isn't even what she was *fighting* for. Her act of defiance is essentially a child's temper tantrum — no, I don't wanna, you can't make me! "I'm not going to be like you!" she screams. "I'd rather die than be like you!" But *why*? What is it that Merida wants other than for her mom to quit bothering her? It's not the declaration of a girl on the brink of womanhood, asserting her independence from her parents.

Merida and her mother have a huge argument over what should happen next which culminates in each of them destroying something that represents the other. Merida rips the tapestry that Elinor has painstakingly woven, and Elinor throws Merida's bow into the fire. This *should* be Merida's first step toward separation. Her mother's inability to recognize the independence that Merida asserted in winning her own hand *should* catapult Merida out of the home and out into the world. But that's not at all what happens.

"The princess's relationship to her mother is the central focus," writes Kristy Puchko of *CinemaBlend*. "*Brave* has an uplifting message about improving communication between mothers and daughters," writes Ebert. But that isn't an end in and of itself. Not for a girl on the verge of adulthood. The girl's job is to grow up and become her true self. This requires separation from her mother. Once she's achieved that, she can return, show her family how much better and happier she is now, and hopefully win them over. Making mother-daughter communication the focus, necessarily means that Merida can't grow up.

If we needed any more evidence of this, we need look no further than what Merida does to try to solve her problem. She finds a bear-obsessed witch in the woods (what is *with* all these *bears*?!) and makes a request: change my mom. "That will change my fate!" she says. Wrong! (Wrong, wrong, OMG, so wrong!) If Merida was on a journey towards finding her true self, she would ask to change *herself*. Ariel didn't ask Ursula to change King Triton's mind, she asked for legs. Merida doesn't see that her way forward necessitates doing something her mother might disapprove of. She can't accept that there might be a rift between them. She doesn't even ask, like Jasmine, to change the law so she can marry whoever she wants — or not at all. She asks to change her *mother*. Ack!

So the witch changes Merida's mother . . . into a bear. Why a bear? No one knows. The movie is just randomly full of bears. But, for our purposes, a bear is a *beast* and that's basically what's happened. Elinor is now a beast — for the sin of wanting her daughter to marry someone so that their whole kingdom didn't devolve into war — and Merida's job is to turn her back. The witch explains that the spell can only broken if Merida can "mend the bond torn by pride." And she's only got until the "second sunrise" to do it. (Until the last petal falls, basically.) But was it actually pride that caused Merida to turn her mom into a bear? I'd say it was more like childish stupidity! She couldn't separate from her mother enough to see that it wasn't her mother who needed to change — it was herself. Like a child, she sees her mother as an extension of herself and can't see how something could change for *her* without changing her mother. But, instead of helping Merida realize that this isn't true, the movie sets Merida and Elinor up to come back together again, rather than split apart.

In the woods — where they have gone so that Fergus doesn't mistake Elinor for a real bear and kill her — Merida has to teach her mother how to live outdoors. Elinor wants to maintain her queenly manners and etiquette, but has no idea what's edible in the forest, and has the appetite of a real bear. Merida — who has spent time roaming the forest — shows her mother what she can eat and teaches her how to fish. The two bond over this role reversal and Elinor is able to appreciate her daughter's skills for the first time. But, honestly, are we meant to feel that the thing Merida is good at is being a *bear*? Do Merida's interests in wilderness survival make her an animal? Does Merida actually want to *be* a bear? Is that her life's dream? We have no idea, really. But, as it plays out, Elinor's appreciation of Merida comes from Merida's ability to teach her how to be a bear. Not exactly, "Look mom, I'm my own person with a real life I've forged for myself!" When Elinor turns back into person (spoiler alert!) are we meant to feel that she will now appreciate Merida's foraging and fishing abilities? How do *those* represent her true self?

While Merida and Elinor are bonding over bear stuff, full-on warfare has erupted at the castle with no women there to keep the men from brawling. Merida thinks that the "bond torn by pride" is the tapestry she ripped in anger and so she and Elinor (who is still a bear) return to the castle to try to sew it up. The men are fighting because, without the promise of a marriage between Merida and one of the clansmen, the clans won't stay united. So, essentially, Merida's decision not to marry any of them is incredibly selfish. As a Disney princess, we don't want her to marry without love, but we do need her to not be totally self-absorbed. She's got to find a way to unite the clans without getting married.

Reading Elinor's makeshift bear sign language, Merida makes a speech to the clansmen. She says that the law will now be changed so that everyone — including the sons of the other clansmen — can "find love in our own time." But what has caused Elinor to come to this conclusion? She's seen that Merida knows how to survive in the wild, but what does that have to do with love? She's basically dismissing the fairy tale shorthand of Merida's transformation to adulthood. Is Merida still too much of a child to marry and Elinor sees that? It isn't

Jasmine's victory of marrying whoever she chooses. It's a postponement — or maybe even a cancellation — of Merida's adulthood. Merida's great triumph is that she gets her mother to understand that she doesn't want to grow up.

Merida sews up the tapestry but Fergus finds Elinor and thinks she's a real bear. He ties her up in the forest and locks Merida in a tower room to keep her safe from the bear. And thus begins the movie's final sequence which is, almost beat for beat, the same as the final sequence of *Beauty and the Beast*.

Belle, locked in the cellar by Gaston, struggled to break free to save the Beast from people who want to kill him. Merida, locked in the tower by her father, struggles to break free to save her mom from people who want to kill her. But, whereas the person who wanted to kill the Beast was another suitor, the person who wants to kill Elinor is Merida's father. Gaston didn't see Belle for her true self, he only wanted her for her outer beauty. Belle was rushing to the man who really did see her for her true self in order to recognize him as *his* true self so they could be together. Fergus has always accepted Merida and Merida is rushing to her mother so she doesn't lose her mother who she needs desperately because she's still a child.

"I won't let you kill my mother!" yells Merida when she arrives in the woods. "I won't let you do this!" yelled Belle when Gaston announced his intention to kill the Beast. Belle was asserting her allegiance to the Beast, who represented her separation from her family and the man everyone expected her to marry. Merida is asserting her allegiance to her mother who represents her childhood. Now, obviously, Merida shouldn't allow the clansmen to kill her mother, but since we are now operating within the realm of fairy tale shorthand it's worth making the comparison.

Fergus and the clansmen finally accept that the bear is Elinor and allow Merida to run forward and throw the sewn up tapestry over her. But, of course, the *tapestry* was not the "bond" that needed mending and nothing happens. The sun of the "second sunrise" begins to rise and Merida throws herself onto her mother, sobbing. (The last petal of the rose begins to fall and Belle throws herself on the Beast, sobbing). "I'm sorry, this is all my fault," says Merida. ("This is all my fault," says Belle.) "I love you!" says Merida. ("I love you" says Belle.) The clansmen stand arrayed around them, looks of shock and sadness on their faces. (The household objects stand arrayed around them, looks of shock and sadness on their faces.) The sun rises, all hope seems lost. (The petal falls, all hope seems lost). But then — what's this? — something is happening! Elinor is changing! Merida's love has broken the spell! (But then — what's this? — something is happening! The Beast is changing! Belle's love has broken the spell!) The lovers are reunited.

Flynn writes that *Brave* "shows how the mother-daughter relationship can be mended through patience, courage, and love." But the fact that this final sequence is nearly identical to *Beauty and the Beast* makes it more than that. Yes, a daughter can (and *should*) endeavor to mend a broken relationship with her mother. But if you place it within the context of the *Beauty and the Beast* transformation, you necessarily make that comparison. *Brave* places Elinor in the role of romantic lover for Merida. Not that Merida should now *marry* her mother, but she holds that significance. Rather than forming a bond with someone who will allow her to move from her childhood family to her adult one, Merida is now tied to her childhood family indefinitely. Her major, transformative realization was how important her bond with her mother is. And it certainly *is* an important bond, but it's not the bond you need to solidify in order to grow up. And sometimes, it's the bond you need to break.

Brave makes a mockery of fairy tale shorthand and gives us a princess who refuses to grow up. *That* is modern feminism. Dray writes that Merida "teaches us that our fate lives within us – we just have to be brave enough to see it." But Merida's fate — whatever that means in this movie — doesn't live within *her*. It lives within her willingness to remain at home indefinitely, relying on her mother and father to protect her and keep her safe. "I just wanted a princess who is perfectly content to be #TeamSingle," writes Flynn. But a #TeamSingle princess is not a princess — she hasn't completed her journey to adulthood. And, honestly, a *person* who is literally #TeamSingle, in that they never want to find a partner to settle down with, is also stuck. Romantic love is a part of the human experience. It completes us and fulfills us in ways that nothing else can, and it facilitates the transition to parenthood which also expands and enriches our lives in innumerable ways. In trying to convince us that a woman doesn't need a man to *do* everything for her — which no one ever said she did — princess critics had, with *Brave*, finally asserted that a woman doesn't need romantic love at all. And *that's* a dangerous, and terribly sad, thing to teach little girls.

*

Fans of *Brave* (of which, strangely, there are some), or people who've seen the movie recently, may complain that I've left out a lot of the story. Like the part where Merida falls in a hole and realizes a series of long complicated events about a history that has nothing to do with her — but lots to do with bears. Or the part where the evil bear Mor'du turns out to be a dude, cursed like Elinor. Or the part where Merida's brothers turn into bears too. And all I can say is that this was the best I could do — in that all-night diner all those years ago — to fix the plot of *Brave*. You have to get rid of the bears. The bears made no sense.

Brave did very well at the box office, but I can't help but wonder how much of that was people like me who assumed — given that it was Pixar, and given the quality of the previous two princess movies — that it was going to be good. It's a movie that subverts the fairy tale wisdom of thousands of years without even knowing what it's doing. It tells us not to grow up. It tells us not to find love. It tells us that, in order to change our situation, we must change the people around us instead of ourselves. Merida is a walking encyclopedia of terrible advice. But because, by 2012, the concept of fairy tale as allegory and fairy tale shorthand was gone with the wind, no one even knows how corrupt this movie really is.

Parents, take note: Merida is not your friend. Replace your daughter's pretend glass slipper with a pretend bow and arrow at your own risk. The slipper sets your daughter on a path towards finding her true self. The bow sets her on a path to living in your basement for the rest of her life. Your little girls hold the key to bringing back the princesses of yesterday and rekindling the symbolism that speaks to us through the ages. Don't let them down.

Chapter Twelve: Elsa and Anna

Ask a little girl between the ages of two and six to tell you her favorite princess and you're likely to get the same answer: Elsa. Sing a few lines of "Let It Go" in the general vicinity of girls in the pre-kindergarten set and you're likely to set off a full-on karaoke session. If you happen to live with little girls this age, you've probably been wondering what has happened to every blue item of clothing you own and why your ice cube tray is missing. *Frozen*, which came out in 2013, has become a legitimate cultural phenomenon due, in large part, to the absolute fanaticism of little girls for the character of Elsa. What's a little less clear — though there is no shortage of theories — is why *Elsa*.

Merida is the last inductee into the official Disney princess club. Elsa (who fans are quick to point out is actually a *queen*) and her sister Anna haven't yet made the cut. But that's not because they're not worthy. In fact, it's the exact opposite. *Frozen* is the highest grossing animated film of all time. In the months after the film's release, *Frozen* toys were selling out at Disney stores across the country and parents had to enter a lottery for a chance to purchase an Elsa costume. By the time *Frozen* came out on DVD in March of 2014, Disney had already sold over half a million Elsa and Anna dolls. Elsa and Anna are so lucrative on their own that they don't yet need to be a part of the franchise. When that stops being the case, they'll join their princess sisters — but it doesn't look like that'll be any time soon.

Disney studios were completely blindsided by the success of *Frozen*. "*Frozen* is a global phenomenon that has truly exceeded expectations on every level," said Margita Thompson of Disney Consumer Products. In fact, when the studio made the film, it was simply trying to finally bring to life a story that Disney had been wanting to produce since the 1940s. Walt Disney himself had a great appreciation for Hans Christian Andersen's *The Snow Queen* and wanted very much to create a feature film about the villainous queen who freezes the heart of a young boy. But no one — neither during Disney's time, nor in the intervening seven decades — could come up with an adaptation that seemed to work. The problem was with — believe it or not — Elsa herself. No one could come up with a convincing story arc for this character who, in the original fairy tale, was just sort of randomly villainous and never even got her comeuppance. Disney lore has it that no one actually remembers who it was that asked the fateful question that green-lighted the film. "What if Elsa and Anna were sisters?"

After *Brave* had shifted the princess narrative away from lovers and focused on mothers, the studio felt they'd hit on another great idea with the suggestion to focus on sisters. They even had a "Sisters Summit" where female Disney employees got together to talk about their relationships with their siblings to collect data for the film. The filmmakers firmly believe that this focus on sisterhood is what explains the success of Elsa as a character. "The ending has always been about, no -- it's not a man's love, it's the love between these sisters, it's family love," said Robert Lopez, half of the husband-and-wife songwriting duo whose songs undoubtedly put Disney musicals back on the map. "This is about nuanced, three-dimensional women, dealing with leadership, love, and their own relationships," added Lopez' wife, Kristen Anderson-Lopez.

But little girls aren't prancing around playing out the scene where Anna's act of "true love" towards Elsa unfreezes her heart. In fact, their love of the icy heroine has nothing to do with her relationship to her sister at all. No. These little girls are warbling "Let It Go" — Elsa's big number about *distancing* herself from everyone, including her sister — like their lives literally depend on it. This moment, in which Elsa makes the truly terrible decision to live all alone in her ice palace wallowing in misanthropy and self-pity, ignited something in the hearts of little girls everywhere and catapulted Elsa to rock star status. The movie may be about sisters, but its success comes from this one moment of Elsa's very solitary transformation.

What are we supposed to make of this? What does it mean that little girls identify so strongly with a character singing a power ballad about shirking responsibilities, letting her inner force for destruction run rampant, and condemning her entire kingdom to eternal winter? I mean, sure, little kids pretty much *are* forces of chaos in and of themselves, but I don't think that's what's going on here.

"Let It Go" is a scene of pure princess transformation — Cinderella's rags becoming a beautiful ball gown, her inner self made manifest — that happens for all the wrong reasons. The scene has all the symbolism of the fairy tale princess who has had to hide her true self all her life suddenly transformed into her true self for all the world to see. And it comes with a song so catchy — so filled with teen angst and rock star power — that, if you don't listen too closely, you could believe that this is what Elsa's singing about too. But it isn't. It really isn't at all.

It's *Anna*, Elsa's sister, who actually possesses the inner attributes of a true princess. She is kind, brave, and loyal, and she understands the power of love. But, at every turn, the characters in the movie reprimand Anna for being this way. A running gag has everyone close to Anna berating her for agreeing to marry a man she just met — something that *would* be a bad idea in real life, but is symbolic of the transition to adulthood in a fairy tale. So, while *Elsa*

225

gets the big princess transformation scene, it's *Anna* who's really the "princess" in the fairy tale sense of the word.

But let's not forget why the symbolism of fairy tales exists in the first place: it's to convey complex concepts to small children in ways they can intuitively understand. A little girl doesn't need to verbalize what's happening to Cinderella when her rags turn into a beautiful dress — they just *get it.* So, when the exact same thing happens to Elsa, it doesn't matter to them that the *plot* doesn't match with the symbolism. All that matters is that a girl who felt like she couldn't be herself is doing all the things she's supposed to do (symbolically) to embrace her true self. Because that *matters* to little girls.

Frozen's director, Jennifer Lee, said that "Anna represents love and Elsa represents fear." In essence, they are not so much sisters as they are two aspects of *one* person — one Disney princess. The filmmakers kind of acknowledge this — in talking about each character as an attribute, rather than a full-fledged person — but they don't seem to understand what it all means for the plot and symbolism of the film. What ends up happening is that Anna embodies the inner attributes of a Disney princess, and Elsa struggles with a Disney princess problem: how to be herself in a world that won't accept her. This setup means that Elsa gets to be the one to transform, so Elsa is the one who speaks to little girls.

But this is a problem. Because *Elsa* isn't actually all that great a role model. She's self-absorbed, fearful, closed-off, and makes a lot of really bad choices. *Anna* is actually the one who does all the emotional (and literal) work. And, for her trouble, she gets ridiculed, her first boyfriend turns out to be a sociopath, and she gets iced in the heart. She's goofy, and wide-eyed, and overly trusting — a parody of a Disney princess — and this makes us overlook her in favor of the much darker, more complex-seeming Elsa. But *Anna* is really the one with the strength of character worthy of a princess (because her main attribute is love). All this proves, yet again, how important symbolism is in fairy tales and how powerfully little girls respond to it. And it's what makes this movie such a complicated — and potentially detrimental — addition to the canon.

It doesn't help that princess critics understand none of this. They, of course, think it's feminism that draws little girls to Elsa. "Frozen is one of the few Disney Princess movies in which none of the key plot points revolve around the protagonist getting wifed up," writes Chelsea Mize of *Bustle*. Jane Merrick, of *The Independent*, says it's Elsa's awesome ice powers that draw little girls to her. "She is the female equivalent of a superhero like Batman or Spider-Man. And little girls, who haven't quite yet had society's norms thrust upon them, just want the same as little boys – they want to emulate superheroes, not the demure and subservient princesses waiting for their prince to come." If this were true, though, wouldn't little girls be obsessed with the scenes where Elsa uses her ice powers to create big snow monsters, and spiky walls of icicles, and fight soldiers who are threatening her (all of which are also in the movie)? Dorian Lynskey, of *The Guardian*, calls Elsa "the movie's X-factor" for not just being "more of the same." And the fact that Elsa has no love interest at all in the film has caused a princess critic led movement to #GiveElsaAGirlfriend in the *Frozen* sequel.

This movie simultaneously gives little girls all the key elements of a traditional princess fairy tale, *and* talks a big feminist game. It gets away with this by splitting the princess up into two people. In one sense, it has something for everyone — the princess critics and the traditionalists — but, on the other hand, in doing this it dilutes, dismisses, and dismantles the princess narrative. And it does it insidiously, with hardly anyone noticing, which makes it worse. There is no doubt that *Frozen* is a cultural phenomenon, and that Elsa is beloved by little girls, but I think it's worth examining why. The princess critics — and even the filmmakers themselves — don't actually seem to understand what's going on in this movie. But if we're going to restore the reputation of the traditional princesses, and expose the feminist ones as frauds, we've got to be able to explain *Frozen*. So let's get started.

*

We all know the premise of the movie, right? Elsa and Anna are the children of the King and Queen of Arundel. Elsa is born with ice powers, Anna is not. Elsa accidentally ices Anna in the head so the rock trolls (don't ask me, *I* didn't write this movie) remove all Anna's memories of Elsa's ice powers in order to cure her. Now Elsa has to hide her powers from everyone (including Anna) so the sisters grow up isolated in the castle, away from the outside world, and Elsa and Anna grow apart. But when their parents die in a shipwreck, Elsa, as the older child, has to take the throne. So we've got one princess who is basically a normal person who's grown up totally isolated and lonely and just wants to see the world and find love — like Rapunzel — and we've got one princess who has grown up with a part of herself that she's been told is dangerous and is doing her best to keep it under wraps at the expense of a real life — like Ariel.

Elsa and Anna's reactions to opening up the castle to visitors for Elsa's coronation are, predictably, totally different. Elsa is terrified that her subjects will discover her ice powers and brand her a witch and unfit to rule. Anna, on the other hand, is thrilled to finally meet other people and hopes to find "true love." What if Ariel, instead of doing everything in her power to follow her dreams, had tried to do as her father asked and stop visiting the human world and collecting human things? And what if Rapunzel didn't really care about seeing the floating lights and figuring out who she really was but just wanted to meet people and fall in love? Anna is missing Elsa's internal need to be accepted for who she really is, and Elsa is missing Anna's inner optimism, hope, kindness, and heart. It's like they are *one* princess, each possessing parts of the other to make a complete and complex character.

But they can't have *one* love interest (that would be weird). And that's actually a big part of what makes this movie problematic.

Frozen takes great pains to mock the traditional fairy tale trope of love at first sight. Immediately upon emerging from the castle for the first time since childhood, Anna bumps into a handsome prince and falls head over heels in love. Prince Hans seems like your run-of-the-mill Prince Charming — handsome, courteous, love-struck. Anna and Hans sing the movie's only love song, "Love Is An Open Door," and, after that, they are engaged. Just like "Let It Go," this musical number happens in the wrong place in the character's journey. Hans (spoiler alert) is *not* Anna's true love — and Anna eventually *will* have a true love, unlike Merida. The fact that she sings her love song to someone who turns out to actually be a murderous psychopath (more on that later) is meant to tell us something: love at first sight isn't real (oh, and don't trust a guy who tells you it is). Whether or not love at first sight actually *is* a thing in real life (since becoming someone who writes about Disney princesses I can't tell you how many real people have told me it's happened to them), doesn't matter. It's a *symbol* in a fairy tale and really doesn't deserve the treatment it gets in *Frozen*.

When Anna tells Elsa — who is basically a stranger to her at this point — that she's going to marry Hans, Elsa informs her, "You can't marry a man you just met!" This is meant to be a punch in the gut to all the traditional princesses. Mize says that Elsa "keeps her dumb, more prototypically Disney princess sister from marrying the first man to hair flip his Justin Bieber flow in her direction." But Anna's response, "You can if it's true love," is actually pretty interesting. The *filmmakers* obviously meant for Anna to come across as totally naive here. She really doesn't *know* Hans at all (as we discover later) and has definitely rushed into something she probably shouldn't have. (Although given that this was her one day to get out there in the world and meet people, we can't really blame her for jumping on the first nice-seeming guy she saw.) But, the thing is, Anna is actually right. In a fairy tale, you *can* marry a guy you just met, *if* it's true love — if the princess has been transformed such that her true self is visible to the world, and the prince sees her true self and acknowledges it, then she *can* marry him.

Elsa is so upset that Anna would even suggest marrying someone she just met that she literally unleashes eternal winter on her entire kingdom. For at least a decade, Elsa has kept her powers hidden. She even got through her coronation in front of her whole kingdom without icing anyone. But *this* — the idea that someone might fall in love at first sight — is so horrifying to her that she spontaneously ices all of Arundel.

Jennifer Lee said of Anna, "I wanted a girl whose only journey was sort of coming-of-age, where she goes from having a naive view of life and love — because she's lonely — to the most sophisticated and mature view of love, where she's capable of the ultimate love, which is sacrifice." But this isn't what we get. We get a girl whose view of "true love" shifts from being about romantic love to being about sisterly love. But that sends the wrong message. There's nothing wrong with a movie about sisters. The *problem* comes when you try to make a connection between romantic love and sisterly (or motherly) love.

It's creepy! If Anna is meant to be "coming of age" then she needs to break away from her nuclear family — like every other traditional Disney princess. That's what the "age" part of "coming of age" is all about. She has to grow up. And growing up means — like we discussed with Merida — breaking away from your family. Purposely creating a character whose arc shifts her from looking for a husband to finding a *sister* is a really weird and, frankly, kind of icky message. The fact that the filmmakers made Hans turn out to be evil doesn't negate this. It's just their way of trying to sell their point when really, in another — fairy tale — context, Anna would be A-okay.

So then Elsa runs off to steal every little girl's heart by singing "Let It Go." It's a weird place for a transformation number, right? This *should* be the place for what's known as the princess "I Want" song. The song where she reveals her inner dreams and the things she wants from life. "Someday My Prince Will Come," "A Dream Is A Wish Your Heart Makes," "Part of That World," "Belle, Reprise," you get the idea. Nothing has happened to Elsa to really change her situation. She has ice powers she wishes she could control, she lost control of them. Nothing is different — except that everyone now knows about them. But, instead of singing a song called something like "I Wish I Could Control My Powers," she sings "Let It Go."

"Let it go / Let it go, / Can't hold it back anymore," Elsa (voiced by the truly once-in-a-lifetime talent of Idina Menzel) sings from her isolated mountaintop. "No right, no wrong, no rules for me / I'm free." I mean, sure, what little girl can't relate to that? No rules? Awesome! But we adults know that this is a legitimately awful philosophy for a Disney princess — or anyone else — to hold. The "it" of "Let It Go" are Elsa's powers. Powers that are dangerous and, if uncontrolled, can hurt, curse, and kill the people around her — even the people that she loves. Elsa is not a "badass" woman who's been oppressed by the patriarchy, and this song doesn't represent her releasing all her badassery for all the world to see. Elsa is a teenager on the brink of womanhood. There is a force within her — her womanhood, perhaps? — that *is* a part of her, but which, if allowed to burst forth unchecked, will lead to a life of isolation and pain. Like a female version of the Beast, Elsa has to learn to *control* — and channel — what's already inside her. So "Let It Go" is not the big empowerment number it's cracked up to be.

Songwriter Anderson-Lopez said, of "Let It Go," that the song's message is, "screw fear and shame, be yourself, be powerful." And that's how princess critics have taken it too. Beatriz Serrano, of *Buzzfeed*, writes that Elsa leaves Arundel "so she can be free. She leaves so she doesn't have to listen to other people's constant criticism. She leaves to live like she wants to live, surrounded by what makes her happy. She leaves to be herself." This is the generally accepted reading of this song. It sure seems to be what the filmmakers wanted to convey. But it just isn't true. Yes, for one rebellious moment, Elsa may believe that living alone on a mountaintop in an ice palace will make her happy. But anyone who's ever been — oh I don't know — *alive* knows that living alone and isolated won't make you happy. Neither will giving in to every emotional whim you feel. And, the funny thing is, even though the filmmakers talk a big game about the empowerment implications of this song, Elsa ultimately decides that this life of isolation and uncontrolled powers, is *not* what she truly wants. This *isn't* who she truly is.

But, even so, this *is* the moment in which Elsa's big transformation takes place. And *that* is why little girls love her. With a wave of her icy hand, Elsa's long sleeved, dark-hued dress transforms into a slinky ice-blue number which sparkles in a way that's reminiscent of Cinderella's ball gown. Her white-blonde hair comes tumbling down from her modest updo and becomes a long, undulating braid infused with sparkling snowflakes. And what's on her feet? Ice slippers that sparkle like — you guessed it — glass. Dana Stevens, of *Slate*, finds this moment problematic, calling it "a vision of female self-actualization as narrow and horizon-diminishing as a makeover." She'd probably say the same thing about Cinderella's transformation. And she'd be wrong, as we've already discussed, many times (with glee).

In "Let It Go" Elsa is telegraphing all the symbolism of the Cinderella transformation, while singing a rocking ballad and ending up dressed like a Barbie doll. What's not to like? Throw off your rags, little girls everywhere, and become who you truly are! And that's all well and good except for the fact that that's not what Elsa's doing here. In fact, she's making a really bad decision and acting like it's her final transformation. And while that may be relatable — who hasn't fully embraced some lifestyle that turned out to be harmful? — it isn't *good*. And what's *worse* is all these little girls going around singing "Let It Go!" as if that meant "Be Yourself." Because Elsa, without Anna, is a terrible role model. Her journey is far from complete. Out there in the world somewhere, Anna is doing all the hard work.

After Elsa unleashes eternal winter and runs away, Anna does what a traditional princess does. She goes on a journey — a journey that will lead her out of childhood and into womanhood. She leaves Hans — who, so far, has done nothing at all to show his true nature, even acting kind and considerate when Anna's not watching — in charge of Arundel and runs off to try to find her sister. If the traditional Disney princess narrative *was* what princess critics think it is, then Anna's journey to try to rescue her kingdom and reunite with her sister would be a radical feminist deviation. Instead of going off on a journey to find a husband — or sitting around waiting for one to appear — Anna's journey is about her love for her sister and the people of Arundel. But a traditional princess's journey is *not* about husband-hunting. It's about looking for the one thing that will make you whole — be that becoming human, or getting out from under your abusive mother's thumb, or changing an unfair law. And so Anna is doing a very Disney princess thing here — a thing that *Elsa* really ought to be doing. She is stepping up and protecting her people, the way a ruler should. And, just like a Disney princess, she meets a man along the way, and the man helps her achieve her goals. Anna is the one on the journey. And she's the one who will grow up. But the actual problem — needing to be recognized and accepted — is Elsa's, and Elsa is the one who gets the transformation. As one princess, they might make sense. As two, not so much.

Anna — who still believes she's in love with Hans — finds her *real* love interest in Kristoff, a cranky, dirty, loner who cuts ice for a living and carries on long conversations with his reindeer, Sven (who can't talk, Kristoff talks for him). The point (which we are basically hit repeatedly over the head with) is that the man for you might not look like Prince Charming, and he might not initially seem like the kind of guy you want to date. But . . . hold on a minute . . . wait . . . I think we may have actually heard of this before . . . wasn't there . . . oh, that's right: BEAUTY AND THE BEAST!! This is *not* a new concept, and we don't need a Prince Charming look-alike psycho killer to bring it home for us. Nor do we need Kristoff — whose own life choices are rather questionable — to lecture Anna about marrying a guy she just met. "You got engaged to someone you just met that day??" he asks. "What if you hate the way he eats? What if you hate the way he picks his nose? And eats it!" (Gross, thanks for *that* image, Kristoff.) Kristoff is, as his adoptive parents the rock trolls (remember them?) say, "a bit of a fixer-upper." He needs a feminine touch — *Anna's* feminine touch — to make him whole. So Anna is on a very traditional princess journey. The only problem is, the part of her that is actually going to undergo the transformation — who *needed* a transformation in the first place — happens to live inside the body of her sister Elsa.

When Anna finds Elsa and tries to convince her to come back and save Arundel from the eternal winter she created, Elsa refuses. "Yes I'm alone, but I'm alone and free," Elsa says. Even when she learns that the winter she created is permanent and her people are in danger, Elsa says "I belong here, alone, where I can be who I am without hurting anybody." She doesn't know how to undo the harm she's caused and she refuses to face up to her mistake and come back and try. This is unequivocally *not* a person who has come to embody her true self. Elsa is lost, scared, alone, and in need of intervention. The part of her that knows who she truly is and what must truly be done lives in *Anna*. Anna has to make the journey for her. And, because she hasn't yet completed it, Elsa still isn't willing to come back. When Elsa accidentally ices Anna in the heart, Anna has bigger problems than convincing Elsa to return. She's got to figure out a way to un-ice her heart, or turn to ice completely.

"Only an act of true love can thaw a frozen heart," the rock trolls tell her. And this is where the movie begins its final "gotcha" twist which is meant to radically shift the princess narrative and rip thousands of years of fairy tale symbolism to shreds. Because *what*, pray tell, constitutes *true love*? Anna, of course, immediately thinks she's got to get back to Hans who will administer true love's kiss and

unthaw her heart. In the big reveal of Hans as a crazy axe murderer —
okay fine, not an *axe* murderer, but a murderer — you can practically
hear the filmmaker's gleeful laughter and the rasp, rasp, rasp of their
rubbing together hands. The *prince* is a *bad guy*! Get it! Because *men* are
bad guys! Because Prince Charming is too good to be true! Because
we're bitter, and sad, and alone, and . . . moving on. When Kristoff —
who has fallen in love with Anna — rushes her to Hans and lets her go
(like the Beast letting Belle go because he loves her) Anna appeals to
Hans for a kiss. But Hans — gotcha! — reveals himself to only be in
it for the throne.

 This man who, even while Anna was away, has been a good,
kind prince — handing out blankets to people, opening the castle up
to freezing villagers — suddenly says he's planning on murdering Elsa,
marrying Anna, and then murdering her too. Whoa! Holy psycho
boyfriend! Gina Dalfonzo, of *The Atlantic*, calls foul on this revelation
saying it "feels so abrupt that it seems more like a poor writing choice
than like a clever concealment of the truth." And she points out that
"there is something uniquely horrifying about finding out that a
person—even a fictional person—who's won you over is, in fact,
rotten to the core. And it's that much more traumatizing when you're
six or seven years old." But here's the thing: for feminists, Hans' true
nature *was* telegraphed beforehand. It was telegraphed by the fact that
he seemed to fall for Anna at first sight, by how handsome and kind he
seemed to be, by his very Prince Charming-ness. Because *that* is *not* a
way that a person can really *be*.

 But *duh* you crazy, crazy princess critics! *Duh!* Prince
Charming is symbolic! He represents the woman's final
transformation to womanhood and her true self. He *sees* her true self
and is worthy of it. Sure, in real life, you might want to be wary of a
guy who proposes marriage after one night — even a *really* great night
— but *that* guy wouldn't be a prince in a fairy tale. The big reveal about
Hans is also a statement: Prince Charming is dead. Feminism killed
him because they didn't understand him. Talk about a victim.

"We're not saying you can change him cuz people don't really change / We're only saying that love's a force that's powerful and strange." This is what the rock trolls tell Anna about Kristoff. (You could imagine Mrs. Potts saying the same thing, right?) There *is* a man for Anna in this movie. And it's Kristoff. And that's fine. He's a nice enough guy. But even *he* isn't the "true love" that will save Anna. And here, again, we're being played. Because Anna, upon realizing she almost married a murderer, suddenly figures out that she *actually* loves Kristoff and rushes off across the ice to find him. And why shouldn't she? The movie *told* us that her love could change him. *Him*, specifically. Kristoff was the "fixer-upper" that Anna's love would save. It's *there* in the movie. Which is why what actually happens isn't fair, plot-wise. The final reveal is *just* there to make us all feel like suckers for thinking that maybe romantic love was more important — for a Disney princess — than sisterly love.

With Anna almost entirely turned to ice, and Kristoff just a few feet away, Hans draws his sword on Elsa (who his soldiers have forced down from her mountain). Anna must choose: save herself with true love's kiss, or save her sister. And she chooses her sister. She throws her body in front of Elsa at the exact moment her own body turns to ice, shattering Hans' sword and protecting Elsa. But, of course, *this* was the act of true love that Anna needed to unthaw her heart. And, just as soon as she's turned to ice completely, she becomes human again. Stephanie Merry, of *The Washington Post*, calls this a "surprising and poignant ending, which subverts so many fairy-tale stereotypes." And that's exactly what it's trying to do. Ha ha ha, you terrible misogynists, the movie seems to be saying, we *tricked* you. *Romantic* love isn't what's important. *Family* love is.

But we've got to finish the transformation. Anna did all the heavy lifting, but it's *Elsa* that needed to change. She needed to find a way to live with her powers without letting them consume her. And it's *Anna's* act of selflessness towards her that convinces her that *love* is the way to control her powers — specifically the love she feels for

Anna. But, hold the phone, Elsa has *always* loved Anna and always *acted* out of that love for her. "I'm just trying to protect you," Elsa says to Anna in her ice palace. Elsa's love for Anna is the whole reason she hid from Anna for their entire childhood. She loved her so much she didn't want to hurt her with her uncontrollable powers and gave up their relationship — which was a good one — in order to do that. Her entire life has been a series of sacrifices for love of Anna. This moment shouldn't be transformative for *Elsa*. It should be transformative for *Anna*, who didn't know that her sister loved her — who thought she *hated* her and wanted nothing to do with her all those years. But, whatever, the filmmakers are trying to make a point, not tell a *story*.

So Elsa learns the lesson she needed to learn — that controlling your powers is better than letting them overtake you — and finally becomes who she truly was meant to be. It's a fairy tale ending — in terms of symbolism — except for the fact that she has no partner to spend her life with. *Anna* gets the partner instead. Anna is the sister who actually did all the work to enact Elsa's transformation, so *she* gets the reward. (Do the filmmakers even know what they're doing, or did they just get so excited about their big the-prince-is-a-bad-guy-and-true-love-is-between-sisters reveal that they accidentally left *in* the fairy tale ending?) Anna gets to be with Kristoff, because Anna has "fixed up" the "fixer-upper" — meaning Kristoff, but also *Elsa*, the part of *herself* that needed a transformation.

Roger Ebert said the movie "seems so cynical, this attempt to shake things up without shaking them up too much," continuing that *Frozen* "seems to be at odds with itself." And it is. And it's cynical too. But not necessarily in the way that Ebert means. *Frozen's* filmmakers tried to create a fairy tale that actively subverts fairy tale symbolism. The prince is a bad guy, true love is between sisters, the real love interest is dirty and talks to reindeer. But they couldn't *subvert* fairy tale symbolism because they didn't *understand* it. *Frozen* isn't about two sisters — it's about *one* princess. A princess who, at the end, comes to love *herself* — like Cinderella, Snow White, or Ariel — and, in loving herself (or *being* herself, if you will) she finds a man who loves her too. It's all there. There's only one problem: Elsa.

At the end of the movie, while Anna gets to grow up and move away from Elsa by being with Kristoff, Elsa gets to (yay!) make a skating rink for everyone using her powers. She's like the castoff part of Anna — the girl who Anna must leave behind in order to grow up. But that's problematic, because it's *Elsa* who got the big glittery-dressed transformation sequence. So it's *Elsa* that little girls want to *be*. And now, I hope, feminist parents ought to be sort of horrified that they've allowed their little girls to dress as Elsa but banned Cinderella.

*

The fact that Elsa is ultra-popular with little girls is undisputed. What *is* still an open question is: why? Princess critics and *Frozen* filmmakers are convinced it's the sister aspect. But ask an actual little girl and you're sure to get something along the lines of "Her sparkly dress! Her pretty hair! Her awesome song!" And, while princess critics take answers like this as evidence for the ways in which the patriarchy still has its evil claws deep into our girls, we know that they're really responding to a symbolism that is thousands of years old. It's a symbolism that goes beyond dresses and hair, but also beyond sisterhood, or family rifts, or misunderstandings. It's a symbolism that represents a girl breaking free from her childhood and emerging gloriously into her future as a woman. Failing to acknowledge this — forcing little girls to shift their attention away from it — does us all a disservice.

There is no doubt that Disney is on a path set by the princess critics. They are more concerned with their princesses' external qualities — their race, their body type, their sexual orientation — than their inner beauty. But the thing that gives me hope — that should give us all hope — is that little girls aren't buying it. They still gravitate towards the symbols and ideas that Disney princesses — and fairy tale princesses in general — have always offered. They care about transformation, about love, about inner courage, kindness, and strength. Sure, they might grow up to be princess critics — trying to explain away their love of these princesses with nonsense about "gender norms" and "social constructs" — but they'll still love the princesses. If Elsa is Cinderella 2.0, then we're in trouble. But if Elsa reminds us why Cinderella matters, well then we might be getting somewhere.

Epilogue

"So this is love," sang Cinderella all those years ago. "This is what makes life divine . . . the key to all heaven is mine . . . So this is the miracle that I've been dreaming of, so this is love." Love has always been the force of transformation in Disney princess movies. It's love that lets us see that who we truly are has been recognized by the world. It's love that pushes us to achieve our dreams. It's love that draws the man from the beast. Love is the magic carpet that carries us up and out of our childhoods and into the bright blue sky of the life we were meant to live. Not because a woman's only dream is to find a husband, and not because a woman needs a man to achieve her dreams for her. But because — both realistically *and* metaphorically — love gives us the wings we need to fly.

In a very real sense, finding a partner to share your adult life with is the thing that unlocks heaven. Because *that's* the thing that shows us that we're going to be okay. That we *can* leave our parents, and go out into the world, and do the things we want to do. It shows us that someone other than our parents *can* love us. Someone will want to make a life with us. Someone will be there. We will not be alone.

In a symbolic sense, as we've seen throughout this book, the prince — and the connection he and the princess share — represent the princess's readiness to take on this new phase of her life: adulthood. In films like *Snow White* and *Cinderella*, the prince and princess come together at the moment when the princess's journey has led her to assert her inner self to the world and emerge out of childhood into her new womanhood. The prince is the symbolic representation of that transformation. In films like *The Little Mermaid* and *Beauty and the Beast*, the prince and princess come to know one another in a more realistic way, but the symbolism is the same — the princess joins with her prince at the moment when she has achieved her goals and become her true self.

Taking the symbolism of romantic love out of fairy tales and replacing it with family love — as Disney has done with *Brave* and *Frozen* — literally corrupts the message of fairy tales. It tells little girls that staying home with mom and dad is more important than finding your own way in the world. It tells them that, if they feel different from their parents — if they feel that they were *born* to be something their parents disapprove of — it's much more important to be obedient than it is to break free. Stay home, this kind of fairy tale tells them, do as you're told without question, "never ask to leave this tower again."

If we are going to take the princesses back from the feminists — and we *can* — we have to remind them of what a fairy tale truly is. It's an allegory for growing up, following your dreams, and becoming who you truly *are*. The symbols are *symbols*, and they tell a story that we can all agree on. A story of a girl who knows who she is and what she wants and goes out there and gets it.

And if we and the princess critics reach a stumbling block when it comes to the importance of romantic love in the lives of women, all I can say is this: when your life is done — when you've

242

achieved all the career success and life advancement your heart desired — and you turn to the chair beside you to share your happiness, won't you want that chair to have someone sitting in it? Someone who's been with you through thick and thin? Who's comforted you when you stumbled, and rejoiced with you when you were strong? In the words of Belle and the Beast in the stage version of *Beauty and the Beast* that changed my life: "Two lives have begun now / Two hearts become one now / One passion one dream, one thing forever true: / I love you!"

Don't take this away from little girls. Give them back the role models they need — the princesses they love. We can do it. Together, we can do it. Because, "No matter how your heart is grieving / If you keep on believing / The dream that you wish will come true."

I believe. Do you?

Acknowledgements

This book wouldn't even exist if it hadn't been for my mother, Ellen. She called it into being with her gentle suggestion – "You should write a book about Disney princesses" – and she nurtured it (and me) every step of the way. One by one, she edited each chapter of this book, unfailingly making them better. All that this book is I owe to her.

I also want to thank my father, Andrew, for his wisdom, guidance, and support – not just for this book, but always and all my life. It is his voice inside my head that tells me both that I can do this and also that I can strive to do it even better. He, more than anyone else, knows what it's like to be me, which – among so many other things – has always been a wonderful gift.

Thank you also to my brother, Spencer, for his encouragement, insight, and thoughtful comments along the way. A big thank you to him for reading the book in its entirety and offering excellent feedback. And, in particular, for his guidance on the Christian elements of the Cinderella chapter.

A very special thank you to Minna Ninova for designing the cover for this book. Her kindness in donating her considerable talent and skill far exceeds the cup of tea I still owe her in payment.

Thank you to my husband, John, for putting up with my princess obsession. Thank you for taking me seriously when I wanted to discuss the themes of a cartoon, or the symbolism of a children's movie. He is, without a doubt, my very own Prince Charming.

And, of course, thank you to my son, Peter, who thinks that all mommies own their own tiaras.

About The Author

Faith Moore is a free-lance writer, stay-at-home mom, and a self-proclaimed Disney Princess Addict. She has been published in The Wall Street Journal, The New York Daily News, Acculturated, and The Federalist, and is a regular columnist at PJ Media. She has published many articles challenging the feminist critiques of Disney princesses, and exploring the consequences of denying the existence of gender roles. She also has a blog and a YouTube channel. Before becoming a stay-at-home mom to her son, Faith taught elementary school for ten years.

Website: www.FaithKMoore.com
Twitter: @FaithKMoore
Facebook: @DisneyPrincessAddict
YouTube: Princess State of Mind

Made in United States
Troutdale, OR
10/07/2024